DESIGN METHODS

DELFT

DELFT UNIVERSITY OF TECHNOLOGY

DESIGN

FACULTY OF INDUSTRIAL DESIGN ENGINEERING

GUIDE

Annemiek van Boeijen

Jaap Daalhuizen

Jelle Zijlstra

Roos van der Schoor

BIS PUBLISHERS

Students at work
in the faculty building of
Industrial Design Engineering
at the Delft University
of Technology.

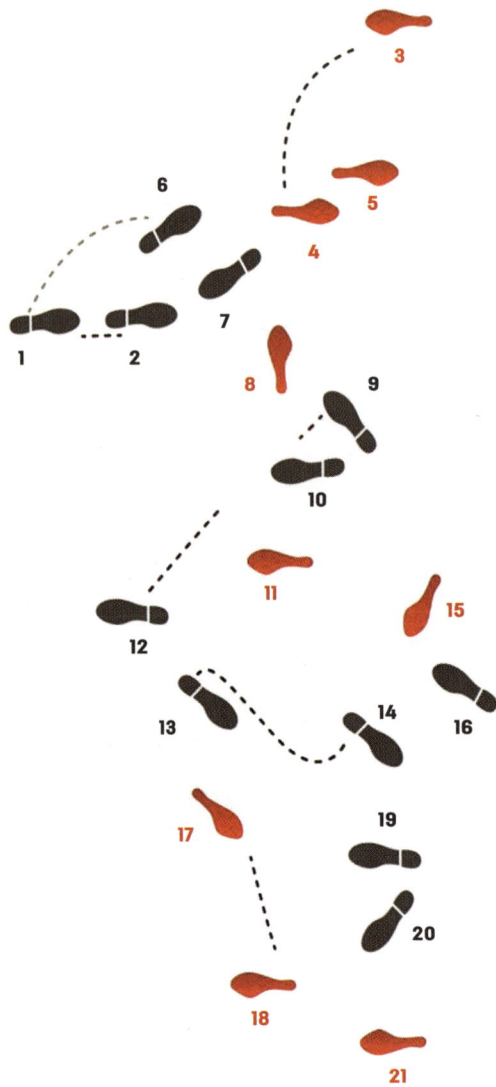

FOREWORD

Ever since its founding in the 1960s, the Delft Faculty of Industrial Design Engineering has taken a methodical approach to design education. But the methods were never uncontroversial. The Dutch writer Godfried Bomans asserted:

"In the realm of the mind a method is comparable to a crutch; the true thinker walks freely."

Many designers share his thoughts. Good designers seem to need no methods. They tend to attribute their successes to intuition, creativity and expertise, and not to the use of particular methods.

Now, nobody believes anymore that designers can do without intuition, creativity and expertise, as research into the problem-solving behaviour and thought processes of designers has convincingly shown how essential these capacities are. But that does not mean that methods have no role to play in design.

Despite criticism and doubt – some godfathers of the 'design methods movement' of the 1960s became critics of their own work – methods have not disappeared from the scene. Methods are often used as means of teaching design. The development of better methods is probably the most important driver of design research. And it is not uncommon for design consultancies to advertise themselves on the basis of their specific methodological approaches.

Since 1991, industrial design students at the Delft University of Technology have been raised with the book Product Design: Fundamentals and Methods that I wrote together with Johannes Eekels. The genesis of this book goes back to our lectures in the 1970s, but much of its content is still relevant. However, the field of design has changed greatly. Nowadays, industrial designers also design services and social and economic artefacts. In product development, the social and behavioural sciences have come to play a major role alongside engineering. Our awareness of the limits of production and consumption has increased enormously and unprecedented technological possibilities have emerged for the development of design tools.

Such developments have led to numerous new methods. I am extremely excited that finally a new Delft textbook that also addresses these new methods has been published. But there is more to it. Methodological textbooks usually focus on detailed descriptions of methods and barely address their application. The authors of this book have explicitly opted for the latter perspective. As good descriptions of methods are sufficiently available, they confine themselves to short characterisations of methods and refer to relevant sources for more information. How should a project plan be designed given specific objectives and available resources, when and in what situation and how should a particular method be used, and what can and cannot be expected from the use of a method? This book gives answers to these and other such questions.

Thanks to this specific focus, this book provides an important contribution to the literature on design methods. Given the success of its digital forerunner, accessible on the TU Delft OpenCourseWare website, this book has a promising future ahead.

Norbert Roozenburg

Associate Editor of the International Journal Design Studies.
First graduate at the Delft Faculty of Industrial Design Engineering in 1971.

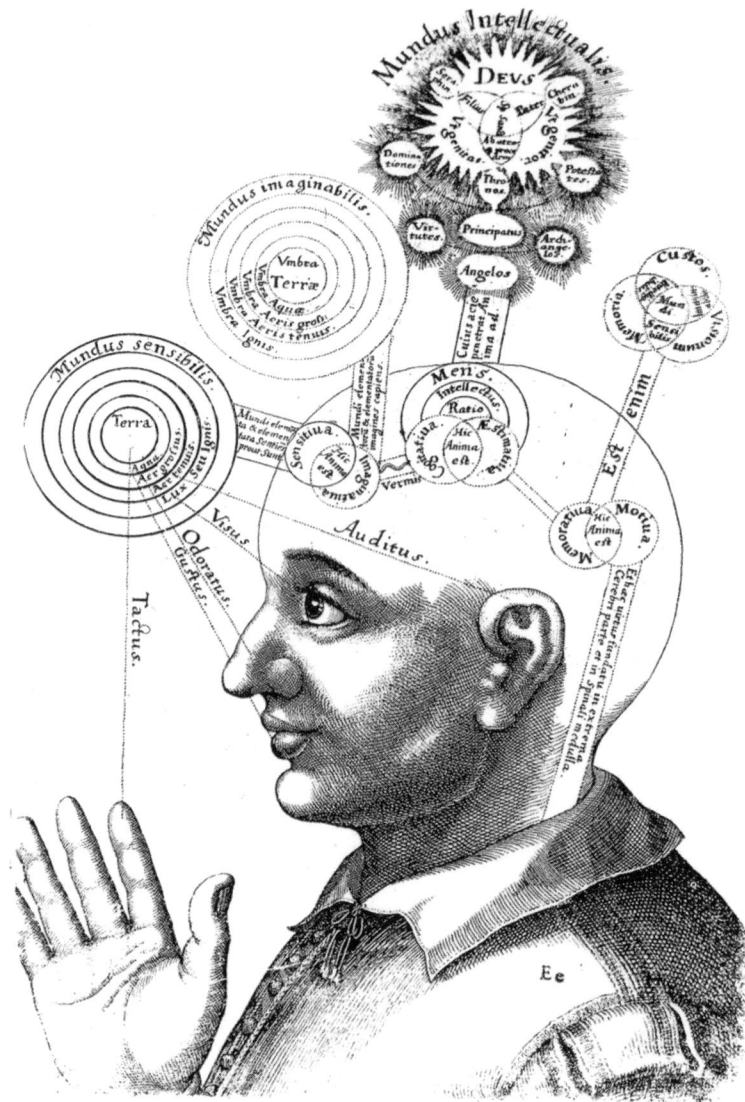

Microcosm diagram of the mind designed by physician Robert Fludd, beginning 17th century; 3T pocketradio designed by Dieter Rams in 1958 and the Apple iPod designed by Johnatan Ive in 2001.

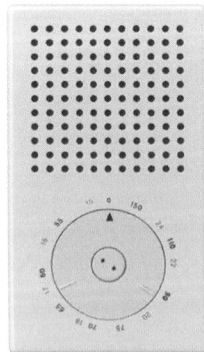

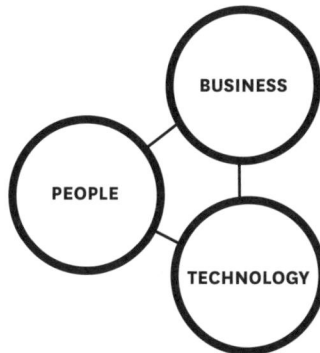

DELFT UNIVERSITY OF TECHNOLOGY
FACULTY OF INDUSTRIAL DESIGN ENGINEERING

ACKNOWLEDGMENTS This book could not have been written without the expertise, inspiration and skills of design researchers and design educators and the support of the faculty management team. Our special thanks go to the contributors of this book who all worked as staff members, former staff members or students in the faculty of Industrial Design Engineering in Delft. The editors hope that the book will justify their dedicated work. Cheers! In References and Further Reading we refer to their work with an asterix*.

Special thanks go to *Petra Badke-Schaub* and *Remco Timmer* as advising members of the editorial board.

Arjen Jansen	*Froukje Sleeswijk Visser*	*Marc Tassoul*	*Pieter Desmet*
Bert Deen	*Gert Pasman*	*Marcel Crul*	*Pieter Jan Stappers*
Carlos Coimbra Cardoso	*Gulia Calabretta*	*Marielle Creusen*	*Pinar Cankurtaran*
Conny Bakker	*Ingrid de Pauw*	*Matthijs van Dijk*	*Renee Wever*
Corné Quartel	*Jan Buijs*	*Nazli Cila*	*Stefan van de Geer*
Corrie van der Lelie	*Joost Vogtländer*	*Norbert Roozenburg*	*Stella Boess*
Erik Roscam Abbing	*Koos Eissen*	*Nynke Tromp*	*Sylvia Mooij*
Frido Smulders	*Lilian Henze*	*Paul Hekkert*	*Wouter van der Hoog*

CONTENTS

How is the book structured?
The methods in the Delft Design Guide are structured according to the type of activity they typically support. The structure in this book has been inspired by work of the Design Council on describing the design process.

STAGING A PROJECT
This section can help you to 'stage' your design project using the methods provided in this book.

MODELS, APPROACHES & PERSPECTIVES
This section contains models of design, approaches to design and perspectives on design.

DISCOVER
This section contains methods that can help you to discover insights and create understanding while designing.

DEFINE

This section contains methods that can help you to define for whom and for what problem or challenge you are going to design.

DEVELOP

This section contains methods that can help you to develop ideas and concepts while designing.

EVALUATE & DECIDE

This section contains methods that can help you to evaluate design proposals and make decisions while designing.

ARTICULATE & SIMULATE

This section contains methods that can help you to articulate and simulate design proposals while designing.

You can also search for content by using the index in the back of the Guide on page 167.

'We shape our tools and thereafter our tools shape us.'

MARSHALL MCLUHAN

HOW TO USE THIS GUIDE

The Delft Design Guide presents design methods and approaches that can be useful to you as a designer, both during your time as a student and as a practitioner. We hope you will use the guide as a source and reference. It will help you to gradually build a rich repertoire of ways to approach the design of products and services.

An important recommendation It is crucial to be aware of two issues before you start using the book. First, design methods are not recipes for success, just like strictly following a cooking recipe is not a guarantee of a good meal. Methods will help you to structure your thinking and actions. In this guidebook, we present the essential steps that will enable you to work efficiently and achieve your goals without too many detours. Furthermore, the methods will help you to communicate with your team or client. Consequently, you will not lose your way in complex design processes. You will mostly learn by experience, reflecting critically on your chosen path and methods.

Second, there are many ways to accomplish something. Your task is to find an appropriate approach for each new situation. To perform well, you need to adapt any method to the specific situation. The selection of an appropriate approach depends on your goal or task, the circumstances, your personality, background and experiences. For every 'designer - design problem - environment' combination there are multiple applicable methods that all have their benefits and limitations. The more methods you have experienced, the better your knowledge of which ways of working are suitable for you in tackling design problems effectively and efficiently.

Who is the book written for? The Delft Design Guide is first and foremost intended for design students. It complements the teaching materials provided in design courses. The book also supports design tutors by serving as a reference. Furthermore, course developers can use the book to make selections and divide the methods in the curriculum. And finally the Delft Design Guide serves as a reference for design practitioners.

When might you need this book? Designing distinguishes itself from other disciplines in that it combines a number of activities, such as visualising, creative thinking, empathising with the intended users and reasoning from values via functions to forms. In essence, designing is an activity that is intended to lead to new possibilities and an embodiment of those possibilities. Designing requires you to cope with uncertainty and to play with possibilities, leading to new insights that can result in innovations. As a designer you have the difficult task of understanding the world around you while creating new products that will change your world. Questions that you may ask yourself are:
· Is there a specific way a designer thinks and acts?
· What questions do I need to answer? How and when?
· What activities do I need to perform? When and in which order?
· How do I determine the boundaries of the context I am designing for?
· How can I map the 'world' of my intended users?
· When can I stop analysing and start creating and how do I generate ideas?
· How do I choose between solutions?
Design methods and tools can help you answer these and many other questions.

What is in the book? Design education at Delft University of Technology focuses on the design process. By teaching design methods we aim to train students to achieve fluent control of design processes and thereby manage and execute design projects successfully. The models, approaches, perspectives and methods and tools presented in this book are taught at the faculty of Industrial Design Engineering in Delft. Much of the content has been developed at Delft. Some of the content has been adopted – and sometimes modified – from outside sources. Together they represent the three main 'pillars' of Delft design education: People, Business and Technology. As the field of design is continuously evolving, the guide's contents are a snapshot of the majority of methods we currently teach. New design methods are developed continuously. Nonetheless, this collection offers you a rich variety of resources to assist you in dealing with the challenges of designing.

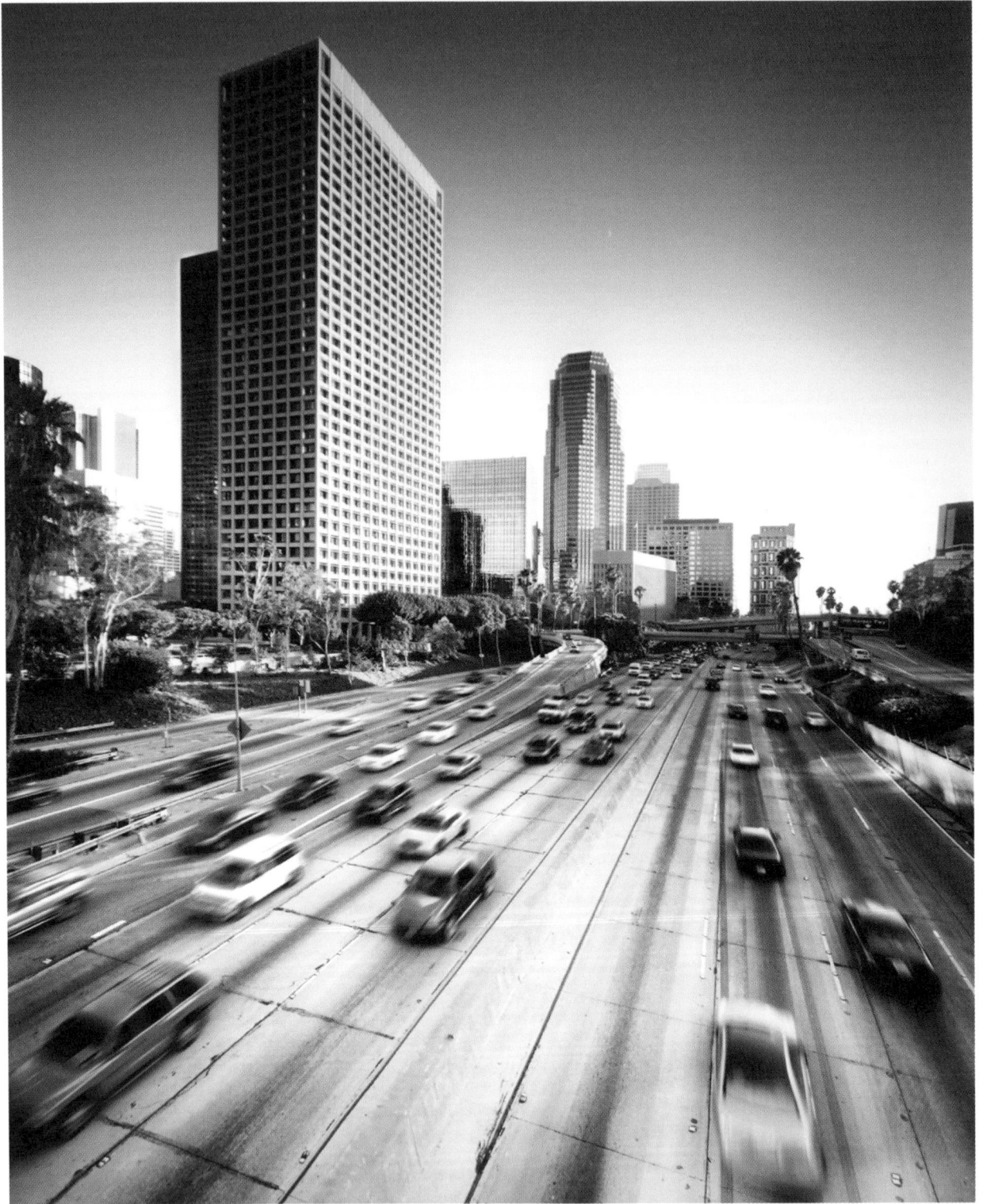

'How often I found where I should be going only by setting out for somewhere else.' (Richard Buckminster Fuller)

STAGING DESIGN ACTIVITY

When staging your project, the aim is to come up with an approach that fits your goal and ambitions, the resources that are available and the interests and expectations of your stakeholders. In the Delft Design Guide we present a large variety of methods that you will find useful, both as a student and later as a practitioner. We hope that you will use the guide as a source and reference during and after your education and that over time you will develop and expand your repertoire of ways to approach designing products and services. One of the main purposes of the Delft Design Guide is to provide you with resources that you can use to stage your projects. By building a rich repertoire of ways to approach design projects, you will be better able to stage different projects in an appropriate and timely manner.

Different roles of methods when staging design Methods can play different roles for you and in your project. Obviously, staging is about determining which activities are necessary for coming up with a good design outcome for the specific project you are working on. Methods can help you to do that. For example, when you know you require information about user needs, specific user research methods can give insight into how you could do that. But staging also involves making sure that you can coordinate and manage both your efforts and those of your team. For example, when you work in a team and need to agree on task division and milestones, methods can help to distinguish and define activities. And staging is about making sure that you can justify and account for your efforts to your external stakeholders, for example your client or your design teacher. Last but not least, staging is about creating an overview for yourself and giving you the flexibility to adapt – and experiment with – different approaches as you go along. For example, by mapping your activities onto a process model of product innovation, it becomes

Designing is a complex activity that can take many forms. Therefore, staging your project in an appropriate and timely manner is a prerequisite for developing successful design outcomes. Staging is about planning and preparing for doing the right things, before you start to do those things right. It is sometimes also about rethinking the things you are doing during your project when unexpected things happen.

easier to 'position' yourself in a project and manage your expectations of what things you should be doing now and what things you can leave for later. In this light, methods can help you to design with confidence, spurring you to create valuable and innovative results. When staging your project you should ask yourself three basic questions:

1. Which approach is most likely to help me *realise* my design goal?
In order to answer this question you will need to clarify a number of issues. What is the design goal? What resources are available in terms of time, budget, expertise, infrastructure, etc.? Which stakeholders are supposed to benefit from the outcome of the project? What are their needs, desires and wishes? Who will be working on the project and what are their (combined) skills, attitudes and ambitions? What approach would fit my own background, expertise and ambitions? Based on the answers to these questions, you can start to synthesise an initial approach that fits the project and its circumstances.

2. Given that approach, how can we *organise* the work that needs to be done? In order to answer this question, you will again need to clarify a number of issues. How can the work be divided amongst the team members? What are the dependencies between the individual activities? Which milestones are necessary? What intermediate results need to be delivered? Which qualities should these intermediate results possess? Based on the answers to these questions, you can adapt and optimise your approach.

3. How can we *justify* and account for the work to project stakeholders?
In order to answer this question, you will need to clarify the following issues: who are the stakeholders that directly influence the project process in terms of resources, support, decision making? What are their interests and needs? What value do the different activities add to the project and outcome? How can the planned efforts be justified beforehand when pitching the project? How can the efforts be justified during the project? What kinds of information and intermediate results can help to elicit buy-in and support from stakeholders to enhance the success of the project? How can the project be justified afterwards?

MODELS, APPROACHES & PERSPECTIVES

This section contains models of design, approaches to design and perspectives on design.

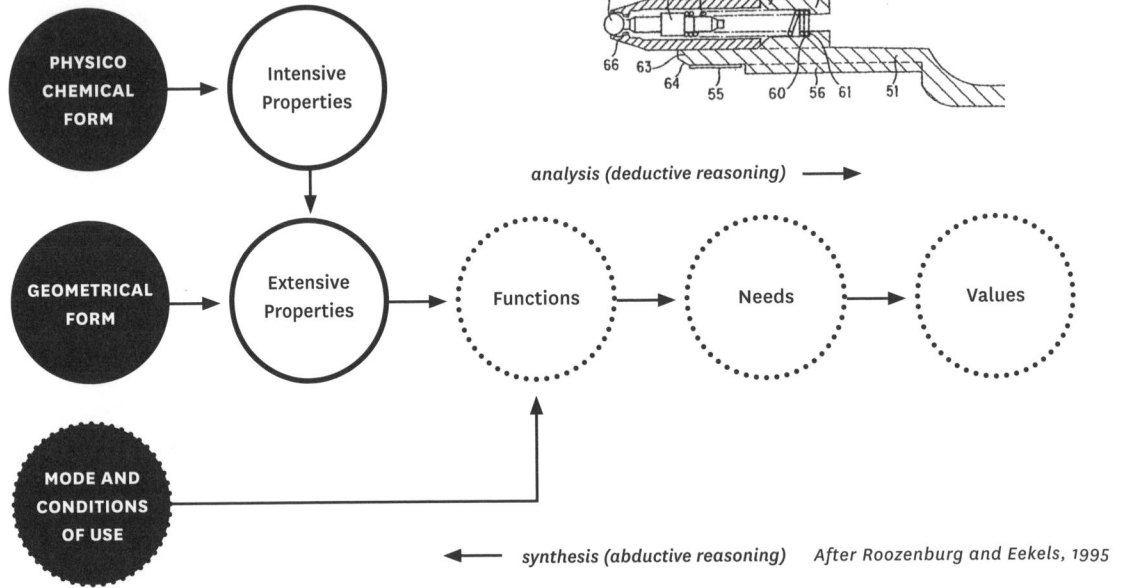

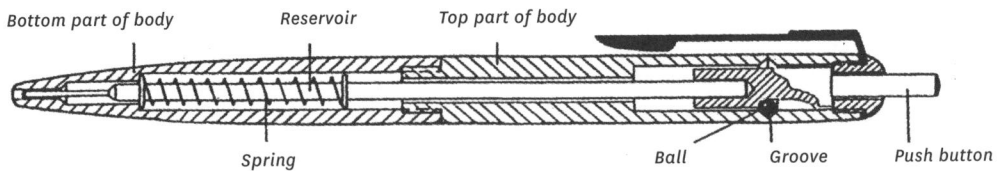

analysis (deductive reasoning) →

synthesis (abductive reasoning) ←   After Roozenburg and Eekels, 1995

Bottom part of body   Reservoir   Top part of body

Spring   Ball   Groove   Push button

FORM	PROPERTIES	FUNCTIONS	NEEDS	VALUES
geometrical form (shape of parts)	*weight*	*writing*	*expression*	*profits*
physico-chemical form (materials)	*stiffness*	*brand promotion*	*communication*	*education*
	colour	*pinning up hair*		*status*
	comfort			

REASONING IN DESIGN

What is the purpose of the model?

Products are designed and made to serve functions. By fulfilling functions a product can satisfy needs of people and realize their values. To design a product is to conceive its use and to find a suitable geometrical and physio-chemical form for it. Seen this way, the kernel of designing a product is reasoning from values, via needs, functions and properties to the final form of the product and the mode and conditions of its use. In order to understand the nature of designing one must understand the nature of that reasoning process.

The functioning of a product depends on its form, use and context of use. This means that if you know the geometrical and physio-chemical (material) form of a product, you can in principle predict its properties. If you also know in which environment and how the product will be used, you can predict whether it will function as intended and whether the related needs and values will be realised. This kind of reasoning, from form and use towards function and needs, is called 'analysis'. Analysis is a deductive process. If it is done properly analysis will lead to particular conclusions with great certainty. However, for designers the essential mode of reasoning is to reason from function to form, which is called 'synthesis' – this starts with the values and needs of the potential user and ends with ideas for the form of a product and its use. Synthesis is not a deductive, but an abductive process. In synthesis creativity is the driving force and there may exist many different solutions.

Model description

FORM

The geometrical and material form of a product is specified in its design. The design is what you as a designer will determine and document during the design process. The parts that make up a design are realised in the production process.

The Reasoning in Design model is a generic representation of how designers reason when designing. The model is primarily based on the design of tangible products. The model helps you to be aware of and reflect on the different levels of your reasoning.

MODE AND CONDITIONS OF USE

A product does not function until it is used. Use always finds place in a specific environment. Both the form of the product and its use affect the manner in which a product will actually function.

PROPERTIES

Due to its form, a product has certain properties, like weight, strength or colour. Properties describe the expected behaviour of a product under certain circumstances. Properties can be intensive or extensive. The former are completely determined by the material of a part, for example its weight. The intensive properties and the geometrical form determine the latter. For example, the material and the geometrical form together determine the strength of a part. As a designer you typically focus on the extensive properties, as they most directly determine the functioning of a product. By choosing a certain material, you often set many intensive properties all at once. These properties have both desirable and less desirable consequences. For example, steel is stiff, but is heavy and rusts, while aluminium is light and does not corrode, but is less stiff. The art of designing is to give the product such a geometrical form that it has the desired extensive properties, given its intensive ones.

FUNCTION

Properties and functions both say something about the behaviour of things. Statements on properties are objectively true or false. This is not so for functions.

Functions express what a product is for, its purpose, and this depends on the intentions, preferences, objectives and goals of human beings. Different users might have different functions for the same product; for example, a ballpoint pen can be used to write a letter or to pin up long hair. Functions can be technical, ergonomic, aesthetic, semantic, economic, societal, etc.

NEEDS AND VALUES

By fulfilling functions, products can satisfy needs and realise values. For example a ballpoint pen can satisfy the need to express oneself in writing and thereby realise aesthetic, cultural or economical values.

Tips & Concerns

· In design intuition and creativity have an indispensable role to play. Notwithstanding the importance of scientific knowledge, systematic approaches and modern possibilities for simulation, without intuition and creativity design processes would come to a standstill. Producing new ideas requires intuition and creativity, not only in the domain of product design but in all design domains.

· Not only the form but also the mode and conditions of use determine how a product will actually function. The context of use counts as much as the product itself and therefore designers should pay equal attention to both of them. Thus, designing a product includes designing its use.

REFERENCES & FURTHER READING: Roozenburg, N.F.M. and Eekels, J.*, 1995. *Product Design: Fundamentals and Methods*. Chichester: John Wiley & Sons. / Roozenburg, N.F.M. and Eekels, J.*, 1998. *Productontwerpen: Structuur en Methoden*. 2nd ed. Utrecht: Lemma.

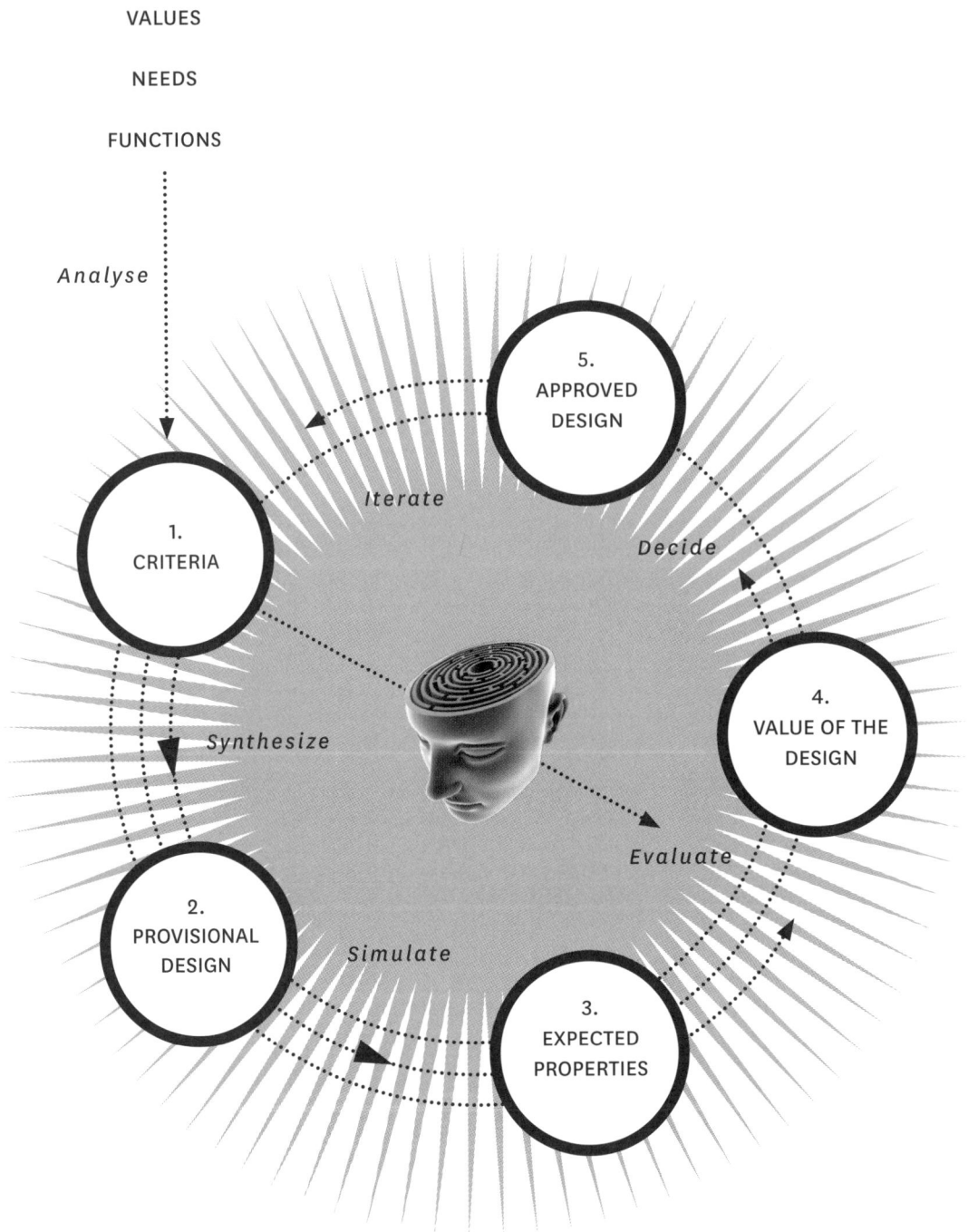

VALUES

NEEDS

FUNCTIONS

Analyse

5.
APPROVED
DESIGN

1.
CRITERIA

Iterate

Decide

4.
VALUE OF THE
DESIGN

Synthesize

Evaluate

2.
PROVISIONAL
DESIGN

Simulate

3.
EXPECTED
PROPERTIES

The basic building block of the design process is this circle of thought, action and decision. Designing is like a fractal: zooming in or out results in a similar image. Designing is an iterative process where you sometimes have to take a few steps back – 'back to the drawing board!' – in order to go a step forward later on. Being aware of the basic cycle that you are going through, up to a few times per minute, helps you as a designer to organise your thoughts and design activities. After Roozenburg and Eekels, 1995.

BASIC DESIGN CYCLE

What is the purpose of the model?
The model describes the different stages a designer goes through when solving a design problem. Theoretically you can go through just a single cycle, but usually you will perform many iterations.

The Basic Design Cycle is a model that represents the trial-and-error process of design. It consists of a sequence of empirical cycles. The knowledge of both the problem and the solution increases with each cycle.

This thinking process comes naturally to us – even Stone Age people created products, such as tools and weapons, and thus went through this cycle of thoughts. You go through this 'design' cycle every morning when you are deciding what to wear. However, if you lose sight of where you are in this cycle, confusion might set in – even for professional designers. Ideally, you spiral from problem to solution, from abstract to concrete, from function to product geometry. Usually this is an iterative process where you sometimes have to take a few steps back – 'back to the drawing board!' – in order to go a step forward later on. Being aware of the basic cycle that you are going through, up to a few times per minute, helps you as a designer to organise your thoughts and design activities.

Process description
The model describes five stages, each with a related outcome/result.

ANALYSE:
In this stage you analyse aspects related to your design goal or a design problem. The processed information will yield the design criteria. For example, when thinking about what to wear, you consider the weather and the social context.

SYNTHESISE:
In this stage you generate possible solutions. This ideation will result in ideas or designs. For example, you come up with possible ensembles of clothing, shoes and accessories.

SIMULATE:
In this stage you draw and model your ideas so that you can estimate and define the expected properties of your design. For example, you try on several ensembles.

EVALUATION:
In this stage you bring in your design criteria to evaluate your design. For example, you check how you look in the mirror and consider whether you are dressed suitably for the weather.

DECISION:
In this stage you decide whether your design is acceptable or not. If it is not, you go back to one of the earlier stages. For example, you decide that your jacket is too warm and that you should wear a thinner one instead.

Tips & Concerns
· Do not confuse the five stages with the phases of the design process. The design process does not involve just one creative phase or one analytical phase; these activities are ongoing continuously. This means that there is not one creative phase after which you can stop being creative.
· You must engage in creative thinking throughout the process, also during the engineering of details and when determining the production processes.
· When you 'get lost' in your ideas and thoughts, you might find it helpful to consider which stage of the basic cycle you are in and to discuss this with others.

Limitations of the model
· As analysis is the first stage of the model, this suggests that it should also be your point of departure. However, that step is not necessarily your preferred point for starting your design cycle. If you prefer the doing style (one of the four learning styles defined by David Kolb) you may feel most comfortable with synthesis as your point of departure – in that case, start by designing solutions.

REFERENCES & FURTHER READING: Kolb, D.A., 1984. *Experiential Learning: Experience as the Source of Learning and Development.* Upper Saddle River, NJ: Prentice Hall. / Roozenburg, N. F.M. and Eekels, J., 1995. *Product Design: Fundamentals and Methods.* Chichester: John Wiley & Sons. / Roozenburg, N. F.M. and Eekels, J., 1998. *Product Ontwerpen: Structuur en Methoden.* 2nd ed. Utrecht: Lemma.

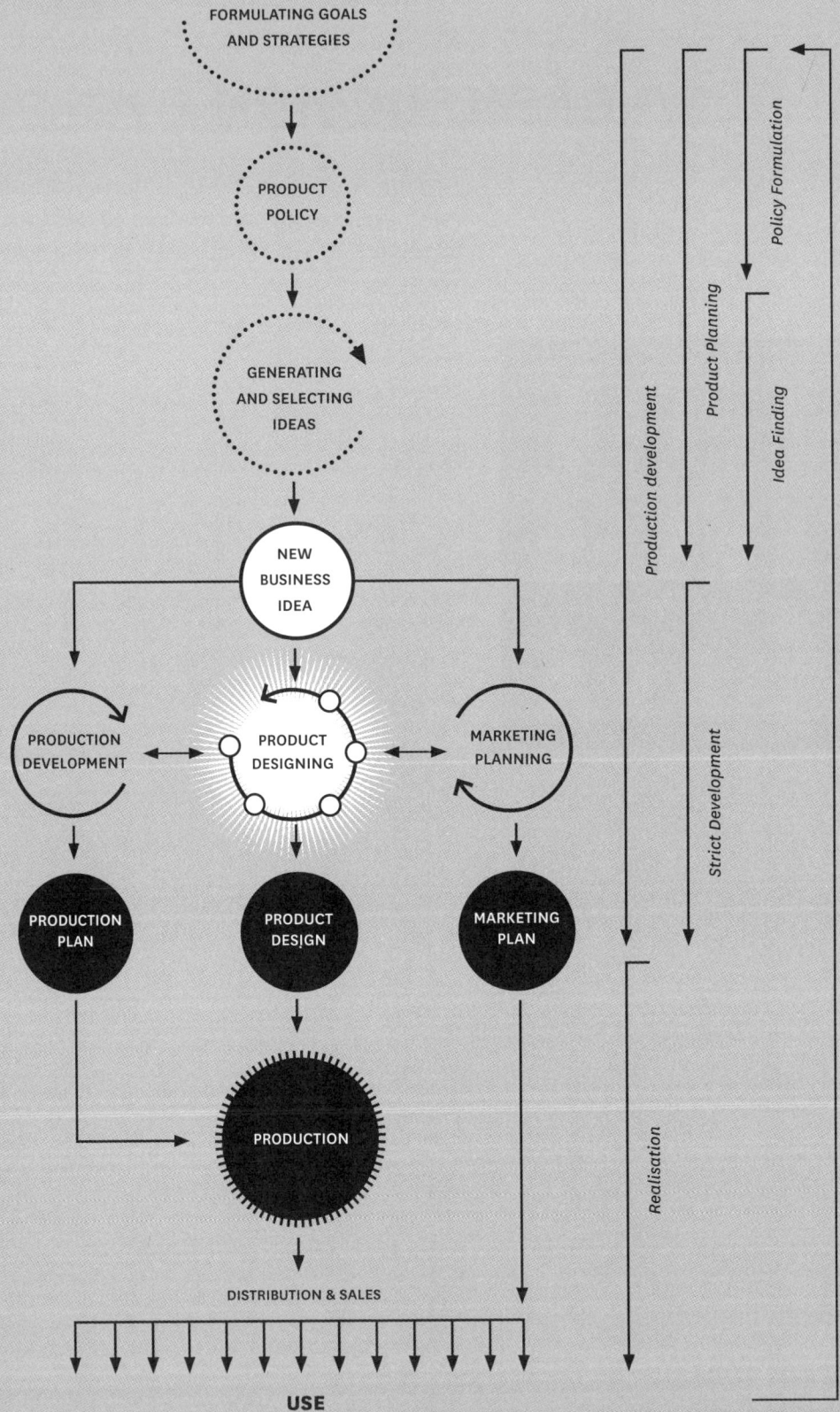

FORMULATING GOALS
AND STRATEGIES

PRODUCT
POLICY

GENERATING
AND SELECTING
IDEAS

NEW
BUSINESS
IDEA

PRODUCTION
DEVELOPMENT

PRODUCT
DESIGNING

MARKETING
PLANNING

PRODUCTION
PLAN

PRODUCT
DESIGN

MARKETING
PLAN

PRODUCTION

DISTRIBUTION & SALES

USE

Policy Formulation

Product Planning

Idea Finding

Production development

Strict Development

Realisation

In this model the circle is pulled straight to indicate the passing of time. It depicts the entire process of one innovation loop from company strategy to market introduction. After Roozenburg and Eekels, 1995

PRODUCT INNOVATION PROCESS - 1

What is the purpose of the model?
If you want to successfully innovate, you must produce fruitful ideas, work them out skilfully into comprehensive plans for action and then realise those plans tenaciously yet flexibly. The Product Innovation Process model shows how product design is embedded as a phase within the larger industrial innovation process. The process distinguishes two phases: the product development phase, entailing all the activities that lead up to a new product design, and the realisation phase. At the core of the model is strict development, which encompasses product design, production planning and marketing planning in parallel. Strict development is preceded by product planning activities, entailing policy formulation and idea finding, which define the kind of product that will be designed. During the strict development phase, the product is prepared for production as well as distribution and sales. The development of a new product will be successful insofar as these activities are in synch.

Process description
PRODUCT PLANNING
In the product planning phase you determine what product(s) will be developed and when. During policy formulation you articulate the innovation strategy and goals. Particularly in larger organisations, you will plan more than one product: a product mix. For this, you draft a product-market strategy, which defines the intended product domain as well as the target market(s). A well-crystallised product development policy is the basis for idea finding and can also provide normative information for making choices later on in the product development process.

The Product Innovation Process model created by Roozenburg and Eekels describes how product design is embedded in the overall product innovation process. The model helps you to plan and manage your project and to keep an overview while designing.

When searching for new product ideas it is wise to demarcate the areas in which you want to be active – these are called 'search areas'. They represent strategic ideas for future activities of a company. In a new product idea at least two elements come together: a technical possibility and a market need. It is important to arrive at a proper balance between the two elements, as they are both needed.

STRICT DEVELOPMENT
In the strict development phase, you develop promising ideas for new products into detailed plans for the product, production and sales. The ideas are vague at first, developing into concrete plans. The plans are typically organised iteratively and in parallel. It is important that in each cycle all aspects of the new product (function, appearance, use, manufacturing, cost, environment, etc.) are taken into consideration.

REALISATION
In this phase the detailed plans developed in the strict development phase are transformed into reality. This covers the production, distribution, sales and the actual use of the product.

Tips & Concerns
· Product development needs to be organised concentrically, with iterative cycles of development in which partial design proposals are clarified so that their technical and commercial feasibility can be evaluated. The number of cycles is arbitrary, yet it is essential to take all aspects of development activity into account in each cycle. Concentric development – or integrated product design or concurrent engineering – prevents your organisation from spending more money and time than necessary on failing ideas. It also increases the quality of the design and decreases lead time.

Limitations of the model
· The model describes product innovation at a rather abstract level in terms of activities and the outcomes of those activities. The model can help you to plan and manage the innovation process, but should be accompanied by more operational methods and practices that guide concrete activities.

REFERENCES & FURTHER READING: Roozenburg, N.F.M. and Eekels, J.*, 1995. *Product Design: Fundamentals and Methods*. Chichester: John Wiley & Sons. / Roozenburg, N.F.M. and Eekels, J.*, 1998. *Productontwerpen: Structuur en Methoden*. 2nd ed. Utrecht: Lemma.

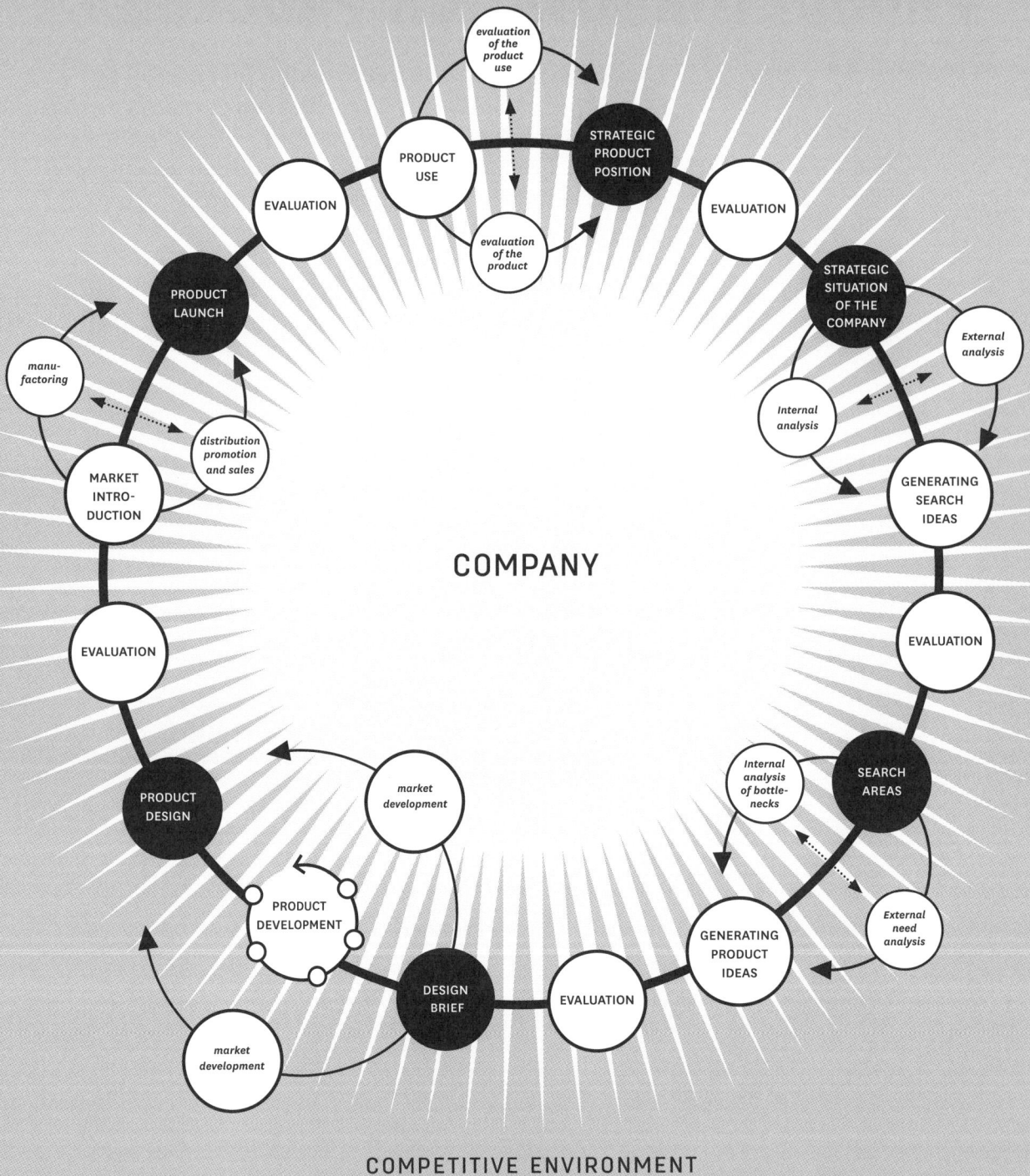

evaluation of the product use

STRATEGIC PRODUCT POSITION

PRODUCT USE

EVALUATION

evaluation of the product

EVALUATION

PRODUCT LAUNCH

STRATEGIC SITUATION OF THE COMPANY

External analysis

manu-factoring

Internal analysis

distribution promotion and sales

MARKET INTRO-DUCTION

GENERATING SEARCH IDEAS

COMPANY

EVALUATION

EVALUATION

SEARCH AREAS

PRODUCT DESIGN

Internal analysis of bottle-necks

market development

PRODUCT DEVELOPMENT

External need analysis

GENERATING PRODUCT IDEAS

DESIGN BRIEF

EVALUATION

market development

COMPETITIVE ENVIRONMENT

It never ends: the Product Innovation Process is a continuous circular process. A company moves through the cycle all the time, developing new products and redeveloping existing products, sometimes simultaneously. After Buijs, 2012

PRODUCT INNOVATION PROCESS - 2

What is the purpose of the model?

A company responds to its changing competitive environment by developing new products and services. The Product Innovation Process model describes the continuous process of developing innovations; from the use of existing products to a company's strategic product position, via three other stages back to product use. The model is characterised by five elements: a circular process view, similar to an experiential learning process; five stages; each stage is visually similar in terms of building blocks, shape and size; seen from the company's viewpoint; and connected to the company's external environment. The five-stage Product Innovation Process model consists of product use, strategy formulation, design brief formulation, product development and market introduction. The model helps you to properly align all these activities.

Process description

PRODUCT USE

The use of the company's existing products is seen as the starting point for the next innovation round. This stage involves connecting the last step, 'product use', with the first step, the 'strategy formulation' of the company, but now in order to start the next innovation cycle.

STRATEGY FORMULATION

You can explicate the strategic need for innovation by predicting the future corporate situation if no strategic changes are made. Then you determine the current strategic situation of the company and perform an internal analysis and external analysis of the company. The former will allow you to identify the strategic strengths and the core competences. The latter will

The Product Innovation Process model developed by Buijs describes the overall product innovation process with an emphasis on the fuzzy front end. The model can help you to plan for and manage innovation and to keep an overview while innovating.

allow you to identify the opportunities and threats outside the company. In combining these you can formulate 'search areas', which are strategic ideas for innovation and potential new business opportunities. When evaluating these search areas, you can check their validity in a number of ways, for example by interviewing experts, looking at patents or observing potential customers and users.

DESIGN BRIEF FORMULATION

In this stage the selected search areas are transformed into product ideas, formulated in the design brief. The brief describes the ideas in such a way that an internal or external design team can start developing the product and/or service. The brief can include a vision statement, program of requirements and other guidelines and means to steer the design direction.

DEVELOPMENT

This stage involves traditional design activities related to the product and/or service design, including also the development of the market, for example a marketing plan, and technology for the product and its production. This stage results in, among others, working prototypes, technical documents and assembly schemes.

MARKET INTRODUCTION

This stage entails the further development of a full-scale manufacturing process and marketing, encompassing full-scale sales, promotion and distribution. The final result is the product and/or service launch.

Tips & Concerns

· Product innovation processes are intended to help companies design and introduce new products that customers are willing to buy and use. Therefore, the innovation process ends in product use – but at the same time, this forms the starting point of a new product innovation process.

· Visualising the innovation process as a circular model suggests that there is neither a beginning nor an end, which is true in the sense that introducing a new product on the market will lead to reactions from competitors. These in turn will cause the original innovating company to start the next new product innovation process in order to regain its competitive advantage.

Limitations of the model

· The model describes product innovation at a rather abstract level in terms of activities and the outcomes of those activities.

· The model can help you to plan and manage the innovation process, but should be accompanied by more operational methods and practices that guide concrete activities.

REFERENCES & FURTHER READING: Buijs, J.A.*, 2012. *The Delft Innovation Method; a design thinker's guide to innovation*. The Hague: Eleven International Publishing. / Buijs, J.A. and Valkenburg, R.*, 2005. *Integrale Productontwikkeling*. 3rd ed. Utrecht: Lemma. / Buijs, J.A.*, 2003. *Modelling Product Innovation Processes: from Linear Logic to Circular Chaos*. Creativity and Innovation Management, June, 12(2), pp. 76-93.

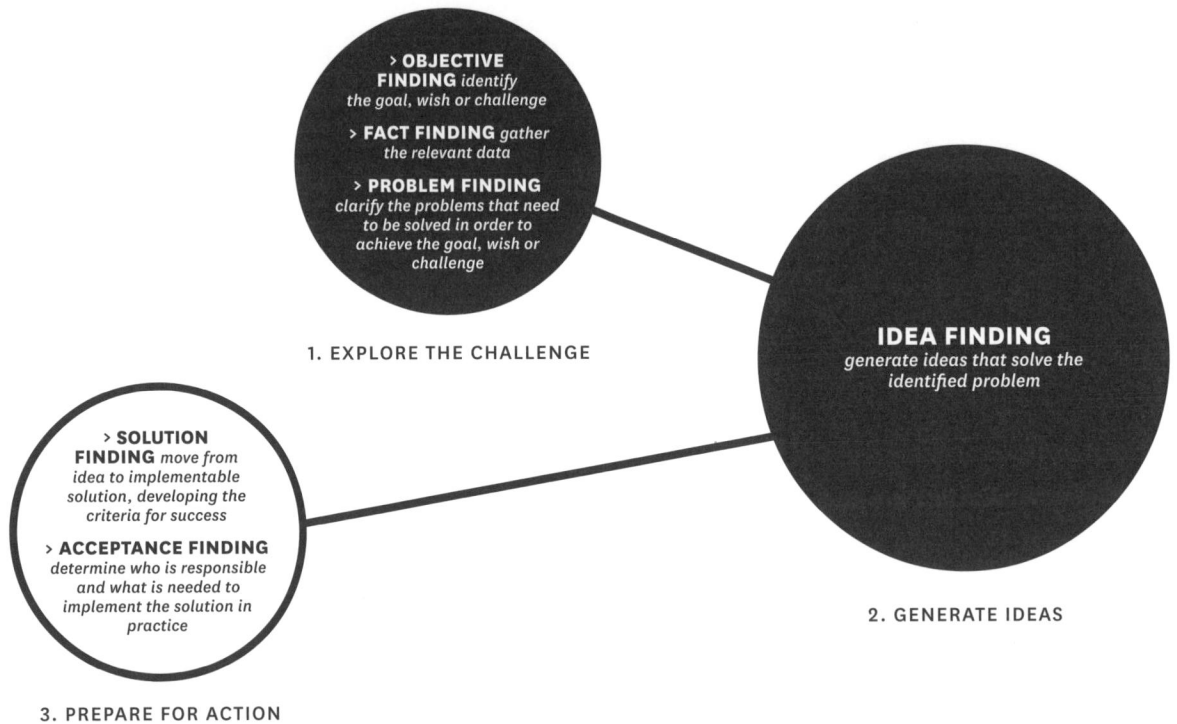

> **OBJECTIVE FINDING** *identify the goal, wish or challenge*

> **FACT FINDING** *gather the relevant data*

> **PROBLEM FINDING** *clarify the problems that need to be solved in order to achieve the goal, wish or challenge*

1. EXPLORE THE CHALLENGE

IDEA FINDING *generate ideas that solve the identified problem*

2. GENERATE IDEAS

> **SOLUTION FINDING** *move from idea to implementable solution, developing the criteria for success*

> **ACCEPTANCE FINDING** *determine who is responsible and what is needed to implement the solution in practice*

3. PREPARE FOR ACTION

Thelonius Monk like many other Jazz musicians develops his music during improvisational sessions. Ideas are implemented immediately, tested and improved until the music 'works'. Solutions need to be found for musical problems like expressing a certain mood or feeling or for going from one tempo to another. During solos, individual musicians are given the floor to show their skills and creativity. Creative processes are all about postponing judgement, fresh ideas need a safe environment and time to grow into better ideas. Photo: Eugene Smith 1959.

CREATIVE PROBLEM SOLVING

What is the purpose of the approach?
The purpose of Creative Problem Solving is to help you to unleash your creativity by freeing your mind of limitations. CPS stimulates you to find 'out-of-the-box' solutions through free association and/or free idea generation. The ideas you come up with do not have to logically connect to the given problem or situation.

Process description
CPS consists of a three-stage process that mimics your natural creative process, following six explicit steps:

STAGE 1: EXPLORE THE CHALLENGE
STEP 1
Objective finding > identify the goal, wish or challenge
STEP 2
Fact finding > gather the relevant data
STEP 3
Problem finding > clarify the problems that need to be solved in order to achieve the goal, wish or challenge

STAGE 2: GENERATE IDEAS
STEP 4
Idea finding > generate ideas that solve the identified problem

STAGE 3: PREPARE FOR ACTION
STEP 5
Solution finding > move from idea to implementable solution, developing the criteria for success
STEP 6
Acceptance finding (plan for action) > determine who is responsible and what is needed to implement the solution in practice

Creative Problem Solving (CPS) is a structured approach for generating novel and useful solutions to problems. The approach helps you redefine your design problems, come up with breakthrough ideas and then act on these new ideas.

During the second phase, you can employ several heuristics to stimulate creativity and fuel the idea generation process:

1. INVENTORY:
   collect and recall all existing information concerning the issue
2. ASSOCIATIVE:
   expand ideas by making associative links to new ideas, for example by brainstorming in a design team
3. CONFRONTATIONAL:
   identify and break down assumptions to get to new ideas, then force-fit these into the problem at hand, such as by using Synectics
4. PROVOCATIVE:
   ask 'what if not …?' or 'what else …?' You can spark new insights by using analogies, metaphors and random stimuli, such as picking a word from the newspaper
5. INTUITIVE:
   look at your problem or challenge in a non-structured and non-rational way, using your experience and direct and personal inspiration
6. ANALYTICAL-SYSTEMATIC:
   systematically make an inventory of possible solutions and make systematic variations and combinations.

Tips & Concerns
· In order to apply CPS successfully you should create a 'safe' environment where team members and other stakeholders can come up with out-of-the-box ideas.
· Criticism should be postponed and associations stimulated. If for instance a client states that he would not like to venture into a certain strategic direction, he might obstruct the creative process and block designers by demanding that they look for the right solution in the direction that he *does* like.
· An 'undesirable' idea can act as a steppingstone towards a 'desirable', implementable solution.
· In general, all rules for creative techniques apply here, such as a warm up and postponing criticism.

Limitations of the approach
· CPS requires a genuine interest in out-of-the-box solutions. Do not use the approach to justify existing ideas.

REFERENCES & FURTHER READING: De Bono, E., 1973. *Lateral Thinking: Creativity Step by Step*. New York, NY: Harper & Row. Osborn, A., 1953. *Applied Imagination: Principles and Procedures of Creative Problem Solving*. Buffalo, NY: Creative Education Foundation Press. Tassoul, M.*, 2006. *Creative Facilitation, a Delft Approach*. Delft: VSSD Delft. / Roozenburg, N.F.M. and Eekels, E.*, 1998. *Product Ontwerpen: Structuur en Methoden*. 2nd ed. Utrecht: Lemma.

8 steps of the process embedded in the VIP model. After Hekkert and van Dijk, 2011.

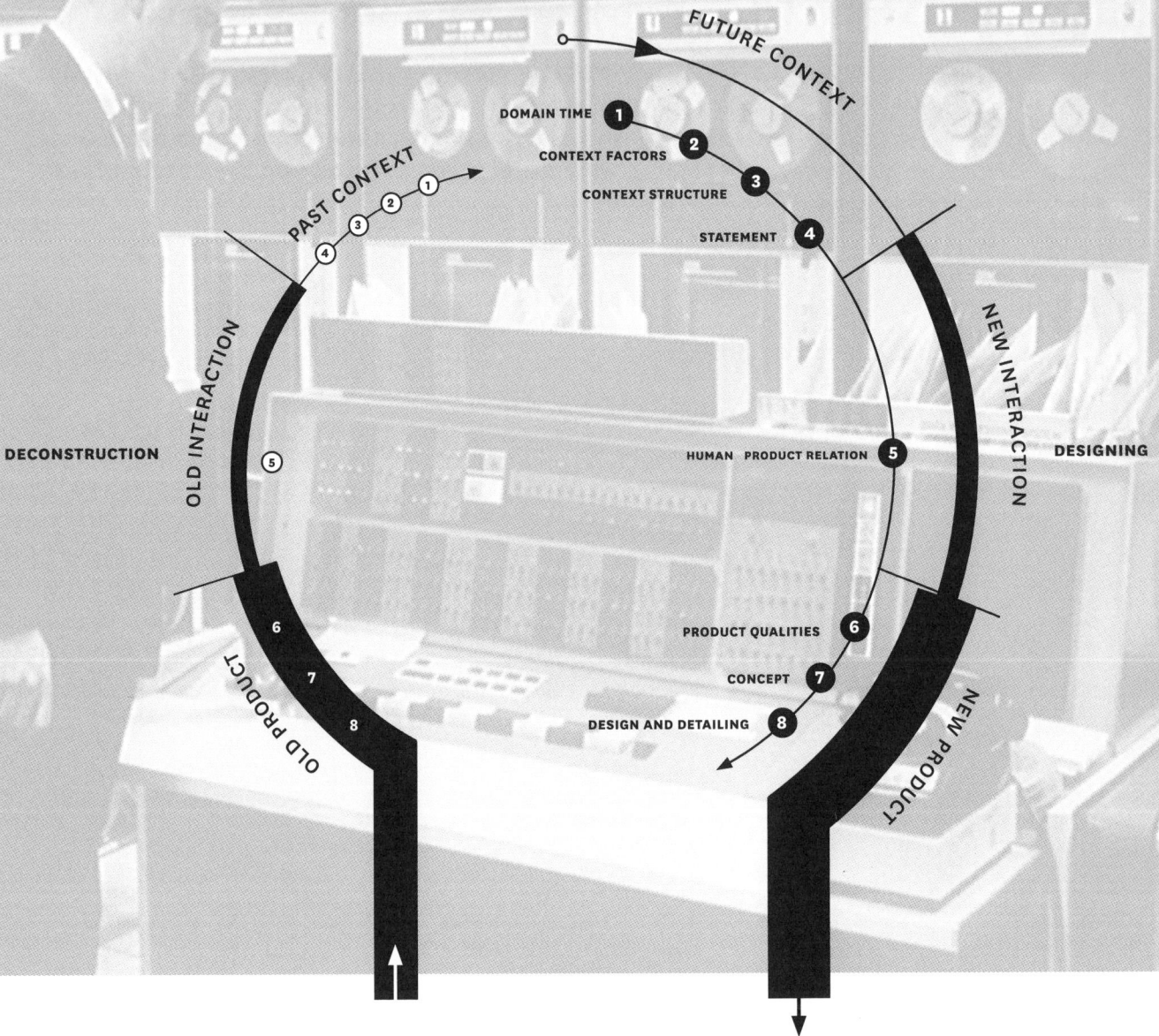

FUTURE CONTEXT

PAST CONTEXT

DOMAIN TIME **1**

CONTEXT FACTORS **2**

CONTEXT STRUCTURE **3**

STATEMENT **4**

NEW INTERACTION

OLD INTERACTION

DECONSTRUCTION

HUMAN PRODUCT RELATION **5**

DESIGNING

OLD PRODUCT

PRODUCT QUALITIES **6**

CONCEPT **7**

DESIGN AND DETAILING **8**

NEW PRODUCT

How personal is your relationship with your PC? The ViP approach focuses on the relationship between user and product and how it changes when moving into the future. For example, IBM was the main manufacturer of large mainframe computers during the Seventies. Extrapolating from their business at that time, they predicted that a handful of their machines per country would be enough to do all necessary calculations. They did not realise that the relationship between people and computers would become much more personal, as Microsoft and Apple proved.

VISION IN PRODUCT DESIGN (VIP)

What is the purpose of the approach?

ViP is a context-driven and interaction-centred approach that offers you a way to come up with products that give people meaning or value. These are designs with a soul: authentic products that reflect the vision and personality of their creator – you. Given the big impact of products on our society, daily life and well-being, the developers of this method consider this responsibility to be essential. ViP provides you with a perspective on your role as co-shaper of society and a step-by-step approach to developing a responsible and authentic design vision that will steer the conceptualisation. This vision includes the explication of what you wish to offer people in a future context before defining the means whereby the design can achieve this. This aspect of the method makes it suitable for innovation processes of any kind.

Process description

ViP distinguishes between the preparation phase and the designing phase. In the preparation phase the current product(s), product-user interactions and context of those interactions are questioned. In the designing phase, the future context, interactions and design are developed.

When developing a future context, you are confronted with all kinds of considerations. What starting points are interesting and which ones are relevant? What facts lend support to my context and how do I allow personal motives, interests or intuition to play a part? Where and how do I involve the mission of my client and/or developments in the market?

Vision in Product Design is an approach that supports innovators of any kind to 'design' the vision underlying their design or intervention, for example, its reason 'why' or 'raison d'être'.

By carefully selecting and discussing the building blocks of this future context, you shape the worldview underlying the design.

In order to act upon this world, you need to take a position, which is called 'the statement'. In this statement you carefully define the raison d'être of the final solution: what do I want to offer people? What do I want them to understand, experience or do?

This statement is not directly translated into a product. Products are just a means for accomplishing appropriate actions, interactions and relationships; products provide meaning for people only through interaction. Hence, you are encouraged to consider this interaction first. Without knowing what to design yet, you have to conceptualise a vision of the interaction, an image of the way the product is going to be viewed, used, understood and experienced.

After envisioning the interaction between user and product, you define the product character, for example the qualitative characteristics that the product has to embody.

The statement, interaction and product vision together form the basis for further conceptualisation and materialisation.

Tips & Concerns

- It is key to devote attention to the quality of the factors that build the future context as this sets the basis for the remainder of the project. Factors need to be specific, meaningful and original.
- Conceptualising an interaction is not an easy task. Here, ViP makes a strong appeal to your skills in conceptual and abstract thinking. It helps you to come up with analogies – for example, comparable situations in which similar interactions exist.
- Although the structure of the method reflects a clear rationale, it helps you to move back and forth through the steps: statement, envisioning interaction and product vision.

Limitations of the approach

- ViP postpones the development of product ideas as it supports designers to consider its meaning to people first. You should be willing and able to set aside enough time to do so.
- ViP does not provide answers to questions, but rather asks you to pose the right questions. It is up to you to take a position and argue for this position consistently and convincingly.

REFERENCES & FURTHER READING: Hekkert, P.P.M. and Van Dijk, M.B.*, 2011. *Vision in design: A guidebook for innovators.* Amsterdam: BIS publishers.

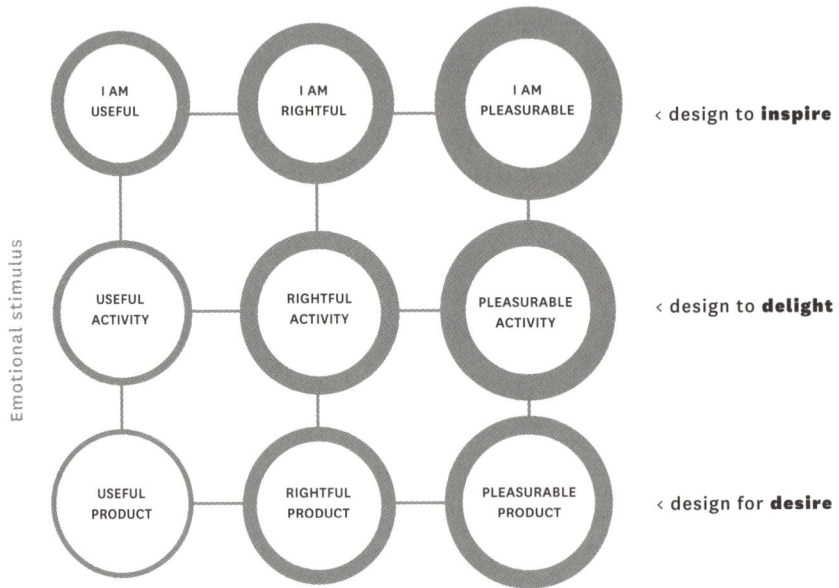

I AM USEFUL	I AM RIGHTFUL	I AM PLEASURABLE	‹ design to **inspire**
USEFUL ACTIVITY	RIGHTFUL ACTIVITY	PLEASURABLE ACTIVITY	‹ design to **delight**
USEFUL PRODUCT	RIGHTFUL PRODUCT	PLEASURABLE PRODUCT	‹ design for **desire**

Emotional stimulus

Appraised personal significance

After Desmet, 2002

DESIGN FOR EMOTION

What is the purpose of the approach?
Design for Emotion is a systematic approach to designing products with predefined emotional intentions. The approach can be used to:
a) Define an appropriate emotional effect.
b) Gather relevant user information so that this emotional effect can be achieved.
c) Envision concepts that evoke the intended effect.
d) Measure to what extent the design concept evokes the intended emotion.

The approach is based on a basic model of emotion in design, which distinguishes different layers of emotion that should be taken into consideration in design processes. The key variables in the model are Stimulus and Concern. Products can act as emotional stimuli in three different ways: object, activity and identity. Three types of user concerns are relevant: goals, standards and attitudes. These two variables combine to form a matrix of nine sources of product emotion (left).

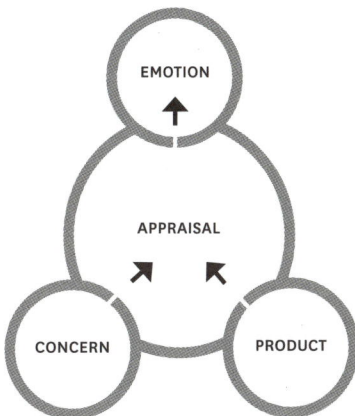

Design for Emotion is an approach that enables you to take the intended emotional impact as the leading principle in the design process.

Process description

STEP 1
Determine the underlying concerns of the user. You should ask three questions.
· What are their goals (for example, things they want to accomplish or see happen)?
· What are their standards (expectations and beliefs about how they, others and objects should behave or act)?
· What are their attitudes (dispositional likings or dislikings for qualities of objects, people or activities)?
These concerns should be formulated not only in relation to objects – the product to be designed – but also in relation to the activity that is enabled or supported by using the product and in relation to the people (including the user) involved in the context of use.

STEP 2
Observe current emotional responses in the context of use. This can help you determine user concerns. These existing emotions are used as entry points in interviews to understand underlying concerns.

STEP 3
Formulate possible conflicts between user concerns. These conflicts are then used to formulate new design solution spaces. The emotional impact of concepts can be tested with the use of PrEmo (Product Emotion Measurement Instrument).

Tips & Concerns
· Concerns should be formulated as: 'I want ...', 'I, someone, a product should ...' or 'I like ...' The formulation should be concrete, and concern sets should include not only goals but also standards and attitudes.
· At least 25 different positive emotions can be experienced in human-product interaction. In the design process, the intended emotions should be defined because different emotions require different designs.
· Design for Emotion is design for concerns; and therefore this approach always requires a research stage in which user concerns are determined.

Limitations of the model
· Design for Emotion focuses on emotional effects of design but does not necessarily take other relevant aspects and/or requirements into consideration. The approach should therefore be incorporated into regular design approaches rather than used in isolation.
· Although the basic concepts in the approach are easy to understand, using them in design processes does require some experience.

After Desmet, 2008

REFERENCES & FURTHER READING: Desmet, P.M.A.*, 2012. Faces of Product Pleasure; *25 Positive Emotions in Human-Product Interactions.* International Journal of Design, August, 6(2), pp. 1-29. / Desmet, P.M.A. and Schifferstein, N.J.H.*, 2012. *Emotion research as input for product design.* In J. Beckley, D. Paredes, & K. Lopetcharat (Eds.), Product Innovation Toolbox: A Field Guide to Consumer Understanding and Research (pp. 149-175). Hoboken, NJ: John Wiley & Sons. / Desmet, P.M.A.*, 2002. *Designing Emotions* (doctoral thesis). Delft, NL: Delft University of Technology. / Desmet, P.M.A.*, 2008. P*roduct Emotion*. In: P.P.M. Hekkert, & H.N.J. Schifferstein (Eds.), Product Experience (pp. 379-397). Amsterdam: Elsevier.

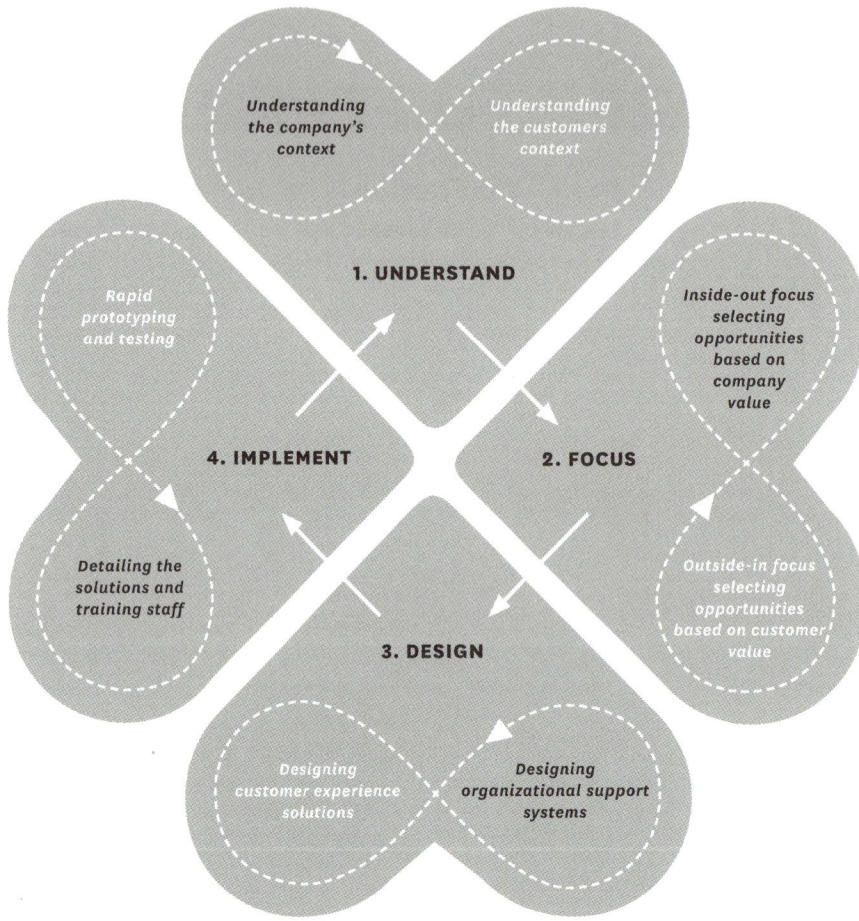

Above: The 8-shaped loops are iterations between internal and external stages of innovation. After Roscam Abbing, 2010
Below: Starting out as a soap and butter manufacturer, the Dutch multinational Unilever developed many household products and brands. Other branding specialists are Henkel, Procter & Gamble, Nestlé and Pepsico.

BRAND DRIVEN INNOVATION

What is the purpose of the approach?

A brand is a holistic framework that combines the various qualities and contextual attributes that are required for radical, meaningful and sustainable innovation. By using Brand Driven Innovation, you can decompose the brand of an organisation. A brand perspective on innovation from the outside in helps you to understand that an organisation cannot please every customer and adopt every new technology. It makes it easier for you to determine which trends are relevant and which are not. Additionally, a brand perspective on innovation from the inside out helps you to understand that not everything the organisation does, knows, wants or is capable of is relevant for its customers.

When you take a Brand Driven Innovation approach, the brand has a process role and a content role. The process role suggests a number of activities for innovative change (how to do it), while the content role gives direction to that change (what to do).

Process description

The Brand Driven Innovation process consists of the following four stages.

STAGE 1. UNDERSTAND:

co-create the brand lens

You will understand the brand as the relationship between the organisation and its customers. Organisations have to demonstrate a clear understanding of the people they are doing business with (outside-in perspective) and they need to have a vision of their role in delivering value to their intended users (inside-out perspective). The creation of a shared understanding of these brand-based issues will form the brand lens.

Brand Driven Innovation supports innovation processes by combining three factors: the central focus of an organisation: vision, what the organisation wants to achieve: ambition, and its possibilities: resources and capabilities. The brand as an overarching concept helps you to combine user/client-centredness: outside-in thinking with organisation-centredness: inside-out thinking.

STAGE 2. FOCUS:

select opportunities

You will use the brand lens to make choices and focus your innovation efforts. The insights from the first stage are used to devise an innovation roadmap that pinpoints those domains of innovation that make sense, looking through both sides of the brand lens.

STAGE 3. DESIGN:

create new solutions

Based on the focus domain(s), you will design new solutions. This entails designing solutions that fulfil the brand's promise by creating value, such as solutions that fit both the organisation's brand vision and the customer's brand expectations.

STAGE 4. IMPLEMENT:

realise the new solution

You will focus on ensuring solutions that reach the market quickly and prepare staff to deliver value through the new solutions. Implementation requires touch-point orchestration. A touch point is any point of contact that the customer has with the organisation's new offering – see Customer Journey.

Tips & Concerns

- In Brand Driven Innovation the brand supports both the process and content of an innovation.
- When developing a brand you combine outside-in with inside-out thinking.
- In 'traditional' branding, marketing communication creates a brand promise. In Brand Driven Innovation, innovation and design *fulfil* this brand promise.
- Brands can be seen as lenses through which external influences become relevant for the organisation and internal influences become relevant for the customer.
- The four Brand Driven Innovation stages are cyclic and iterative and each consists of an internal-and an external-oriented part.

Limitations of the approach

- Brand Driven Innovation requires the organisation to have a brand that is defined and understood in a way that makes it suitable as a driver for innovation (brand usability).
- Secondly, it requires a market situation that provides latitude for this particular type of innovation (innovation potential). If both innovation potential and brand usability are high, BDI is your innovation strategy of choice.

REFERENCES & FURTHER READING: Manning, H. and Bodine, K., 2012. *Outside In: The Power of Putting Customers at the Center of Your Business.* New York: New Harvest. / Martin, R., 2007. *The Opposable Mind: How Successful Leaders Win Through Integrative Thinking.* Boston: Harvard Business School Press. / Roscam Abbing, E.*, 2010. *Brand Driven Innovation.* Lausanne : AvA Academia.

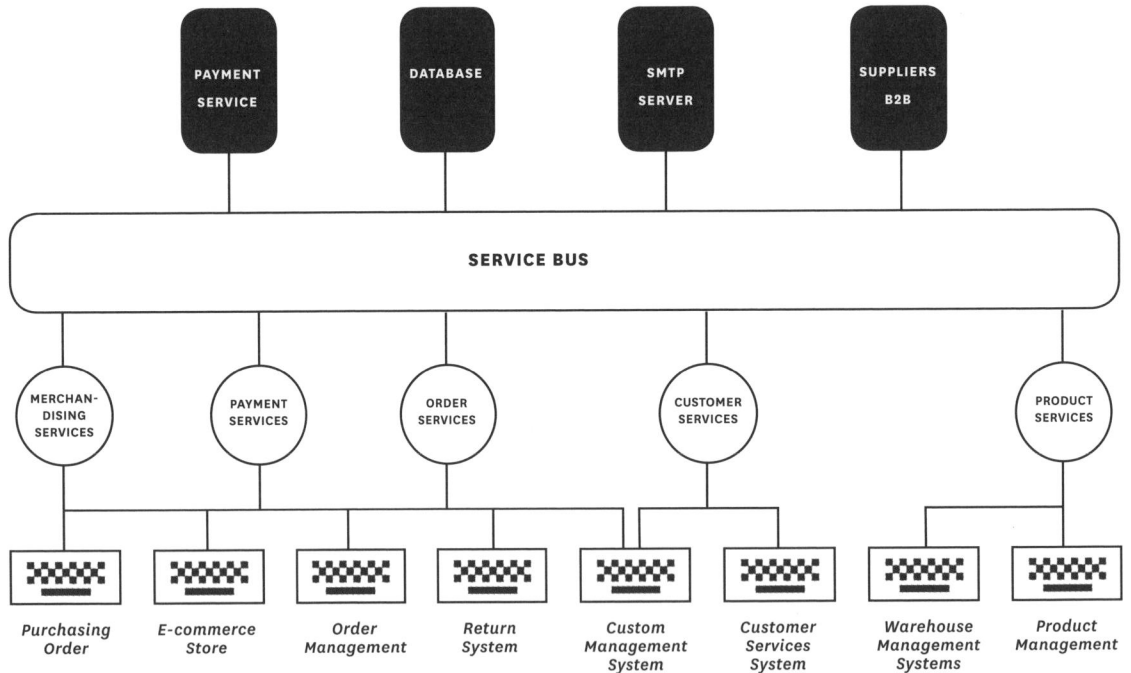

PAYMENT SERVICE	DATABASE	SMTP SERVER	SUPPLIERS B2B

SERVICE BUS

MERCHAN-DISING SERVICES	PAYMENT SERVICES	ORDER SERVICES	CUSTOMER SERVICES	PRODUCT SERVICES

Purchasing Order	*E-commerce Store*	*Order Management*	*Return System*	*Custom Management System*	*Customer Services System*	*Warehouse Management Systems*	*Product Management*

SERVICE DESIGN

Service Design stresses a long-term view. Under this perspective, the design process does not have to end with the sale of a mass-produced, physical object. It may involve designing longer-lasting interactions between provider and consumer, possibly supported with IT, intangible components and services provided by people.

What is the purpose of the perspective?

Service Design attempts to develop the entire system that provides a service to a user. Think of message apps on a smartphone, many of which are meaningless without an Internet connection to a central server or other users, and which start out with minimal functionality but are updated and extended every few weeks. Think of Greenwheels car sharing, which requires an end-to-end system for car maintenance, administration, billing, and providing access to vehicles.

Service Design builds on and integrates earlier design fields such as experience design, interaction design, product design, architectural design and transformation design. In order to understand services, you have to examine them over a longer period of time. Thus, the brand, which is seen as the promise of what the provider and client offer each other, is an especially important element, and business models are more complex than the classic 'cash and carry' of physical products.

The central focus of Service Design is the user experience – it is the end goal that ties all of the system components together. In Service Design, the active participation of users and other stakeholders is often regarded as essential for making sense of the complexities involved. Also, services are often 'grown' during the implementation phase, and although a physical product can be regarded as valuable when it is 'in a box', a service typically only exists during use. This blurs the boundaries between the conceptualisation, implementation and use phases.

Process description

Service Design projects often involve designers and experts from different specialities. Some design skills are more commonly valued in Service Design than in traditional design.

1. *Building a holistic view of the user's life*
   The user context of use, including the user's values, routines, skills and social relations, often play an important part. Many designers regard the users as important participants in the design process.

2. *Visualising the intangible*
   Use over time, multiple touch points and how the service fits into a user's other activities involve many intangible, often abstract and complex, elements to be understood and accounted for in design. This requires appropriate means of visualisation, for example, storyboarding, prototyping, storytelling and role-playing.

3. *Parallel, interacting timelines and roles*
   Services are often conceived as sequences of interactions over time ('touch points').

Tips & Concerns

· Service Design has rapidly developed its own jargon, with terms such as 'customer journey' (a timeline presentation as in the figure), 'front end' (what the user sees), 'back end' (what happens behind the screens) and 'service blueprint' (a graphic way of describing a concept design).

· The final deliverables of Service Design can include not only products, but also interiors, training of service delivery staff, software and more complex business models. The intangible components often require different design skills than the tangible ones. Therefore, Service Design is often teamwork involving a lot of cross-disciplinary communication.

· Iteration is especially important in Service Design. Services often evolve after implementation.

Limitations of the perspective

· Because Service Design is a rather generic perspective, it builds on many other types of design, and does not have a single clear set of methods (or terms) yet.

REFERENCES & FURTHER READING: Kimbell, L., 2011. *Designing for Service as One Way of Designing Services*. International Journal of Design, 5(2), pp. 41–52. / Sleeswijk Visser, F.*, 2013. **Service Design by Industrial Designers**. Delft University of Technology. Obtainable through http://lulu.com. / Stickdorn, M. and Schneider, J., 2011. *This Is Service Design Thinking: Basics–Tools–Cases*. Amsterdam: BIS Publishers.

American office furniture manufacturer Herman Miller developed the Mirra® Chair, which is Cradle to Cradle Certified 'Silver'.
The materials used are free of toxins and 97% recyclable. Each connection between different materials can be taken apart by one person in less than 15 seconds. For its production, the company built a new factory that runs on renewable energy and like the chair itself meets the Cradle to Cradle motto 'waste equals food'.

CRADLE-TO-CRADLE

What is the purpose of the approach?
The Cradle-to-Cradle approach has been applied in the (re)design of a variety of products ranging from carpeting, vacuum cleaners and furniture to buildings. It offers an alternative to eco-efficiency approaches that aim to do 'more with less' in order to minimise environmental damage. Cradle-to-Cradle challenges the belief that products by definition have a damaging impact on their environment. By learning from nature, the strategy provides an approach for designing high-quality products that are truly sustainable.

You can apply Cradle-to-Cradle throughout a design project, especially during the strategic, idea and concept development phase. It helps you in coming up with a vision for your product development strategy, facilitating the development of eco-effective product concepts combining economic and environmental benefits. The approach provides a number of design principles and tools for doing so.

Process description
The Cradle-to-Cradle approach is based on three guiding principles:

· Waste equals food – Eliminate the concept of waste by designing products in such a way that used products can be turned into valuable resources for new products.
· Use current solar income – Apply renewable energy in all processes.
· Celebrate diversity – Gear products towards user needs (not one-size-fits-all), make use of local resources and support biodiversity.

Cradle-to-Cradle is a sustainable design approach. Based on nature-inspired concepts and design principles, this strategy challenges you to develop high-quality products that are 'eco-effective' instead of eco-efficient. This means that the approach promotes the development of truly sustainable products, as opposed to products that merely have a reduced environmental impact.

Several steps are articulated and several tools are available for developing products according to the Cradle-to-Cradle principles. The most important phases are:

PHASE 1
When initiating or planning a project, state your positive quality intentions and ambitions. Imagine a perfect world, and think what your product/process could do for the customer. Additionally, answer this question: what other functions can the product perform to improve the system in which it is used? The three principles provide inspiration for stating ambitions, and the 'C2C Roadmap tool' helps you to set your development strategy (see references).

PHASE 2
For the idea phase, several tools are available. 'Defining use in biological or technical cycles' is a powerful tool for determining whether to use biodegradable materials or technical materials that can be recycled in continuous loops of use (see references).

PHASE 3
In the concept development phase, the three principles and C2C certification criteria can help you to assess the different concepts you develop.

Tips & Concerns
· Cradle-to-Cradle is criticised for a lack of attention to energy consumption. Be careful not to focus only on the 'waste=food' principle. Using a quick scan, such as the Fast Track LCA, to assess your concepts can help you to discover unwanted environmental effects and to choose between specific design alternatives.
· Some companies use the Cradle-to-Cradle certification criteria to develop 'C2C products'. However, these criteria are not intended as design tools, and applying them as such may lead to greenwashing.

Limitations of the approach
· The Cradle-to-Cradle approach is more difficult to apply for complex products, such as fully recycling printed circuit boards.
· The approach can still be applied, as with vacuum cleaners, but a fully Cradle-to-Cradle solution for such products is not feasible in the short term.

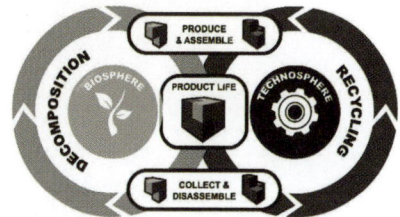

REFERENCES & FURTHER READING: Bakker, C. A., Wever, R., Teoh, Ch. and De Clercq, S.*, 2009. *Designing cradle-to-cradle products: a reality check.* International Journal of Sustainable Engineering, 9 November, 3(1), pp. 2-8. / Braungart, M. and McDonough, W., 2002. *Cradle to Cradle - Remaking the way we make things.* New York: North Point Press. / McDonough, W., Braungart, M., Anastas, P. and Zimmerman, J., 2003. *Applying the Principles of Green Engineering to Cradle-to-Cradle Design.* Environmental Science & Technology, 1 December, 37(23), pp. 434A-441A.

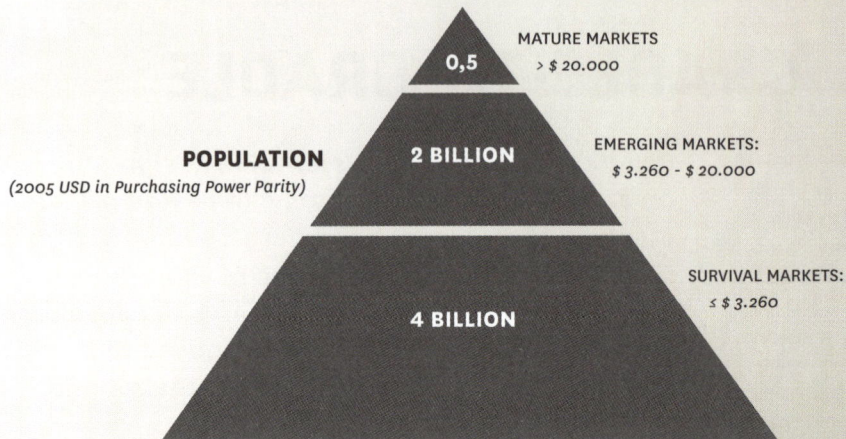

MATURE MARKETS
> $ 20.000

POPULATION
(2005 USD in Purchasing Power Parity)

0,5

2 BILLION

EMERGING MARKETS:
$ 3.260 - $ 20.000

4 BILLION

SURVIVAL MARKETS:
≤ $ 3.260

THE WORLD ECONOMIC PYRAMID: INDIVIDUAL ANNUAL INCOME

Most companies focus on mature and emerging markets, while the huge market of 4 billion people living on less than $ 53,26 a year goes largely unlapped. (source: World Resources Institute)

Many children have no access to computers or the Internet because their families cannot afford it. With the One Laptop Per Child (OLPC) initiative, the Massachusetts Institute of Technology (MIT) developed a rugged and low-cost laptop for low-income families. The aim was to make a '100-dollar laptop'. Eventually the 'XO laptop' was priced at around 200 dollars. It is Linux-based and has a handle to charge the battery by human power, in case there is no power supply. Production and distribution started in 2007.

BASE OF THE PYRAMID (BOP) & EMERGING MARKETS

What is the purpose of the perspective?
Most products are designed for the top of the world's economic pyramid (ToP). These products are unsuitable for the majority of the world's population, who belong to the base of the economic pyramid (BoP). ToP products are typically too expensive, unavailable to the BoP, and are not adapted to local possibilities. Most designers are not familiar with the socioeconomic context of the BoP population. Therefore, contextual research is needed. These methods need to be adapted to local conditions because current design methods do not always work as intended. Another challenge in a BoP design project is to cope with multiple stakeholders: often, such projects involve not only a company, but also parties such as governmental and non-governmental organisations, aid foundations and knowledge institutes with different backgrounds and interests.

The intended users in BoP projects are poor and vulnerable, which raises the additional question of how to cope with sustainability issues. In the case of emerging economies, there is a clear need for knowledge about sustainability and new product innovation, but prior knowledge and resources are limited.

Process description
When designing for a BoP context and emerging markets, extra attention should be paid to the following principles:
- Affordability: The challenge for you as a designer is to propose an affordable product. There are several strategies to make products cheap, but overall a holistic approach is needed, taking into account not only the production costs of a single product, but also the whole system that can benefit from the new product, including entrepreneurs.

Designing for Base of the Pyramid means designing products and product service systems for the world's less fortunate people. Often these people live in nations with emerging markets characterised by rapidly growing production and consumption.

- Accessibility: The products should be accessible to their intended users, who often live in areas with poor infrastructure.
- Availability: If the products are manufactured locally, the availability of materials and skills should be taken into account.
- Reliability: The products should be reliable and easily maintained and repaired locally to avoid dependency on outsiders.
- Sustainability: Solutions need to be sustainable, not harming the often vulnerable living environments of poor people.
- Acceptability: You must have a thorough understanding of the intended users in terms of their own opportunities and preferences, both as part of a cultural group and in general as universal human beings.
- All these issues lead to an integrated, holistic and multi-disciplinary design approach that stimulates local and international entrepreneurship.

Tips & Concerns
- Companies producing for Western markets often have limited insights into requirements related to, for example, product quality, consumer preferences and safety.

- Designers, being 'outsiders', should do their homework first. They need to research the cultural background and current context of their stakeholders, the 'insiders', more extensively than they are used to.
- When you are designing for the BoP, you need more time. Additional aspects that should be taken into account include: building trust, understanding otherness, checking biases, coping with poor infrastructure as well as travelling and communicating.
- Contextual research methods should be adapted to the local context.
- Your contribution to new product development will not automatically be adopted locally. Therefore, local involvement and learning is key.

Limitations of the perspective
- You can only attain a good understanding of the local situation by experiencing the local context, not from desktop research.
- The success of a product/service depends on many factors. As a designer, you cannot control all of them. You need plenty of perseverance, motivation, tolerance for frustration and the conviction that your contribution is worthwhile.

REFERENCES & FURTHER READING: Crul, M.R.M. and Diehl, J.C.* 2006. *Design for Sustainability: A Practical Approach for Developing Economies.* Paris: UNEP. / Jansen, G.J. and Crul, M.R.M.*, 2012. *Sustainable Product Innovation: A Do-it-yourself Toolkit for SMEs in Emerging Economies.* Delft: Delft University of Technology. / Kandachar, P.H., De Jongh, I. and Diehl, J.C.*, 2009. *Designing for Emerging Markets-Design of Products and Services.* Delft: Delft University of Technology. / Prahalad, C.K., 2005. *The Fortune at the Bottom of the Pyramid; eradicating poverty through profits.* Pennsylvania: Wharton School Publishing. / Van Boeijen, A.G.C.*, 2011. *How can Western designers use Contextmapping techniques in non-Western situations?* Proceedings Engineering and Product Design Education conference, 8-9 September.

DISCOVER

This section contains methods that can help you to discover insights and create understanding while designing.

Christo with 'Wrapped Car (Volkswagen), 1963. By wrapping objects, buildings and landscapes, Christo intended to create beauty and the joy of seeing familiar objects and landscapes in a new way – 'revelation through concealment', as an art critic wrote. Other well-known wrapping projects are the Surrounded Islands in Florida, the Reichstag Building in Berlin and Pont Neuf in Paris. He and his wife Jeanne-Claude funded projects by selling his preliminary design drawings. Photo: Charles Wilp.

CONTEXTMAPPING

Contextmapping is a user-centred design approach that involves the user as the 'expert on his or her experience'. By providing the user with generative tools, he or she can express personal experiences in which a product or a service plays a role.

When can the method be used?

Using Contextmapping is most advantageous when a project is in the pre-concept stage, where there is still a lot of latitude for finding new opportunities. Apart from insights for the target project, Contextmapping can yield a diverse range of outcomes, including personas, strategies for innovation, new views on market segmentation and original insights for other innovation projects.

Contextmapping uses generative tools in order to let the users express their experiences in a playful way and at the same time become more aware of their experiences. They are asked to map the context in which they use the product or service. This enables them to express their goals, motivations, meanings, latent needs and practical matters.

A Contextmapping study helps you to understand the users' perspectives and to translate the users' experiences into a desirable design solution.

How to use the method?

Before starting your own Contextmapping session, it is recommended that you first join one as a participant to see what it really means and involves. When you carry out your own session, this will enable you to better empathise with the participants. Also make sure that you plan your Contextmapping session far in advance. Otherwise, it might be difficult to find participants, a date and a space and to prepare your generative tools.

Possible procedure

Preparation:
STEP 1
Define your topic and plan your activities.

STEP 2
Capture your preconceptions in a mind map.
STEP 3
Conduct preliminary research.
STEP 4
Some time before the session, provide the participants with homework activities to sensitise them to the topic and session. This helps them to observe their own lives and reflect on their experiences around your topic. This can be done with the Cultural Probes method.

During the session:
STEP 5
Record the sessions on video or audio.
STEP 6
Do a number of exercises. It is also possible to build a conversation based on stimuli materials.
STEP 7
Ask questions like "how do you feel about it?" and "what does it mean to you?"
STEP 8
Write down your impressions immediately after the session.

Analysis:
STEP 9
After the session, analyse the outcomes to find patterns and possible directions for product design. To this end, select quotes from the transcript and then interpret and organise them. Typically, you will create a rich visual environment of interpretations and categories to analyse.

Communication:
STEP 10
Outcomes need to be communicated to those members of your team who did not attend the session and to other stakeholders of your project.
STEP 11
Good communication of results is necessary because it often supports idea generation, concept development and further product or service development. Your participants are often highly motivated to look at the results again and build on the knowledge they generated, even many weeks after the session.

Tips & Concerns

· The term 'context' is defined as the situation in which a product or service is used. All aspects that influence the experience of product use are considered valuable. These can be social, cultural or physical aspects as well as the internal state of the users – feelings, state of mind and more.
· The term 'contextmap' indicates that the acquired information should work as a guiding map for the design team. It helps the designers find their way, structure their insights, recognise barriers and opportunities. The map is regarded as a source of inspiration, not validation.

REFERENCES & FURTHER READING: Sanders, E.B.N. and Stappers, P.J.*, 2012. *Convivial Toolbox: Generative research for the front end of design.* Amsterdam: BIS. / Sleeswijk Visser, F., Stappers, P.J., Van der Lugt, R. and Sanders, E.B.N.*, 2005. *Contextmapping: Experience from Practice.* CoDesign, 29 March, 1(2), pp. 119-149 / Stappers, P.J.*, 2012. *Teaching principles of qualitative analysis to industrial design engineers.* International conference on engineering and product design education, 6-7 September.

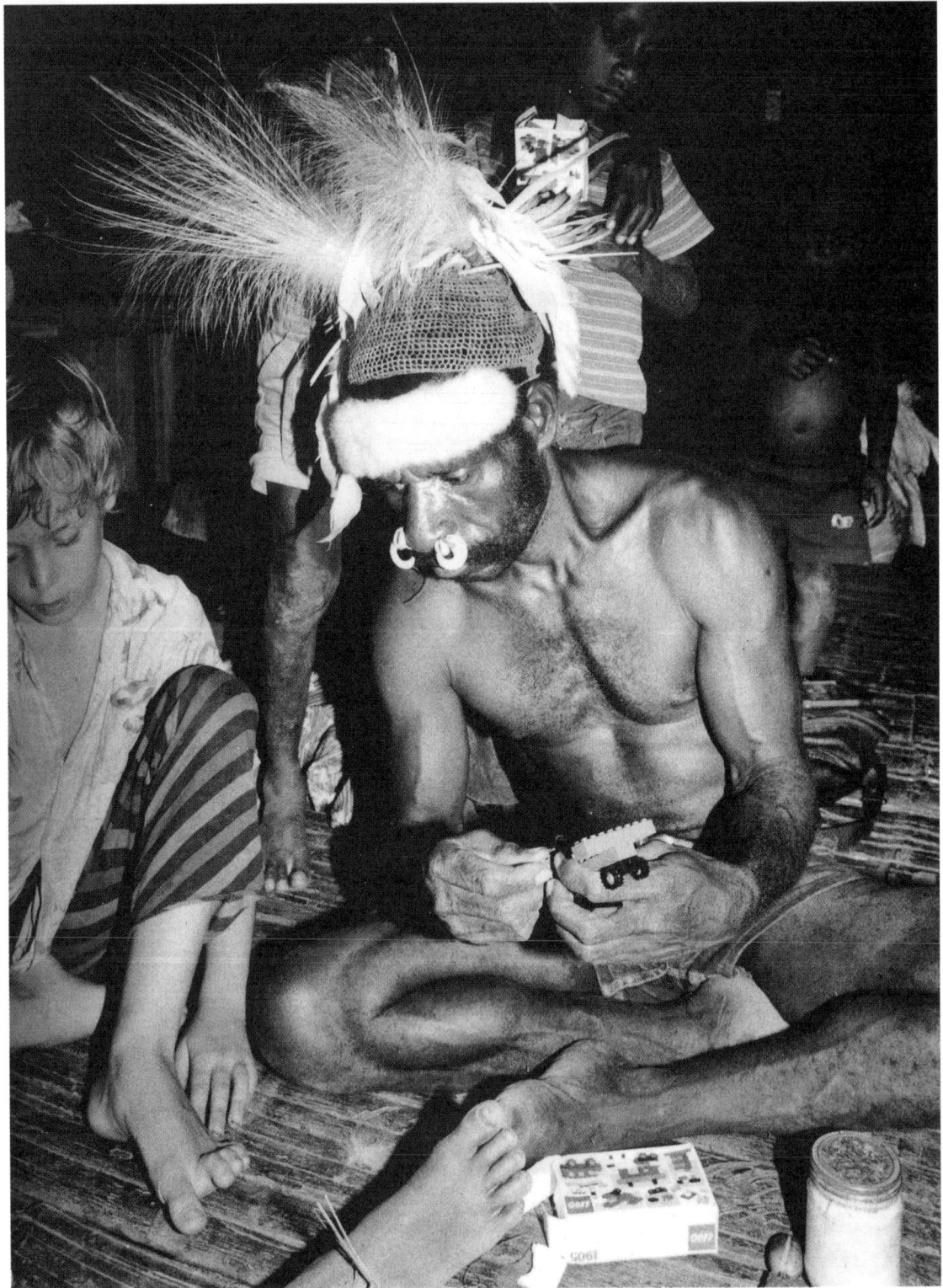

The LEGO brick crosses cultural and language borders with ease. In the photo, a New Guinean father in a remote settlement on the April Rivers tries his hand at building with a set brought by Danish travellers. The man and his children ignored the pictures on the box and designed their own towers and animal figures on wheels. From Henry Wiencek: The World of LEGO Toys, 1987.

CULTURAL PROBES

Cultural Probes is a technique for learning about intended users in a purely inspirational way based on their self-documentation. Intended users are provided with generative packages – that is, probes – which help them to record daily life experiences.

When can the method be used?

Cultural Probes can be used in the pre-concept stage, when there is still a lot of latitude for generating design opportunities. Probes help you to access environments that are difficult to observe directly and to capture the real 'felt life' of your intended users. Probes are 'packages sent into space'. They help you to collect material from a space that you do not know. You do not have any clue about what will come back, and therefore you will study the material with curiosity. This metaphor is essential for the mindset when using probes: You need to be surprised and inspired by the users' self-documentation. You are looking for new insights into their cultural context. For that reason, the technique is called *Cultural* Probes.

The results of a Cultural Probe study help you and your team to keep an open mind, inspired by what the filled in probe packages bring back.

How to use the method?

The development of a Cultural Probe study starts with a creative session with your design team in order to determine what you want to learn about the intended users. A Cultural Probe package can consist of various elements, such as diaries, postcards and audiovisual recording devices – in fact, anything that is playful and encourages the users to tell stories or to express their experiences visually. Typically the probe packages can be sent out to just a few users or up to about 30 people. There is no need to have direct contact with the users, since the material guides the interpretation and inspiration of the designers.

Small variants of probes are often used in sensitising packages for Contextmapping sessions.

Possible procedure

STEP 1
Organise a creative session with your team members to set your goal.
STEP 2
Design the probes.
STEP 3
Test the probes with an intended user and adjust the design.
STEP 4
Send the probe packages to your selected intended users, with a clear explanation about your expectations. Since the probe works on its own and there is no direct contact between designers and users, the probe assignments and materials should be very inviting, inspiring the recipients to use them on their own.
STEP 5
If needed, send a reminder for replies or collect the results yourself.
STEP 6
Study the results together with your team members and use the outcomes in a follow-up session, such as a generative session – see Contextmapping.

Limitations of the method

· Since there is no direct contact between designers and intended users, Cultural Probes will not give you a deep understanding of your intended users. Insights are meant to trigger possibilities, not to validate results. For example, the probe may yield insights about someone's daily grooming experiences, but can neither explain the reasons behind their experiences nor say something about their uniqueness or value.
· Cultural Probes are not suitable if you are looking for answers to specific questions.
· Cultural Probes require an open mindset from the entire design team. Otherwise, the material will not be understood and some team members will not be satisfied with the results.

Tips & Concerns

· Make the probes attractive.
· Give the probes a somewhat unfinished appearance; otherwise participants may be scared to use them.
· Personalise the probes for the participants, for example by adding their photo on the front cover.
· Make the assignments fun and interesting to complete.
· Clearly explain the goals.
· Support improvisation.
· Do a pilot test to ensure that your probes will elicit the preferred documentation.

REFERENCES & FURTHER READING: Gaver, W.W., Boucher, A., Pennington, S. and Walker, B., 2004. *Cultural probes and the value of uncertainty.* Interactions, September-October, 11(5), pp. 53-56. / Gaver, W.W., Dunne, T. and Pacenti, E., 1999. *Design: Cultural Probes.* Interactions, January-February, 6(1), pp. 21-29. / Mattelmaki, T., 2005. *Applying Probes - from inspirational notes to collaborative insights.* CoDesign: International Journal of CoCreation in Design and Arts, 1(2), pp. 83-102. / Mattelmaki, T., 2006. *Design Probes.* Helsinki: University of Art and Design Helsinki.

Collage of photobooths mounted on cardboard, gelatin silver prints, 455 x 585 mm (detail), 1972 Franco Vaccari

USER OBSERVATIONS

User Observation helps you to study what your intended users do in a specific situation. Observations enable you to understand phenomena, influential variables or other elementary interrelations in 'real life'.

When can the method be used?

Depending on the discipline there may be different hypotheses and research questions to be answered, and thus very different data to be assessed and analysed. Human Sciences mainly focus on the behaviour of people and their interactions with the social and technical environment. Using well-defined indicators, you can describe, analyse and explain the relations between observable and hidden variables.

Observations are helpful whenever you have no or hardly any understanding of phenomena, influential variables or other elementary interrelations, or want to see what will happen in 'real life'. Different observations will confront you with both expected and unexpected situations. When exploring the design problem, it is helpful to articulate the aspects that influence the interactions. Observing people in their daily routines leads to a better understanding of what makes a good product or service experience. Watching people interacting with your prototypes will help you to improve your design. You will gain a better understanding of your design problem and how and why concepts work effectively – and also rich illustrations to help you communicate your design decisions to various stakeholders.

How to use the method?

If you want to observe people in their natural setting without intervening, you can do this by acting as 'a fly on the wall' or by observing and asking questions. For subtler research, you observe how people react to situations in real practice or in a lab situation. Video is the preferred means of documenting observation results, but many other methods are also available, such as photos and taking notes. As with

any other research method, it is very useful to add further data sources to triangulate the analysis and interpretation of the data; for example, you may combine observations with interviews to get a better understanding of what was going through people's minds. For analyses all data are grouped in combinations of pictures, remarks and quotes and qualitatively analysed.

Possible procedure

For User Observation to understand usability aspects of your design:

STEP 1
Determine what, who and where you want to observe – the whole situation.
STEP 2
Define criteria for the observation – duration, money, main design criteria.
STEP 3
Select and invite participants.
STEP 4
Prepare the observation sessions – check whether video/photography is allowed; make an observation form, including a checklist of everything you want to observe and questions for interviews; and do a pilot observation.
STEP 5
Execute the observations.
STEP 6
Analyse your data and transcribe the video results.
STEP 7
Communicate and discuss your findings with your stakeholders.

Limitations of the method

When people know that they are being observed, they might behave differently than they would normally. When they do not know, ethical guidelines need to be taken into consideration.

Tips & Concerns

· Always carry out a pilot.
· Make sure that the stimuli, such as models and prototypes, are suitable for the observations and ready in time.
· Ask those you wish to observe for their permission if you want to disclose the observations, or be sure to make them anonymous.
· Think about inter-rater reliability. It is easier to plan this at the beginning of a study rather than later.
· Think of ways to operationalise the data.
· Go through your notes and add impressions as soon as possible after each observation.
· Engage stakeholders by doing at least part of the analyses together. However, be aware that they might take only one or two impressions as a reference.
· The hardest part of observing is to keep your mind open. Do not look for things you already know. Instead, be prepared for the unexpected. For this reason, video is preferred; though it is time-consuming, it provides you with rich illustrations and latitude for multiple observations.

REFERENCES & FURTHER READING: Abrams, B., 2000. *The observational research handbook: Understanding how consumers live with your product.* Lincolnwood, Ill: NTC business Books. / Daams, B.*, 2011. *Product-ergonomie, ontwerpen voor nut, gebruik en beleving.* Undesigning. / Stempfle, J. and Badke-Schaub, P.,* 2002. *Thinking in design teams - an analysis of team communication.* Design Studies, September, 23(5), pp. 473-496.

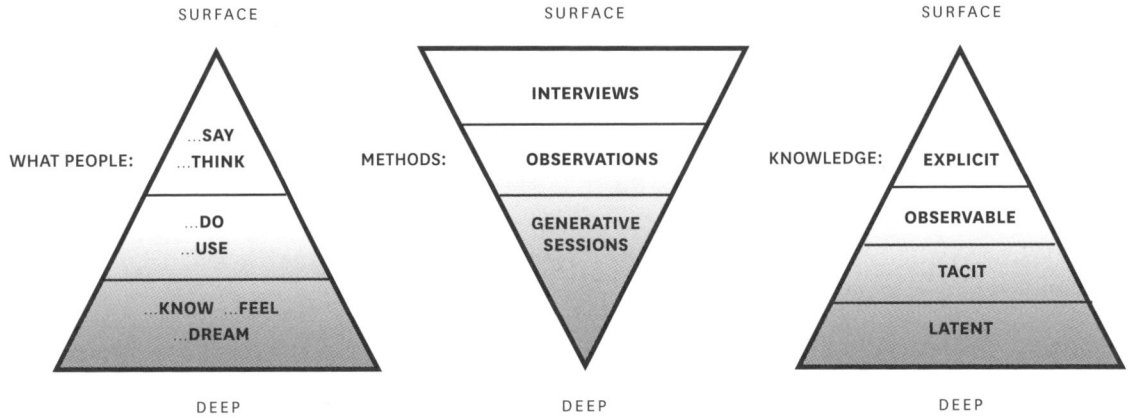

WHAT PEOPLE:	SURFACE	METHODS:	SURFACE	KNOWLEDGE:	SURFACE
	...SAY ...THINK		INTERVIEWS		EXPLICIT
	...DO ...USE		OBSERVATIONS		OBSERVABLE
	...KNOW ...FEEL ...DREAM		GENERATIVE SESSIONS		TACIT
					LATENT
	DEEP		DEEP		DEEP

After Sleeswijk Visser et al., 2005

Getting to know the customer: before he starts, the barber asks his client about his hairstyle wishes. During the creation of the haircut (the barber's product), some superficial and some in-depth issues are discussed via the mirror. Finally he checks if the end result is satisfactory.

INTERVIEWS

Interviews are face-to-face consultations that can be useful for understanding consumer perceptions, opinions, motivation and behaviour concerning products or services, or to gather information from experts in the field.

When can the method be used?

Interviews provide insights and thus enlarge your understanding of a particular phenomenon, a specific context, a problem, certain common practices, extreme and extraordinary situations, consumer preferences, and more.

They can be used in several phases of the new product development process and for different purposes. In a preliminary phase, they can help you to obtain contextual information about product use and opinions about existing products, or to gain expert input about issues. Interviews can also be used during concept testing of products or services in order to collect detailed consumer feedback. This helps you when selecting concepts or improving them. Compared to the focus group method, interviews take more time but provide you with deeper insight, because you can probe further into the answers given by the interviewee.

Interviews are most useful for projects in which the products or services under development are not completely new to consumers. For really new products or services, other methods, such as Contextmapping and Observations, are more appropriate.

How to use the method?

Before an interview, make a topic guide to ensure that you will cover all the relevant issues. This guide can be very structured, such as a questionnaire, or un- or semi-structured, with the questions depending on the answers given. It is recommended to do a pilot interview and to practice first. The general guideline for the number of interviews is to stop when you feel that an additional interview will not yield new information. Research shows that for the assessment of consumer needs, 10 to 15 interviews will reveal about 80% of the needs.

Interviews can be combined with collages or sensitising tasks such as keeping a short diary, as in Contextmapping.

Possible procedure

STEP 1
Make an interview guide, including a list of topics, based on your research questions. Test this guide in a pilot interview.

STEP 2
Invite the right interviewees. Depending on your objective you may interview three to eight people.

STEP 3
Carry out the interviews. An interview typically takes about one hour and is usually voice recorded.

STEP 4
Either make transcripts of what was said or make summarising notes.

STEP 5
Analyse your transcripts and draw conclusions.

Limitations of the method

· Your interviewees can respond only to what they know consciously. Latent or tacit knowledge can be gained by observation or by using generative techniques, such as in Contextmapping, making use of images and other stimuli to evoke stories.
· The quality of the result depends on your own skills as an interviewer.
· Your interview results are qualitative and from a limited number of respondents. To collect quantitative results from a large number of respondents, use questionnaires.

Tips & Concerns

· Perform the interview in a relaxed atmosphere without distractions and provide refreshments.
· Start with general topics such as product usage and experience, and not, for example, by presenting new concepts. In this way you sensitise your interviewees to the context.
· Distribute your interview time among your topics in advance to ensure that you will have enough time left for your final topics, which are often the most important ones.
· When using visuals, such as drawings of your concepts, the quality of the visuals is crucial. First check if your interviewees understand what you are asking from them and if they have questions.

REFERENCES & FURTHER READING: Byrne, M., 2001. *Interviewing as a data collection method.* AORN Journal, Augustus, 74(2), pp. 233-235. Creusen, M.E.H., Hultink, E.J. and Eling, K.*, 2013. *Choice of consumer research methods in the front end of new product development.* International Journal of Market Research, January, 55(1), pp. 81-104. / Griffin, A., 2005. *Obtaining customer needs for product development.* In K.B. Kahn, S.E. Kay, R.J. Slotegraaf, S. Uban (eds.), *The PDMA Handbook of New Product Development.* pp. 211-227. Hoboken, NJ: John Wiley & Sons, Inc. / Rubin, H. and Rubin I., 2005. Qualitative interviewing, *the art of hearing data.* Sage, CA: Thousand Oaks. / Sleeswijk Visser, F., Stappers, P.J., van der Lugt, R., & Sanders, E.B.N. (2005). *Contextmapping: experiences from practice. CoDesign:* International Journal of CoCreation in Design and the Arts, 1(2), 119-149.

Visitors to a theatrical performance in Copenhagen were asked to give their opinion after the show by tearing this flyer to indicate their answer. Designed by Alessia Cadamuro

QUESTIONNAIRES

Questionnaires are research tools consisting of a series of questions and other prompts intended for gathering information from respondents.

When can the method be used?

Questionnaires can be used in several phases of the design process. In a preliminary phase they can be useful for gaining information about the target group, product use and opinions on existing products. Questionnaires are also used for concept testing of products or services. This helps the designer in choosing one out of several concepts and/or assessing consumer acceptance of the concepts.

Quantitative research methods such as Questionnaires can be used in order to gain insight into the frequency with which certain perceptions/opinions/behaviours occur and into the level of interest of consumers in certain product or service concepts. Also, they enable you to determine the most interesting target group for the product or service.

Questionnaires can be administered face-to-face or by telephone, or be filled in by the respondents themselves either on paper or via the Internet.

How to use the method?

Questions in the Questionnaire should follow from your research questions. Asking useful questions is more difficult than it seems, and the quality of the Questionnaire determines the usefulness of the outcomes. It is recommended to read up on Questionnaire construction before using this method.
The end result depends on the goal of the research. Examples are: insight into the frequency of certain opinions or behaviours, the frequency of the perceived advantages and disadvantages of existing solutions, or the occurrence of certain needs. Such insights provide you with

knowledge about the target group and help you to determine what to focus on in the development and design of a solution.

Possible procedure

STEP 1
Based on your research questions, determine the topics you want to address.
STEP 2
Choose the form of response per question, for example, closed, open or categorical.
STEP 3
Formulate the questions.
STEP 4
Determine the question order, group similar questions and make a clear layout.
STEP 5
Pre-test and improve the Questionnaire.
STEP 6
Invite the right respondents depending on the topic: a random sample or selected respondents, for example, those who are knowledgeable about the topic and vary in age and gender.
STEP 7
Present the results by reporting percentages for answer options or using statistics to report mean results and test relationships between variables/questions.

Limitations of the method

· Subconscious or more emotional information cannot be gathered with Questionnaires.
· The quality of the results strongly depends on the quality of the Questionnaire. Longer Questionnaires lead to fewer respondents.

· Designers often criticise Questionnaire results for being too abstract. For example, qualitative methods are better suited for eliciting empathy and deep insights. But for determining whether large groups share certain values and needs, quantitative data are needed.

Tips & Concerns

· Ask yourself whether the Questionnaire will answer all your research questions and whether all of its questions are really necessary.
· You can use Questionnaires to collect qualitative data as well. Sometimes, limited numbers of respondents in combination with deep and open questions result in more useful data than large numbers of respondents.
· Questionnaires are often boring to fill in, making it difficult to get enough responses. Make your research more fun by incorporating visuals, for example; online versions provide possibilities for doing so.
· When testing one or more concepts with consumers, the presentation of these concepts is crucial. The concepts should be clear. Test this before distributing the Questionnaire – see Product Concept Evaluation.

REFERENCES & FURTHER READING: Creusen, M.E.H., Hultink, E.J. and Eling, K.*, 2013. *Choice of consumer research methods in the front end of new product development.* International Journal of Market Research, January, 55(1), pp. 81-104. / Lietz, P., 2010. *Research into questionnaire design - A summary of the literature.* International Journal of Market Research, 1 September, 52(2), pp. 249-272. / McDaniel Jr. C. and Gates, R., 2001. *Primary Data Collection: Survey Research.* In Marketing Research Essentials. pp. 170-208. Cincinnati, Ohio: South-Western College Publishing. / McDaniel, C. Jr. and Gates, R., 2001. *Questionnaire Design. In Marketing Research Essentials.* pp. 287-324. Cincinnati, Ohio: South-Western College Publishing.

Photographer Ari Versluis and profiler Ellie Uyttenbroek systematically document what they call 'Exactitudes': by selecting subjects in the street and registering them in an identical framework and with similar poses, they provide an almost scientific, anthropological record of people's attempts to distinguish themselves from others by assuming a group identity.

FOCUS GROUPS

A Focus Group is a group in which several topics concerning a specific product or issue are discussed. Focus Groups often consist of people from the target group of the product or service that is being developed.

When can the method be used?

Focus Groups are used in several phases of the development process – in the preliminary phase in order to gain contextual information about product use and opinions about existing products, in the idea generation phase, and when testing product or service concepts. A Focus Group can be used to choose one out of several concepts or to gather recommendations for further development. Focus Groups provide a quick overview of consumers' opinions about a subject and insights into the opinions and needs of the target group. Part of its value lies in the unexpected findings that can come from a free-flowing discussion in the group. When deeper and more individual information is needed, interviews should be used – see Interviews.

How to use the method?

At least three Focus Group sessions should be conducted so that outcomes can be generalised to some extent. A Focus Group consists of 6-8 participants, a moderator and someone who is in charge of collecting the data. The moderator has a vital role, so experience in moderating is very helpful. Perform a pilot Focus Group, so that you can improve your list of topics. A Focus Group can be combined with making collages or sensitising tasks such as keeping a short diary – see Context Mapping. Online Focus Group sessions are possible as well. The end result depends on the goals of the sessions – for instance, insights into consumer needs within the product area, ideas for new products, or insights into consumer acceptance and perceived (dis)advantages of certain product/service concepts.

Possible procedure

STEP 1
Make a list of topics you want to address (topic guide), containing broad issues or specific questions.
STEP 2
Test the topic guide in a pilot Focus Group. Make changes if necessary.
STEP 3
Invite the respondents, people from your target group(s).
STEP 4
Perform the Focus Groups. A session typically takes one and a half to two hours and is usually recorded for transcription and analysis.
STEP 5
Analyse and report the findings by indicating the main opinions and the range in opinions for each topic/issue.

Limitations of the method

· If participants do not have experience with the product they are confronted with, Focus Group sessions are less suitable.
· Group processes might influence the results. For example, a dominant person might push his or her opinion on the other participants. That is why the quality of the results depends on the quality of the moderator.

· A session has a small number of participants. If you want to know to what extent people share the same opinions, you should perform quantitative research, such as by using questionnaires.

Tips & Concerns

· Start with general topics, for example product usage and experience, so that participants get into the right context before asking opinions or presenting new concepts.
· When testing one or more concepts with consumers, the presentation of these concepts is crucial.
· The concepts should be clear, so start by asking participants whether they have questions before asking about their reactions.
· Carefully plan how much time to allocate to each topic in order to avoid having to rush through the topics at the end of the session, which are often the most important ones.
· In your report, illustrate the findings with verbatim quotes from the participants – this makes the outcomes engaging.

REFERENCES & FURTHER READING: Bruseberga, A. and McDonagh-Philp, D., 2001. *Focus groups to support the industrial/product designer: a review based on current literature and designers' feedback'.* Applied Ergonomics, 1 Augustus, 33(1), pp. 27-38. / Creusen, M.E.H., Hultink, E.J. and Eling, K.*, 2013. *Choice of consumer research methods in the front end of new product development.* International Journal of Market Research, January, 55(1), pp. 81-104. / Malhotra, N.K. and Birks, D.F., 2000. *Marketing Research: An Applied Approach.* Upper Saddle River, NJ: Pearson Education Ltd.

INTERNAL DISCUSSION
FOUND VIA GOOGLE
ONLINE FORM SUBMITTED
CLIENT MEETING (SALES)
SEQUENCE CHECKED
SAMPLES SUBMITTED
DATA SEND
ANALYSIS

INITIAL CONTACT SALES
TELECON (SALES & TECHNICAL)
CLIENT CONTACT KEEPING INFORMED OF PROCESS (SALES)

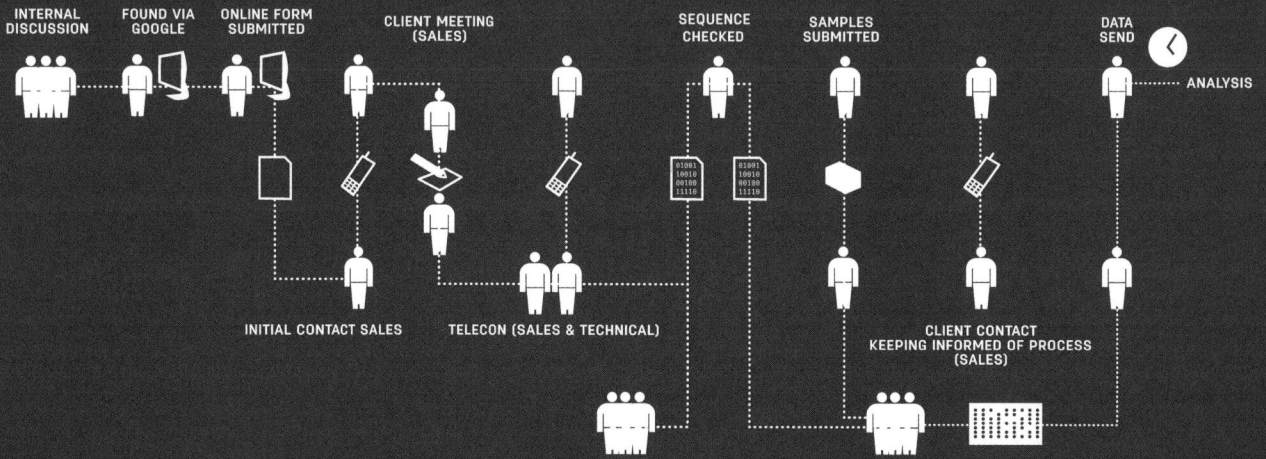

| PRE ENGAGEMENT | COMMERCIAL | CONSULTATION | INITIATION | COORDINATION | COMPLETION |

CUSTOMER JOURNEY

Customer Journey Mapping helps you to gain insight into all the stages a customer goes through while experiencing the use of a product or service. It covers the emotions, goals, interactions and barriers customers experience at each stage.

When can the method be used?

Customer Journey Mapping can be used during the whole project. You start your project by researching the customer and experience, which will lead to your Customer Journey Map; a graphic representation of the stages your customer goes through. During the following phases of your project a Customer Journey is a great way to find out what knowledge you lack. Be sure to acquire that knowledge and add it to the journey later on in the project. Also use it to focus your design efforts and to map the effect of design improvements.

How to use the method?

With Customer Journey Mapping you gain a deep understanding of the process that users go through when using products or services to achieve their aims. A common pitfall for designers is that they design touch points or features that in themselves may function properly, but which do not work in synergy with the product or service as a whole and thus do not help customers to reach their aims in a satisfactory manner. The method helps you to avoid designing isolated 'touch points' or product features that lead to incoherent user experiences. When using the most complex products and services, customers have to take several steps across channels or devices, in a certain time span and with several touch points. Customer Journey Mapping helps you to consider these complex experiences and to design products and services that generate value for both the user and the organisations that provide these experiences.

Process description

STEP 1
Determine the type of customer and give reasons for your choice. Describe him/her as precisely as possible and explain how you know this, such as by drawing on qualitative research.

STEP 2
Map the stages the customer goes through on the horizontal axis. Take the customer's point of view, map activities instead of touch points.

STEP 3
Plot questions on the vertical axis: what are the customer's aims? What does the customer do? From the customer's point of view, what works well? What does not? What emotions does the customer go through?

STEP 4
Add any question that is useful for your specific project. For example: what touch points does the customer encounter? What other people does the customer deal with? What devices is the customer using?

STEP 5
Answer all the questions for each stage, preferably with an interdisciplinary approach.

Tips & Concerns

· Leave the mapping of touch points to the end of the exercise. You want to improve the experience, so do not rely too heavily on what the customer needs to use, but what he/she would like to use.

· Use the vertical axis in a flexible way; for each project the vertical axis looks slightly different.

· Use different visual formats: the journey could have a circle shape, two journeys could meet, the journey could be visualised through a metaphor.

· Ask users to map their own journey by asking them to define the stages and asking how they perceive their own experience, but do not limit your findings to emotional aspects.

· Combine qualitative with quantitative research data and engage managers in your project.

· Be sure to document insights from discussion with users and set aside time for dialogue.

· Do not be afraid to change cells when new insights emerge.

· Use visuals and research data wherever possible.

· Use Customer Journey Mapping at several stages of the design process.

· Take time to sketch and co-create with various stakeholders and leave room for improvements along the way.

REFERENCES & FURTHER READING: Roscam Abbing, E.*, 2010. *Brand Driven Innovation.* Lausanne: AVA Academia.
Stickdorn, M. and Schneider, J., 2012. *This is Service Design Thinking.* Amsterdam: BIS Publishing.

The underground map of a city (in this case Moscow) resembles a mind map structure. This schematic way of representing lines and stations was designed by Harry Beck for the London Underground in 1931. Over the years, the London railway system had become too complex and stretched out to be visualised in a geographically correct map.

MIND MAP

A Mind Map is a graphical representation of ideas and aspects organised around a central theme, showing how these aspects are related to each other.

When can the method be used?

With a Mind Map you can map all the relevant aspects and ideas around a theme, bringing structure and clarity to a problem. It provides an overview and is especially useful for identifying all the issues and sub-issues related to a problem. Mind Maps can also be used for generating solutions to a problem and mapping their advantages and disadvantages. A Mind Map can be used in different stages of the design process, but is often used at the beginning of idea generation. Drafting a Mind Map helps you to structure thoughts and ideas about the problem, and connect them to each other. However, a Mind Map can also be used in the problem analysis phase of a design project. Mind Maps are also effective for outlining presentations and reports. In fact, Mind Mapping can be used in a wide variety of situations.

How to use the method?

Mind Mapping is an excellent technique for developing your intuitive capacity. The main branches of a Mind Map are the solutions. Each has sub-branches, presenting the pros and the cons of that particular solution. Making Mind Maps is a skill that can be trained. Because the Mind Map is supposed to help you to analyse the problem, do not limit yourself when writing everything down. When working in groups, it is also helpful to separately make Mind Maps and discuss them together so that you are all on the same page

Possible procedure

STEP 1

Write the name or description of the theme in the centre of a piece of paper and draw a circle around it.

STEP 2

Brainstorm each major facet of that theme, placing your thoughts on lines drawn outward from the central thought like roads leaving a city.

STEP 3

Add branches to the lines as necessary.

STEP 4

Use additional visual techniques – for example, different colours for major lines of thought, circles around words or thoughts that appear more than once, connecting lines between similar thoughts.

STEP 5

Study the Mind Map to see what relationships exist and what solutions are suggested. Reshape or restructure the Mind Map if necessary.

Limitations of the method

- A Mind Map is a subjective view of a project or subject – essentially it is a map of *your* mind. It is an effective tool when you are working on your own. It is also suitable for use in small teams, though the author may have to provide additional explanations.

Tips & Concerns

- You can find software for Mind Mapping on the Internet. The disadvantages of using computer software are that it slightly limits your freedom compared to working with hand drawings and colours, is less personal, and might be less suitable when sharing the Mind Map with others.
- Make it look good: use drawings, colours, pictures, et cetera.
- You can keep adding elements and thoughts to your Mind Map.
- Vary the type and spacing.
- Use short descriptions instead of long sentences.

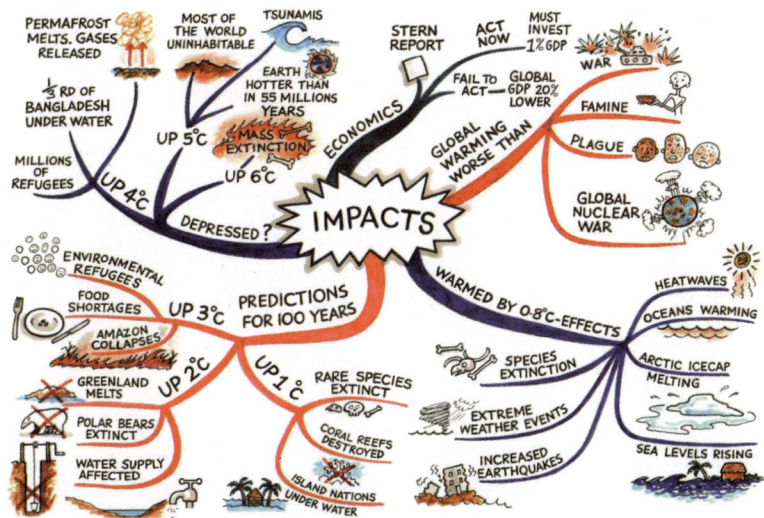

REFERENCES & FURTHER READING: Buzan, T., 1996. *The Mind Map Book: How to Use Radiant Thinking to Maximize Your Brain's Untapped Potential.* New York, NY: Plume. / Tassoul, M.*, 2006. *Creative Facilitation: a Delft Approach.* Delft: VSSD.

Top radar chart

FINANCES

PRODUCT PORTFOLIO

TECHNICAL KNOW-HOW

EXPERT KNOW-HOW

DEVELOPMENT

MANAGEMENT

MARKETING

ORGANISATION AND PERSONNEL

Bottom radar chart

1 Architecture / Built Environment
1 Art & Design
1 English Language & Literature
1 Geography & Area Studies
1 History
1 Linguistics
1 Modern Languages
1 Performing Arts
1 Philosophy
2 Computer Science
2 Engineering - Chemical
2 Engineering - Civil & Structural
2 Engineering - Electrical & Electronic
2 Engineering - Mechanical, Aeronautical & Manufacturing
3 Biological Sciences
3 Medicine
4 Agriculture & Forestry
4 Chemistry
4 Earth & Marine Sciences
4 Environmental Sciences
4 Mathematics
4 Metallurgy & Materials
4 Physics & Astronomy
5 Accounting & Finance
5 Business & Management Studies
5 Communication, Cultural & Media Studies
5 Economics & Econometrics
5 Education
5 Law
5 Politics & International Studies
5 Psychology
5 Sociology
5 Statistics & Operational Research

Scale: 0 5 10 15 20 25 30 35

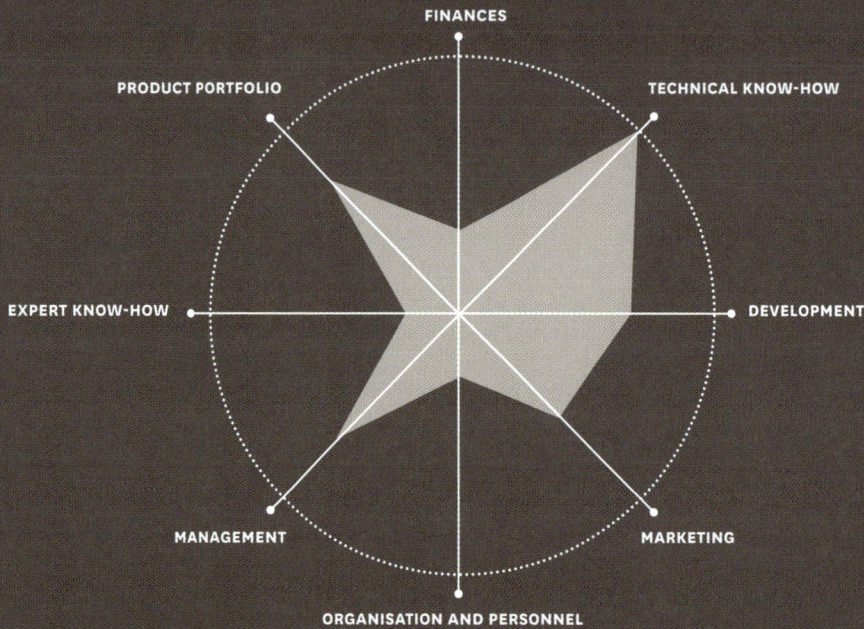

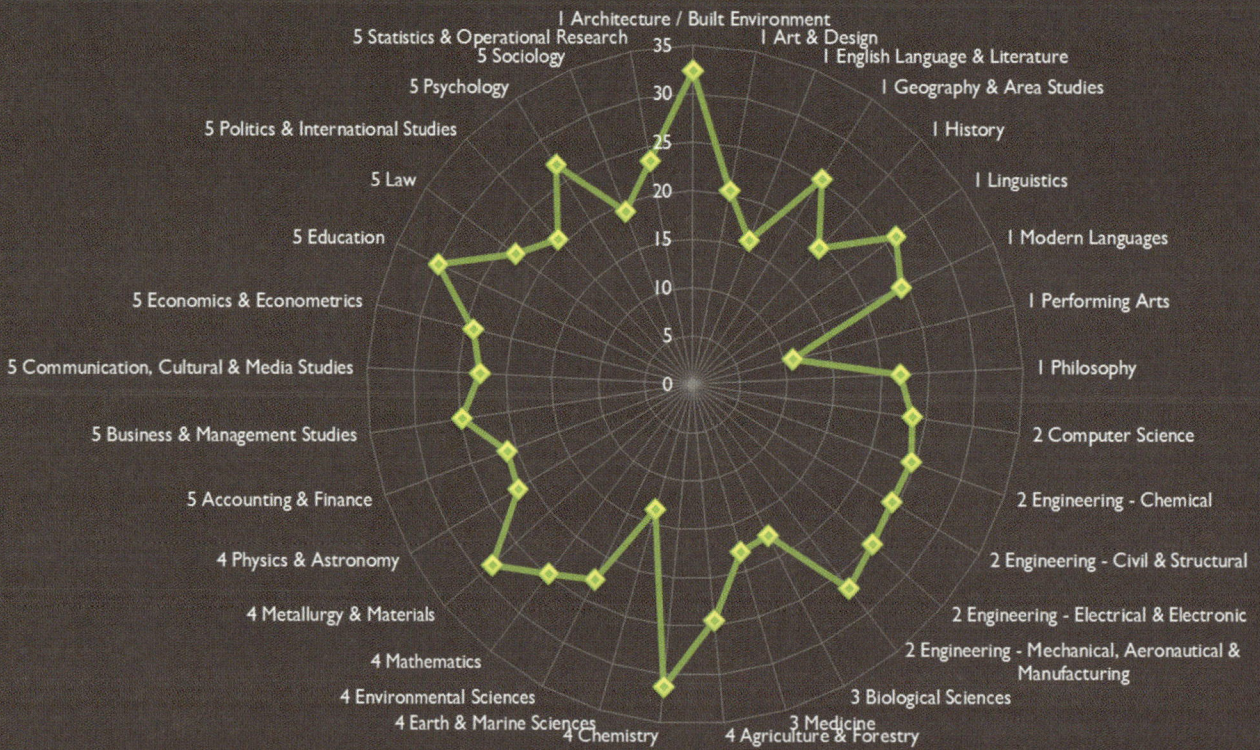

An institution's competency map by discipline. This particular university has key strengths in Architecture, Education, Metallurgy and Chemistry and perform solidly in the Engineering & Technology area. QS World University Rankings® by Subject

STRATEGY WHEEL

When can the method be used?

A Strategy Wheel is usually applied at the beginning of a new product development process to present the strategic strengths of a company. By using the diagram, you obtain a quick understanding of the company's strategic strengths. Often it is also useful to construct Strategy Wheels of a company's direct competitors.

A product innovation process starts with a clear understanding of the current situation of a company. The need for a new product arises from an understanding of a company's strategic strengths and weaknesses, and the opportunities in the market. A thorough analysis of the current situation of a company yields an understanding of the company's strategic strengths, such as technical know-how, product portfolio, development, financial position, export know-how, marketing, organisation, personnel, and management.

How to use the method?

The results of an internal analysis form the starting point for the use of the Strategy Wheel: a clear understanding of the company's strategic strengths in relation to its direct competitors.

The outcome of the use of the Strategy Wheel is a visual representation and a better understanding of the company's strategic strengths.

A Strategy Wheel is a visual representation and a quick tool to review a company's strengths. The Strategy Wheel represents the company's competencies and the scores.

Possible procedure

STEP 1

Determine the company characteristics that you want to evaluate. Examples are: financial strength, in-house technology, R&D knowledge.

STEP 2

Determine a value for each of the characteristics. These values are determined by comparing the company with its direct competitors.

STEP 3

Create a diagram of the scores on the characteristics – this is the Strategy Wheel.

STEP 4

Optionally, put down the values of the competitors' scores on the same characteristics either in the same diagram or in a similar diagram.

STEP 5

Analyse the Strategy Wheel to assess the company's strengths and weaknesses in comparison with its direct competitors.

Tips & Concerns

· The Strategy Wheel is sometimes used to compare other issues, too. For example, design concepts can be analysed and reviewed using the Strategy Wheel.

· The axes represent design requirements on which the design concepts are evaluated. The Strategy Wheel then yields a visual representation of the scores of the different design concepts on the design requirements.

· There are various adaptations of the Strategy Wheel, for example the EcoDesign Strategy Wheel.

REFERENCES & FURTHER READING: Buijs, J.A.* and Valkenburg, R., 1996. *Integrale Productontwikkeling.* Utrecht: Lemma.
Buijs, J.A.*, 2012. *The Delft Innovation Method; a design thinker's guide to innovation.* The Hague: Eleven International Publishing.

TREND ANALYSIS

When can the method be used?

Trends are changes in society that occur over longer periods of time, about 3 to 10 years. They are related not only to people's evolving preferences, for example in fashion or music, but also to wider-sweeping developments in the economy, politics and technology. Trend analyses are usually performed at the beginning of a design project or in the strategic planning process. Not only can they be a rich source of inspiration, they also identify the risks involved when introducing new products.

How to use the method?

With Trend Analysis you try to find answers to the following questions: What developments in the fields of society, markets and technology can we expect over the next 3 to 10 years? How do these developments relate to each other? Where do they stimulate each other and where do they block each other? How do trends influence the strategy of an organisation? What are the resulting threats and what are the opportunities? What ideas for new products and services can we come up with now on the basis of the trends?

For an analysis, a trends pyramid can be used. Trends can be examined at four levels:

· A micro trend is at a product level and has a time horizon of one year.
· A midi trend is at a market level and has a time horizon of one to five years.
· A maxi trend is at a consumer level and has a time horizon of five to 10 years.
· A mega trend is at a societal level and has a time horizon of 10 to 30 years.

A trends pyramid covers a single theme, for example political trends or technological trends.

Trend Analysis methods help you to identify and analyse customer needs and business opportunities in order to develop business strategies, design visions and new product ideas.

Possible procedure

STEP 1
List as many trends as possible. Identify trends from a variety of sources such as newspapers, magazines and the Internet.

STEP 2
Use checklists, such as DEPEST, that help you to ask the relevant questions and to structure your findings:
D = Demographic; E = Ecological;
P = Political; E = Economic; S = Social;
T = Technological.

STEP 3
Remove trends that are similar and identify the hierarchy in trends. Identify whether trends are related and define these relationships.

STEP 4
Place the trends in a trends pyramid. Set up various trends pyramids according to, for example, the DEPEST structure.

STEP 5
Identify interesting directions for new products or services based on trends. Also, combine trends to see whether this would inspire new products or services.

Tips & Concerns

· In the first step, list as many trends as possible and do not pay attention to redundant or similar trends.
· Examining trends is useful for two reasons: it provides a tool that enables you to process and structure the enormous amount of (trend) information generated, and facilitates assessing the consequences of trends.
· You can also use it to identify the preferences of the target group.
· Try to combine trends as much as possible.
· Make use of as many different sources as you can.
· Try to visualise trends just like with scenarios.

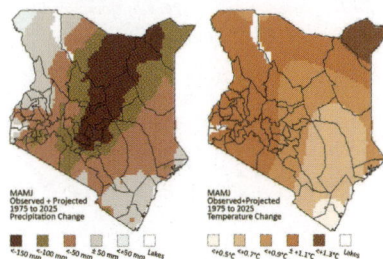

Above: in meteorology, changing rainfall patterns indicate trends that might be connected to global warming. Right: population pyramids visualise trends in birth rates and how a country's population develops over age groups. After World War II, for example, there was a significant baby boom, especially in western countries.

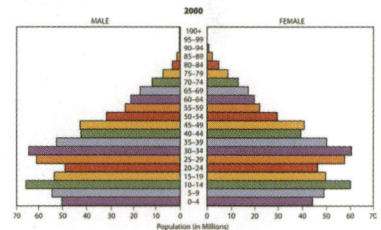

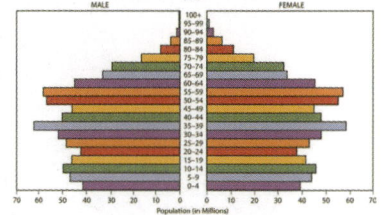

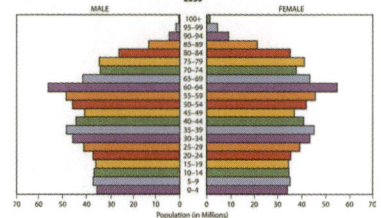

REFERENCES & FURTHER READING: Armstrong, G. and Kotler, P., 1996. *Principes van Marketing.* Hemel Hempstead: Prentice Hall Europe. / Buijs, J.A. and Valkenburg, R.*, 1996. *Integrale Productontwikkeling.* Utrecht: Lemma.

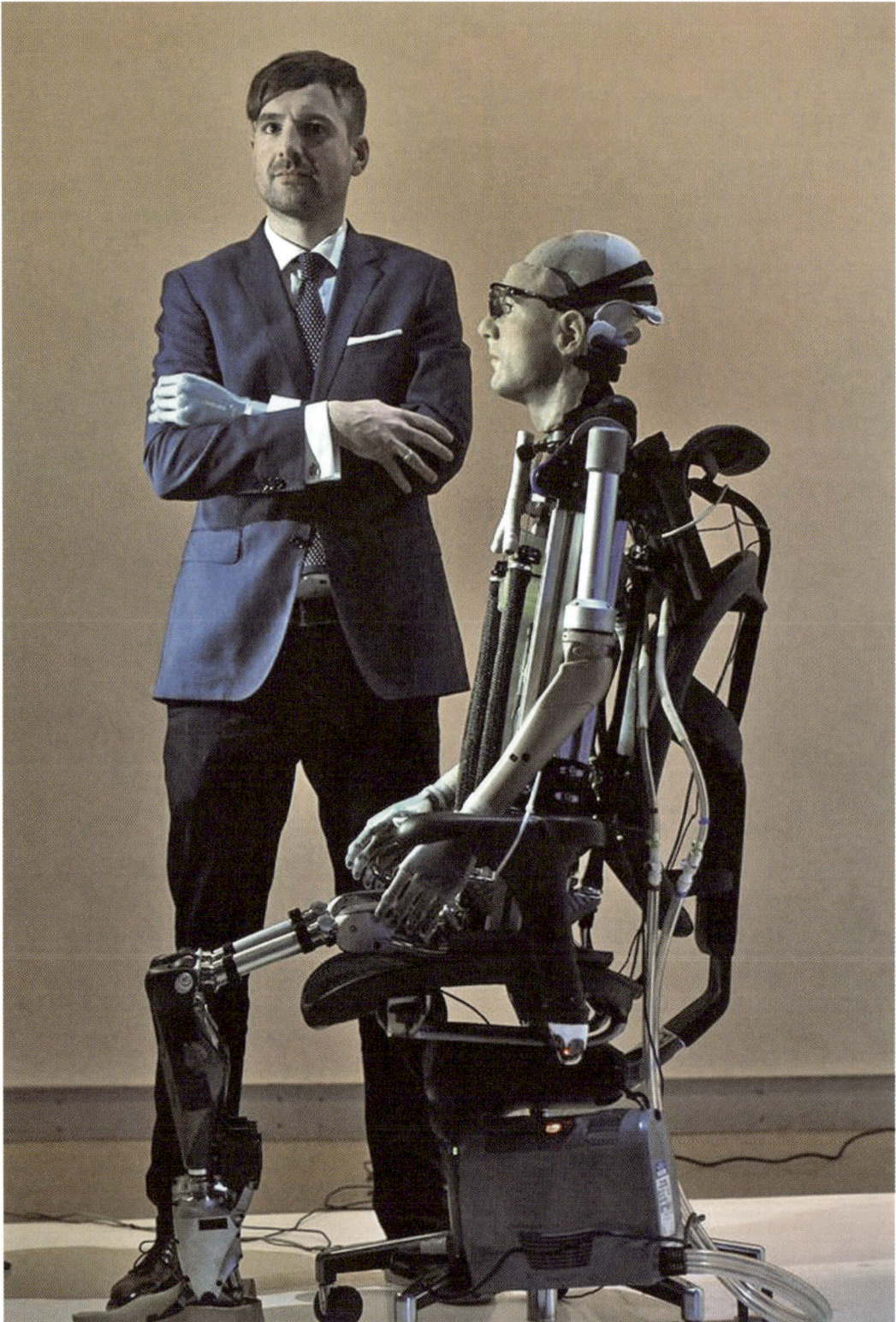

Born with a congenitally missing lower left arm, researcher Bertolt Meyer was fitted with his first prosthetic device when he was only three months old. Inspired by the possibilities of Touch Bionics he presented the Channel 4 documentary 'How to Build a Bionic Man'. At the Science Museum in London he is portrayed next to his bionic self.

FUNCTION ANALYSIS

Function Analysis is a method for analysing and developing the function structure of an existing product or new product concept. It helps you to describe the intended functions of the product and relate them to its parts and 'organs'. A good analysis can help you find and explore new possibilities to embody certain functions in a product or product concept.

When can the method be used?

A Function Analysis is typically carried out at the beginning of idea generation. Functions are abstractions of what a product should do. During this analysis you describe the product or product concept in terms of functions and sub-functions, without material features such as shape, dimensions and materials. The underlying idea is that the function structure may be built up from a limited number of elementary functions on a high level of abstraction. Being forced to think about the product in an abstract way stimulates creativity, and prevents you from 'jumping to solutions', that is to say immediately elaborating on the first idea that comes to mind, which might not be the best. Function Analysis forces designers to distance themselves from known products and components in considering the question: what is the new product intended to do and how could it do that? With this method, you can accomplish a creative breakthrough and come up with unconventional solutions.

How to use the method?

In Function Analysis, a product is considered as a technical-physical system comprising an overall function and its sub-functions, because products usually consist of a number of parts and components that fulfil sub-functions through functional 'organs'. By choosing the appropriate form, materials and composition of parts, a designer can influence how the sub-functions and the overall function are fulfilled. The principle of Function Analysis entails first specifying what the product should do, and then inferring what the parts – which are yet to be developed – should do. The development of a function structure is an iterative process. Of course, you can start by analysing an existing design or with a first outline of an idea for a new solution – but in the course of the analysis you should abstract from it.

Possible procedure

STEP 1
Describe the main function of the product in the form of a black box. If you cannot define one main function, go to the next step.

STEP 2
Make a list of sub-functions. The use stage of a Process Tree is a good starting point.

STEP 3
For a complex product, you may want to develop a function structure. There are three principles of structuring: putting functions in a chronological order, connecting inputs and outputs of flows between functions (matter, energy and information flows) and hierarchy (main functions, sub-functions, sub-sub-functions, et cetera).

STEP 4
Elaborate the function structure:
· Fit in a number of `auxiliary' functions that were left out and find variations of the function structure so as to determine the best function structure.
· Variation possibilities include moving the system boundary, changing the sequence of sub-functions and splitting or combining functions.

Tips & Concerns

· A (sub-)function is always described by a verb and an object (noun):
  - main function of a mirror: reflect light
  - transformer: change voltage
  - blender: cut and mix ingredients
· 'Drive fast' is not a function of a car but something the driver can do with it. 'Fast' is an adjective. 'Enable the driver to drive fast' is a better description of the car's function.
· If you have a function structure, it is recommended you develop variants of it.
· Certain sub-functions appear in almost all design problems. Knowledge of the elementary or general functions helps in seeking product-specific functions.
· Block diagrams of functions should remain conveniently arranged; use simple and informative symbols. Be aware of the different types of functions, such as regular, supporting, unwanted, preventive and technical functions.
· Use drawings.

REFERENCES & FURTHER READING: Roozenburg, N.F.M. and Eekels, J.*, 1995. *Product Design: Fundamentals and Methods.* Utrecht: Lemma.

Conceptual level / Needs analysis

0. NEW CONCEPT DEVELOPMENT
- Dematerialisation
- Shared use of the product
- Integration of functions
- Functional optimisation of product (components)

Product Component Level / Production and supply of materials and components

1. SELECTION OF LOW-IMPACT MATERIALS
- Clean materials
- Renewable materials
- Low energy content materials
- Recycled materials
- Recyclable materials

2. REDUCTION OF MATERIAL USAGE
- Reduction in weight
- Reduction in (transport) volume

Product Structure Level / In-house production

3. OPTIMISATION OF PRODUCTION TECHNIQUES
- Alternative production techniques
- Fewer production steps
- Lower / cleaner energy consumption
- Less production waste
- Fewer / cleaner production consumables

Product Structure Level / Distribution

4. OPTIMISATION OF THE DISTRIBUTION SYSTEM
- Less / cleaner / reusable packaging
- Energy efficient transport mode
- Energy efficient logistics

Product Structure Level / Utilization

5. REDUCTION OF IMPACT DURING USE
- Lower energy consumption
- Cleaner energy source
- Fewer consumables needed
- Cleaner consumables
- No waste of energy or consumables

Product System Level / Recovery and disposal

6. OPTIMISATION OF INITIAL LIFETIME
- Reliability and durability
- Easy maintenance and repair
- Modular product structure
- Classic design
- Strong product-user relation

7. OPTIMISATION OF THE END-OF-LIFE SYSTEM
- Reuse of product (components)
- Remanufacturing / refurbishing
- Recycling of materials
- Safer incineration

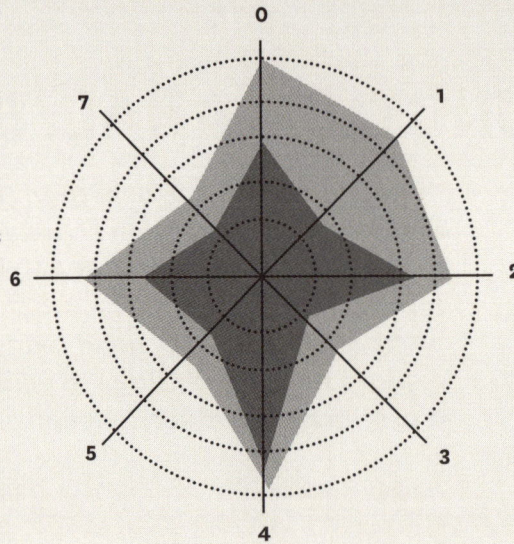

EcoDesign Strategy Wheel. After Brezet and Van Hemel, 1997.

The Green Guru makes bags, wallets and small accessories out of recycled materials like inner tubes from bikes, trucks, tractors and more.

ECODESIGN STRATEGY WHEEL

When can the method be used?
The EcoDesign Strategy Wheel is best applied in the first stage of a product design process, the problem analysis phase, possibly with a general product idea in mind. It is often used in combination with the EcoDesign Checklist.

The EcoDesign Strategy Wheel distinguishes one special strategy on a conceptual level and seven strategies on three product-related levels:

CONCEPTUAL LEVEL
0. New concept development

PRODUCT COMPONENT LEVEL
1. Selection of low-impact materials
2. Reduction of materials usage

PRODUCT STRUCTURE LEVEL
3. Optimisation of production techniques
4. Optimisation of distribution system
5. Reduction of impacts during use

PRODUCT SYSTEM LEVEL
6. Optimisation of initial lifetime
7. Optimisation of end-of-life system

Most of them concern the product life cycle, except for the first strategy, which relates to an innovative strategy.

The EcoDesign Strategy Wheel, also called Lifecycle Design strategies (LiDs), helps you to select and communicate strategies to minimise the environmental impact of your product designs.

How to use the method?
The starting point of the EcoDesign Strategy Wheel is information from the EcoDesign Checklist and a first view of the direction for product design, including the initial product ideas.

During the analysis of the environmental product profile, many improvement options will come up spontaneously. In addition, the EcoDesign Strategy Wheel provides you with eight strategies that can be considered systematically.

By using the EcoDesign Strategy Wheel, you gain a clear understanding of possible strategies for your design. Based on this understanding, you can select the strategy to apply in the conceptualisation phase.

Possible procedure
STEP 1
Define the product idea, product concept or existing product that will be analysed.

STEP 2
Systematically score the product on each dimension of the EcoDesign Strategy Wheel. You can use the answers from the EcoDesign Checklist.

STEP 3
Consider the optimisation options for each of the dimensions, paying special attention to those aspects of the current design that receive poor scores and that have the most relevant environmental impact.

Limitations of the method
· The method is based on qualitative data and personal interpretation of data. The graphic may suggest that the result is objective, which is not the case.

Tips & Concerns
· Use the EcoDesign Strategy Wheel together with the EcoDesign Checklist.
· Do not only consider technical solutions, but also psychological ones. How does the design influence the users and their behaviour with respect to energy efficiency, product lifetime and end-of-life?
· Be aware that some EcoDesign strategies may reinforce each other, but some can be conflicting. The same goes for EcoDesign strategies versus other design and business considerations.
· Recheck your final redesign to see whether it offers the same functionality as the 'old' or reference product, both physically and immaterially.

REFERENCES & FURTHER READING: Brezet, H. and Van Hemel, C.*, 1997. *EcoDesign: A Promising Approach to Sustainable Production and Consumption.* Paris: UNEP. / Remmerswaal, H.*, 2002. *Milieugerichte Productontwikkeling.* Schoonhoven: Academic Service.

ECODESIGN STRATEGIES (0-7)

Conceptual level / Needs analysis

- How does the product system actually fulfil social needs?
- What are the product's main and auxiliary functions?
- Does the product fulfil these functions effectively and efficiently?
- What user needs does the product currently meet?
- Can the product functions be expanded or improved to fulfil users' needs better?
- Will this need change over a period of time?
- Can we anticipate this through (radical) product innovation?

0. NEW CONCEPT DEVELOPMENT

- Dematerialisation
- Shared use of the product
- Integration of functions
- Functional optimisation of product (components)

Product Component Level / Production and supply of materials and components

- What problems arise in the production and supply of materials and components?
- How much and what type of plastic and rubber are used?
- How much and what type additives are used?
- How much and what type of metals are used?
- How much and what other types of materials (glass, ceramics, etc.) are used?
- How much and which type of surface treatment is used?
- What is the environmental profile of the components?
- How much energy is required to transport the materials and components?

1. SELECTION OF LOW-IMPACT MATERIALS

- Clean materials
- Renewable materials
- Low energy content materials
- Recycled materials
- Recyclable materials

2. REDUCTION OF MATERIAL USAGE

- Reduction in weight
- Reduction in (transport) volume

Product Structure Level / In-house production

- What problems can arise in the production process in your own company?
- How many and what types of production processes are used (including connections, surface treatments, printing and labelling)?
- How much and what type of auxiliary materials are needed?
- How high is the energy consumption?
- How much waste is generated?
- How many products don't meet the required quality norm?

3. OPTIMISATION OF PRODUCTION TECHNIQUES

- Alternative production techniques
- Fewer production steps
- Lower / cleaner energy consumption
- Less production waste
- Fewer / cleaner production consumables

Product Structure Level / Distribution

- What problems can arise in the distribution of the product to the customer?
- What kind of transport packaging, bulk packaging and retail packaging are used (volumes, weights, materials, reusability)?
- Which means of transport are used?
- Is transport efficiently organised?

4. OPTIMISATION OF THE DISTRIBUTION SYSTEM

- Less / cleaner / reusable packaging
- Energy efficient transport mode
- Energy efficient logistics

Product Structure Level / Utilization

- What problems arise when using, operating, servicing and repairing the product?
- How much and what type of energy is required, directly or indirectly?
- How much and what kind of consumables are needed?

- What is the technical lifetime?
- How much maintenance and repairs are needed?
- What and how much auxiliary materials and energy are required for operating, servicing and repair?
- Can the product be disassembled by a layman?
- Are those parts often requiring replacement detachable?
- What is the aesthetic lifetime of the product?

5. REDUCTION OF IMPACT DURING USE

- Lower energy consumption
- Cleaner energy source
- Fewer consumables needed
- Cleaner consumables
- No waste of energy or consumables

Product System Level / Recovery and disposal

- What problems arise in the recovery and disposal of the product?
- How is the product currently disposed of?
- Are components or materials being reused?
- What components could be reused?
- Can the components be reassembled without damage?
- What materials are recyclable?
- Are the materials identifiable?
- Can they be detached quickly?
- Are any incompatible inks, surface treatments or stickers used?
- Are any hazardous components easily detachable?
- Do problems occur while incinerating non-reusable product parts?

6. OPTIMISATION OF INITIAL LIFETIME

- Reliability and durability
- Easy maintenance and repair
- Modular product structure
- Classic design
- Strong product-user relation

7. OPTIMISATION OF THE END-OF-LIFE SYSTEM

- Reuse of product (components)
- Remanufacturing / refurbishing
- Recycling of materials
- Safer incineration

ECODESIGN CHECKLIST

When can the method be used?
The EcoDesign Checklist is best applied in the concept generation phase, when you have developed a clear idea of the product. You can also use it to analyse existing products. The Ecodesign Checklist is used in combination with the Ecodesign Strategy Wheel as a tool to avoid overlooking any environmental impacts of a product.

How to use the method?
The starting point for the use of the EcoDesign Checklist is a product idea, a product concept or an existing product. The checklist starts with a needs analysis, which consists of a series of questions concerning the functioning of a product as a whole. The main question asked in a needs analysis is: to what extent does the product fulfil its main and auxiliary functions? You should answer this question before focusing on the environmental bottlenecks in the various stages of the product's life cycle. The needs analysis is followed by a set of questions categorised in terms of the stages of the product life cycle – production, distribution, utilisation, recovery and disposal. The EcoDesign Checklist consists of a set of questions to be asked, coupled to a list of improvement options. These are derived from the Ecodesign Startegy Wheel.

The EcoDesign Checklist is a list of questions that supports the analysis of a product's impact on the environment. It provides relevant questions that enable you to identify the environmental bottlenecks during the product life cycle.

Possible procedure
STEP 1
Define the product idea, product concept or existing product that will be analysed.
STEP 2
Perform a needs analysis, answering the questions from the EcoDesign Checklist.
STEP 3
Provide options for improvement, following the suggestions listed in the EcoDesign strategies. Describe the options for improvement as clearly and precisely as possible.

Limitations of the method
· Checklists aim to be complete, but never are. With some common sense and imagination you can adapt the list to your situation.

Tips & Concerns
· Make sure you answer all the questions in the EcoDesign Checklist.
· Use the EcoDesign Checklist together with the EcoDesign Strategy Wheel – see EcoDesign Strategy Wheel.

These vehicles harvest headwind to move forward during the AEOLUS Competition for Wind Powered Vehicles in the Netherlands. Wind energy is transformed into electricity that powers an electric motor. The competition allows students to develop innovative concepts and challenges them to learn about renewable energy, aerodynamics and building vehicles.

REFERENCES & FURTHER READING: Brezet, H. and Van Hemel, C.*, 1997. *EcoDesign: A Promising Approach to Sustainable Production and Consumption.* Paris: UNEP. / Remmerswaal, H.*, 2002. *Milieugerichte Productontwikkeling.* Schoonhoven: Academic Service.

FOUR MAIN PROCESS GROUPS: ----▶ **1. ORIGINATE** ➔ **2. DISTRIBUTE** ➔ **3. USE** ➔ **4. DISCARD** ----‐

● 1. ORIGINATE

1.1 Study current situation ──────────── 1.1.1 Existing products
1.1.2 Current producers

1.2 Develop product ───────────────────── 1.2.1 Design product
1.2.2 Build prototype
1.2.3 Test prototype

1.3 Search for producers

1.4 Make ready for production

1.5 Produce ───────────────────── 1.5.1 Production step 1
1.5.2 Production step 2
1.5.3 Etcetera

1.6 Check quality

1.7 Package product

1.8 Store products ----‐

● 2. DISTRIBUTE ◀----

2.1 Set price

2.2 Advertise; make publicity ─────────── 2.2.1 Open cupboard
2.2.2 Available space
2.2.3 Close cupboard

2.3 Sell products

2.4 Advise buyers

2.5 Deliver product ----‐

● 3. USE (If applicable: user 1, user 2, user 3, ...) ◀----

3.1 Get product into the house ────────── 3.1.1 Transport (in car, by bicycle, ...?)
3.1.2 Carry
3.1.3 Unpack

3.2 Put in cupboard

3.3 Take out of cupboard ──────── 3.3.1 Open cupboard
3.3.2 Find product
3.3.3 Take product out

3.4 Clean product

3.5 Maintain product ───────────── 3.5.1 Check product
3.5.2 Lubricate; replace battery; ...
3.5.3 Adjust settings

3.6 Repair product ──────── 3.6.1 Open product
3.6.2 Replace broken parts
3.6.3 Close product ----‐

● 4. DISCARD ◀----

4.1 Sell product second hand

4.2 Reuse of parts

4.3 Recycle materials

4.4 Incinerate materials for electricity production

This generic Process Tree can be adjusted for any product or service. Once well structured and complete, it can be used as a framework and checklist for your List of Requirements.

PROCESS TREE

A Process Tree is a schematic diagram of the activities that a product encounters during its life cycle. The method helps you to focus on the whole product life cycle when developing criteria for product development.

When can the method be used?

A Process Tree is typically used during problem analysis and the conceptual stage of product design. During these stages, you make many decisions that influence the activities of stakeholders in later stages of the product development process. For example, your choice of a certain manufacturing technology for the product concept will influence the activities of a production engineer responsible for manufacturing the product later in the product development process. Each stakeholder activity – sub-processes like manufacturing, assembly, disposal, recycling, etc. – during the product life cycle involves certain requirements and wishes for the new product. For example, a production engineer would probably prefer you to use existing manufacturing technology and design simple parts that are easy to manufacture. Making a Process Tree for your concept design forces you to think ahead: in which situations, places and activities will the new product turn up? Who is doing what with the product in those contexts? What problems can be expected? What requirements do these situations necessitate?

How to use the method?

The starting point of a Process Tree is a product or a product group. The outcome of a Process Tree is a structured overview of the important processes and sub-processes that a product encounters. This overview helps in setting up requirements and defining functions.

Possible procedure

STEP 1
Define the product or product group.
STEP 2
Identify the relevant stages in the life cycle of the product. Use the following stages as a start: production, distribution, use, maintenance and disposal.
STEP 3
Use verbs to describe all the activities that a product goes through, using the identified stages as a checklist to generate the relevant activities.
STEP 4
Write down each activity in the form of a verb-noun combination, for example, transport product to store, place product in the store.
STEP 5
Visualise the Process Tree: Create a table for the Process Tree: The column on the left shows the general stages in the product life cycle. For example:
1. originate
2. distribute
3. use (including different users/ stakeholders)
4. discard
STEP 6
After completion, you can use the tree with its list of activities as a checklist to generate criteria.

Limitations of the method

· Although the method helps you to gain a complete picture of the life cycle, you might overlook certain activities, such as non-intended use of the product. These are your blind spots that cannot be avoided simply with a Process Tree.

Tips & Concerns

· You will sometimes identify activities that are preceded by a more important activity. It is important to break down this hierarchy into sub-activities until you have reached a level where further breakdown is not possible.
· Use is typically the stage in which the product fulfils its function. In the stage of use, you can distinguish between activities performed by the user and activities or process steps performed by the product. Ideally, activities performed by the user are user tasks and activities performed by the product are functions of the product. However, they can also be forms of misuse – or unintended use, such as 'standing on a chair' – and malfunction, respectively. It is a good idea to distinguish between these different types of activities.
· For use, do not focus on one-to-one product-user interaction, but also incorporate sociocultural aspects of products. What meaning does the product evoke from a sociocultural perspective?
· Take into account that usually there are various users. For example, when designing a park bench, you can think of loiterers, park visitors, homeless people and municipal officials.
· When identifying requirements from the Process Tree, ask yourself the following question: which criteria must the product satisfy during the process of...?

REFERENCES & FURTHER READING: Roozenburg, N.F.M. and Eekels, J.*, 1995. *Product Design: Fundamentals and Methods.* Utrecht: Lemma. / Roozenburg, N.F.M. and Eekels, J.*, 1998. *Product Ontwerpen: Structuur en Methoden.* 2nd ed. Utrecht: Lemma.

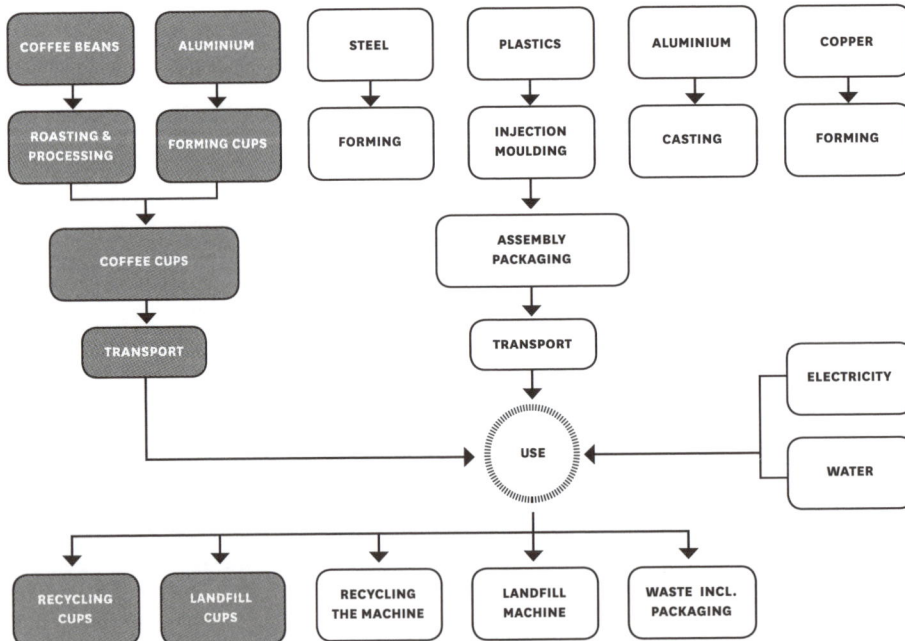

COFFEE BEANS	ALUMINIUM	STEEL	PLASTICS	ALUMINIUM	COPPER
ROASTING & PROCESSING	FORMING CUPS	FORMING	INJECTION MOULDING	CASTING	FORMING

COFFEE CUPS

ASSEMBLY PACKAGING

TRANSPORT

TRANSPORT

ELECTRICITY

WATER

USE

RECYCLING CUPS	LANDFILL CUPS	RECYCLING THE MACHINE	LANDFILL MACHINE	WASTE INCL. PACKAGING

FAST TRACK LIFE CYCLE ANALYSIS

When can the method be used?

It is recommended to use Fast Track LCA in the beginning of the design stage.

· To define possibilities for making use of natural materials or for recycling – see Cradle to Cradle.

· When the main materials for the design are being selected.

· In the concept development phase to optimise the design.

How to use the method?

Although a formal LCA is normally used to determine the environmental impact of the whole product life cycle (cradle-to-grave or cradle-to-cradle), it is also common to make an LCA from cradle-to-factory gate, especially for products which do not require energy in the use phase. In design, a cradle-to-gate LCA should always be combined with end of life data, since end of life has an important impact on the total eco-burden of a product life cycle. You can express the eco-burden –emissions, materials depletion and land use – in terms of eco-costs. These eco-costs can be found in Excel tables with over 6000 materials and processes at www.ecocostsvalue.com under 'data'. These tables make LCA as simple as normal cost calculations: it is a matter of adding up the eco-costs.

A Life Cycle Analysis (LCA) is a method to determine the total eco-burden of a product over its entire life cycle. Fast Track LCA can be carried out when there is a limited amount of time.

Possible procedure

STEP 1
Establish the scope and the goal of your analysis.

STEP 2
Establish the System, Functional Unit and System Boundaries.

STEP 3
Quantify the materials and if applicable the use of energy of the products you compare:

· collect data like weight, material, energy consumption;

· determine accuracy and relevance; establish allocation rules and cut-off criteria.

STEP 4
Enter the data into an Excel calculation sheet or a computer program:

· the eco-audit tool of CES Edupack, a database with eco-costs available at www.grantadesign.com.

· the LCA tool at www.design-4-sustainability.com

STEP 5
Interpret the results. Which parts of the lifecycle are dominant in terms of eco-costs? How can you lower the eco-costs most effectively?

Note: if elements are missing or are not accurate enough, you might have to redo your calculation or parts of it.

Limitations of the method

· If you want to make an LCA on the basis of greenhouse gases only, a Carbon Footprint, you can use the eco-costs tables on the website to facilitate these calculations as well. In Cradle to Cradle calculations carbon footprint analyses do not work well, since the main concern of the Cradle to Cradle philosophy, materials depletion, is not incorporated in the Carbon Footprint indicator. Also it is important to realise that 'social sustainability' is not part of LCA.

Tips & Concerns

· The step-by-step procedure is intended to guide designers in complex cases, but keep your LCA as simple as possible. In the early design stages LCA is not more complex than a cost calculation: instead of costs per kg of material, you apply eco-costs per kg from the Excel tables.

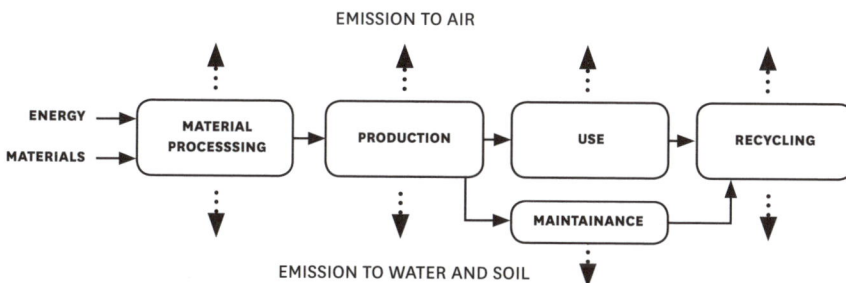

EMISSION TO AIR

ENERGY → MATERIAL PROCESSSING → PRODUCTION → USE → RECYCLING

MAINTAINANCE

MATERIALS →

EMISSION TO WATER AND SOIL

REFERENCES & FURTHER READING: European Commission, Joint Research Centre, Institute for Environment and Sustainability, 2010. *International Reference Life Cycle Data System Handbook: General guide for Life Cycle Assessment - Detailed Guidance.* 1st ed. Luxembourg: Publications Office of the European Union. / Gale, B., 1994. *Managing Customer Value.* New York, NY: The Free Press. / ISO, 2006. ISO 14044 Environmental Management – Life cycle assessment – *Principles and framework.* 2nd ed. Geneva: ISO. / ISO, 2006. ISO 14044 Environmental Management – Life cycle assessment – *Requirements and guidelines.* Geneva: ISO. / Vogtländer, J.G.*, 2013. *A practical guide to LCA, for students, designers, and business managers, cradle-to-grave and cradle-to-cradle.* 2nd ed. VSSD: Delft. / Vogtländer, J.G.*, 2011. *A quick reference guide to LCA DATA and eco-based materials selection.* VSSD: Delft.

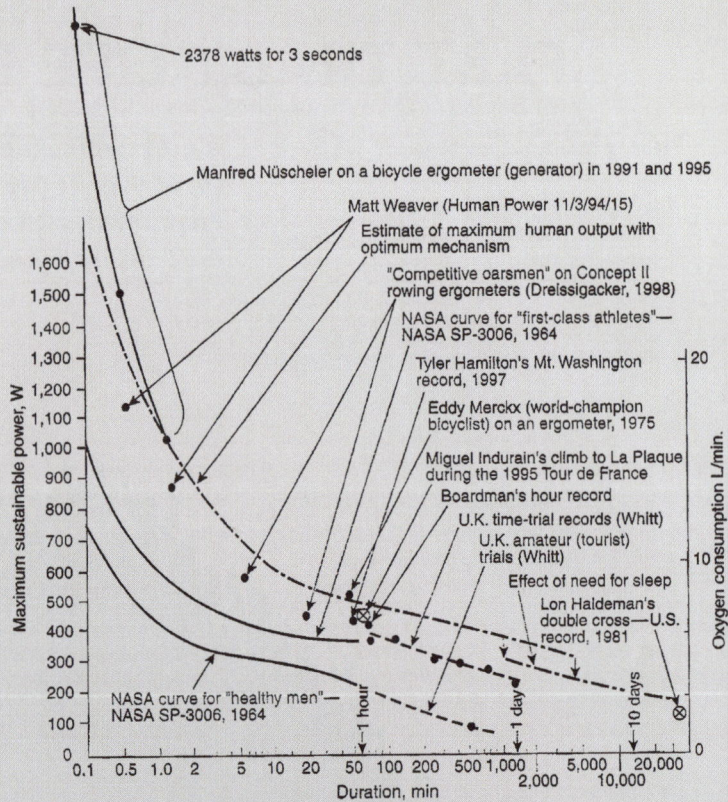

Human power output by pedaling. Curves connect the terminations through exhaustion of constant-power tests. Data collected by Dave Wilson added to an original NASA chart.

Labels on chart:
- 2378 watts for 3 seconds
- Manfred Nüscheler on a bicycle ergometer (generator) in 1991 and 1995
- Matt Weaver (Human Power 11/3/94/15)
- Estimate of maximum human output with optimum mechanism
- "Competitive oarsmen" on Concept II rowing ergometers (Dreissigacker, 1998)
- NASA curve for "first-class athletes"— NASA SP-3006, 1964
- Tyler Hamilton's Mt. Washington record, 1997
- Eddy Merckx (world-champion bicyclist) on an ergometer, 1975
- Miguel Indurain's climb to La Plaque during the 1995 Tour de France
- Boardman's hour record
- U.K. time-trial records (Whitt)
- U.K. amateur (tourist) trials (Whitt)
- Effect of need for sleep
- Lon Haldeman's double cross record, 1981 — U.S.
- NASA curve for "healthy men"— NASA SP-3006, 1964

Axes:
- Maximum sustainable power, W
- Oxygen consumption L/min.
- Duration, min

The Human Power Student Team of the Delft University of Technology attempted to break the world speed record with this aerodynamic recumbent bicycle named Velox. In 2012, they reached a top speed of 129.6 km/h, just 3.7 km/h short of the current world record. Air resistance is their greatest enemy: in 1995, paced by the slipstream of an adapted racing car, Dutch cyclist Fred Rompelberg reached the absolute bicycle world speed record of 268.8 km/h!

HUMAN POWER

When can the method be used?

The Human Power method can be used during conceptual design when you want to consider utilising human power in your product. The method allows you to determine how to utilise human power by mainly looking at a power and energy equation. Human power is often seen as an environmentally conscious alternative to batteries, yet it is not always a feasible alternative. The method therefore also helps you to determine when human power is a feasible option.

How to use the method?

Start by making an inventory of possible opportunities for the use of human power in your product concept. Then, perform a feasibility study for each possibility to find out whether the energy need is appropriate for a human power supply. Finally, verify in what way the user's activity should be transformed to meet the energy need. For example, will the user move his/her legs or arms to generate energy when using your product?

Possible procedure

STEP 1

Identify opportunities: in which ways could human power benefit your product?
· Check whether your product proposal fits any of the following characteristics of human-powered products:
· Is it a product that is used frequently?
· Does your product have a long shelf life?
· Can cost of ownership be reduced by utilising human power?
· Can human power reduce the environmental impact?
· Can human power help raise awareness for other environmental initiatives?
· Can human power provide unique and innovative solutions?

The Human Power method helps you to analyse and decide whether human power is a feasible power source for your design.

STEP 2

Study the feasibility: can the function be realised by human power? Combine the product functionality, human movement and the conversion steps required into a schematic overview (flow diagram) that shows the 'handover' of power. In some cases the benefits of human power become visible only when enlarging the system boundaries beyond the product itself. The environmental and/or cost benefits are not always visible at a product level only.

STEP 3

Match the energy and power requirements: how do they relate? Quantify the efficiency of the individual conversion steps and determine the overall energy system efficiency. To communicate the energy balance, visualise the human muscular work and the product's energy consumption. Note that it is difficult to predict the users' ability and willingness to deliver the added muscular work. In general, users are reluctant to produce over 100 watts of mechanical output, comparable with cycling at 20 km/h on a flat road with no wind, or 25 watts when using their hands and arms. However, for short periods of time, users are able to produce more than this when using their full body weight, such as in emergency situations. It is your challenge to 'seduce' the user to accept this short-term discomfort in order to benefit from the specific product functionality.

Limitations of the method

· Note that human power is often seen as an environmentally conscious alternative to batteries, yet it is not always a feasible alternative.

Tips & Concerns

· Human-powered energy systems can be a good replacement for current systems that damp the motion of (parts of) a consumer product, such as a door closer or knee prosthesis.
· Batteries are relatively cheap, widely available, have a high energy density and can simply be replaced or recharged without specific user knowledge. Do not implement human power as a battery alternative only, but identify additional user benefits.
· If the variation in input force is very large, for example due to use of body mass, the conversion device can be decoupled from the input and therefore protected from overloading by inserting an intermediate storage step between input and conversion device, for example a spring. The energy stored in this intermediate storage device can be converted into electricity during its release.

REFERENCES & FURTHER READING: Jansen, A.J.*, 2011. *Human power empirically explored.* Delft: Delft University of Technology. Jansen, A.J. and Stevels, A.L.N.*, 2006. *Combining eco-design and user benefits from human-powered energy systems.* A win–win situation Journal of cleaner production, 10 January, 14(15-16), pp. 1299-1306. / Reinders, A., Diehl, J.C. and Brezet, H.*, 2013. *The Power of Design: Product Innovation in Sustainable Energy Technologies.* West Sussex, UK: John Wiley & Sons. / Starner, T. and Paradiso, J.A.*, 2004. *Human Generated Power for Mobile Electronics.* Low-Power Electronics Design, 29 November, Chapter 45, pp. 1-35.

S

STRENGTHS

W

WEAKNESSES

INTERNAL ORIGIN
attributes to the organization

HELPFUL
to achieve the objective

HARMFUL
to achieve the objective

O

OPPORTUNITIES

T

THREATS

EXTERNAL ORIGIN
attributes to the environment

SWOT ANALYSIS

SWOT Analysis is a method that helps you to systematically analyse the strategic position of a company's business and to develop a strategic marketing plan. Such a plan can help you to determine directions for product development.

When can the method be used?

A SWOT Analysis is typically performed in the early stages of the innovation process. The outcomes can be used to generate (synthesise) Search Areas. The original idea is to help companies to position their organization in its business context and, based on that positioning, to make strategic decisions. SWOT is an acronym for Strengths and Weaknesses, representing internal factors of the company, and Opportunities and Threats, representing external factors. These factors are related to the business the company is in. The aim of the external analysis (OT) is to understand the company's position related to its competitors, which helps you to understand the company's SW (from internal analyses). A SWOT Analysis results in a set of building blocks to be used to generate Search Areas for product innovation.

How to use the method?

The structure of SWOT suggests a simple and quick effort. However, the quality of your efforts depends on a good understanding of a large variety of factors and is typically done with a multidisciplinary team.
For the external analysis you can use checklists such as DEPEST (Demographic, Economical, Political, Ecological, Socio-cultural, Technological developments – see Trend Analysis) to help you ask relevant questions. An external analysis should result in a thorough understanding of the current market and users, competitors and competing products and services. It should enable you to recognise opportunities and possible threats for the company.
For the internal analyses you need to know the relevant parameters that make the company strong and weak in the context of the business environment and in relation to its competitors. An internal analysis should result in a thorough understanding of a company's strengths and weaknesses.

It should allow you to recognise what kinds of innovations might fit a company's core competences and thus have a higher chance of success.

Possible procedure

STEP 1
Start by determining the scope of the competitive business environment. Ask yourself: what business are we in?
STEP 2
Perform the external analysis by answering questions such as: what are important trends in the market environment? What are people's needs and frustrations regarding current products? What are the prevailing sociocultural and economic trends? What are competitors doing and planning to do? What trends can be seen within the business chain among suppliers, distributors and knowledge institutes? Use checklists such as DEPEST to structure your efforts and do a comprehensive analysis.
STEP 3
Make an inventory of the company's strengths and weaknesses and evaluate them by benchmarking them against competitors. Focus on the company's competitive strengths and core competences and pay less attention to its weaknesses; you are looking for opportunities, not obstacles. Once design objectives have been defined, you might find that some of the weaknesses form a bottleneck for your project and need to be addressed.

STEP 4
Summarise your findings in a SWOT matrix to allow clear communication with your team members or other stakeholders.

Limitations of the method

· The original SWOT method supports you with performing an analysis. However, your interest as a designer is to come up with promising ideas for innovation via Search Areas. To synthesise strategic directions for product innovation you can use the Search Areas method.

Tips & Concerns

· Consider the scope of the company's competitive environment carefully. A successful SWOT Analysis starts with an appropriate scope, which can be very broad or narrow, and there is no rule of thumb to select the appropriate scope.
· Try to formulate Threats as Opportunities. For example, a strict environmental policy can be seen as a threat for a company's current product, but also as an opportunity for product innovation.
· Opportunities are not gifts – they do not simply fall into your lap. You need to make an effort to create them. Threats are gifts that you typically do not want. If you are not careful, they might harm you.

REFERENCES & FURTHER READING: Ansoff, H.I., 1987. *Corporate Strategy.* London: Penguin Books. / Brooksbank, R., 1996. *The BASIC marketing planning process: a practical framework for the smaller business.* Journal of Marketing Intelligence & Planning, 1 July, 14(4), pp. 16-23.

SEARCH AREAS

The Search Areas method helps you to find business opportunities for developing new product ideas. The method supports a synthesising process that is typically based on insights from a SWOT analysis.

When can the method be used?

The method is typically used in an early stage of the innovation process to look for new business opportunities. It builds on a company's strengths (S) and intent to differentiate in the market. Output from a SWOT analysis provides input for the formulation of search fields.

Search Areas or 'opportunity areas' are synthesised from a combination of a company's strengths and opportunities in the market. Strengths are derived from internal analyses of the company and represent its core competences. Opportunities are derived from an external analysis of the market and represent trends such as societal and market developments. Search Areas provide a 'solution space' in which you can generate ideas – as such, they entail a potential set of product ideas.

How to use the method?

Start by collecting the Strengths and Opportunities from a SWOT analysis. Put them in a matrix and search for relevant combinations. Combinations of strengths and opportunities should inspire you to come up with search fields. Generate a large number of Search Areas and then select the ones that are the most interesting for your project. The selection is based on the promise of increasing market size and/ or growth for the organisation's current business or a contribution to the long-term business strategy or vision. Finally you will develop the most promising Search Areas into a design brief. This top-down reasoning, from a generic Search Area to concrete product ideas, can also be reversed to a bottom-up one, for example if you have generated many product ideas in a brainstorming session and you need to evaluate their competitive strength.

Possible procedure

STEP 1
Use the results from a SWOT analysis as a starting point.
STEP 2
Create a large number – about 20 to 60 – of Search Areas by combining the company's internal Strengths with its Opportunities in the external environment. The application of creative techniques is recommended.
STEP 3
Select Search Areas using selection criteria such as the newness and originality of the domain and promise of market size. In the end, valuable Search Areas hold the promise of increasing market size and/ or growth for the organisation's current business or a contribution to the long-term business strategy or vision.
STEP 4
Conduct further contextual user/usage research to check feasibility and formulate a design brief for the selected search areas.
STEP 5
Generate product ideas for each selected Search Area based on the design brief.

Limitations of the method

· Good ideas do not come from a thorough analysis or creative session only. Great ideas sometimes grow as seeds within the company from the efforts of creative and dedicated employees.

Tips & Concerns

· The way you define a company's strengths and the way you observe the external environment and how you translate this into worthwhile strategic objectives is a creative process with many possible outcomes.
· Seemingly strange combinations of strengths and opportunities are interesting because it would be difficult for a competitor to identify them.
· The crux of the Search Area method lies in how a design team is able to come up with innovative ideas, sometimes merely generating marginal advances, but sometimes also tapping into game-changing opportunities that help the company create successful business for years to come.
· The SO combination is a two-dimensional way to find a Search Area. However, in reality the Search Area is multidimensional. You can think of many different search matrixes, so do not look for one overarching Search Area and do not try to fit everything into the Search Area.
· To determine the relevance of Search Areas you can do market research using, for example, the Contextmapping method, literature and experts.

REFERENCES & FURTHER READING: Brankamp, K., 1971. *Planung und Entwicklung neuer Produkte.* Berlin: Walter de Gruyter & Co. Buijs, J.A.*, 1997. *Strategic planning and product innovation - Some systematic approaches.* Long Range Planning, October, 12(5), pp. 23-34. Buijs, J.A.*, 2012. *The Delft Innovation Method; a design thinker's guide to innovation.* The Hague: Eleven International Publishing.

CURRENT MARKETS

MARKET PENETRATION

PRODUCT DEVELOPMENT

CURRENT PRODUCTS ← → NEW PRODUCTS

MARKET DEVELOPMENT

PRODUCT DIVERSIFICATION

NEW MARKETS

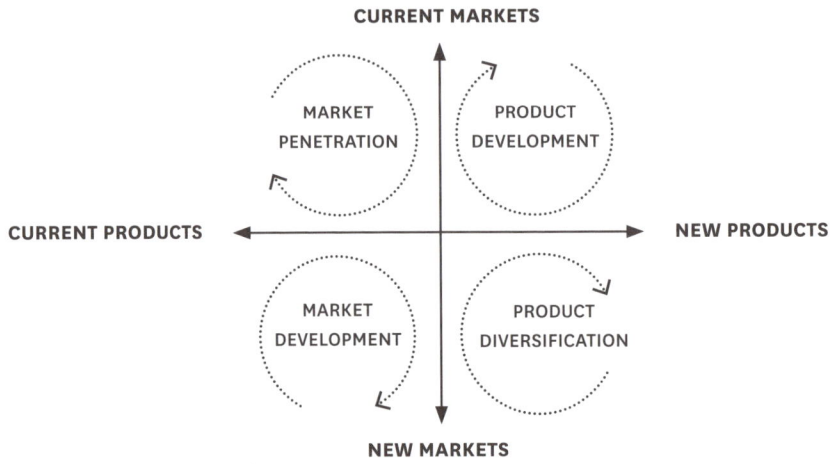

After Ansoff, 1957

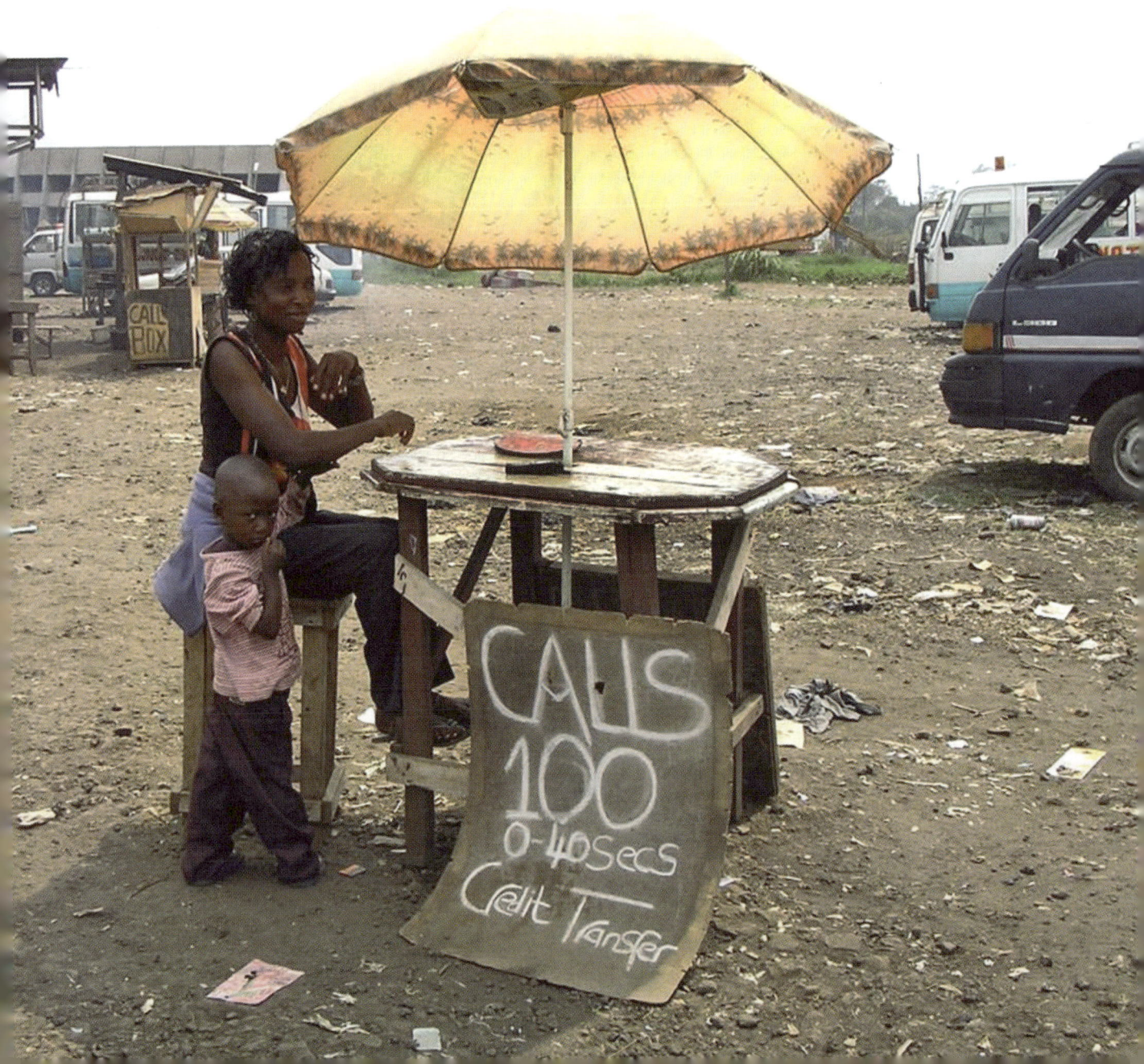

ANSOFF GROWTH MATRIX

The Ansoff Matrix is a strategic marketing tool that specifies four alternative strategies for corporate growth based on different product-market combinations. Its basic premise is that a company's attempts to grow depend on whether it markets new or existing products in new or existing markets.

When can the method be used?

In design, the Ansoff Matrix is typically used to help define a company's strategic objectives in the early stages of product innovation. It is a two-by-two matrix with four quadrants. Each quadrant identifies generic strategies for corporate growth:

1. market penetration, that is, selling existing products to existing customers,
2. market development, that is, selling existing products to new customers,
3. product development, that is, selling new products to existing customers, and
4. diversification, that is, selling new products to new customers. Each strategy is associated with a different level of risk, which increases as one moves into a new quadrant, vertically and/or horizontally.

Accordingly, market development carries the lowest risk and diversification the highest risk. The application of the Ansoff Matrix can help you to evaluate alternative growth strategies and assess which is likely to result in the best possible return. The matrix can support you in making informed decisions regarding the company's product portfolio and its market position. These decisions set the direction for the company's business strategy and have important implications for what kinds of new products you will develop.

How to use the method?

Decisions about the company's growth strategy precede those concerning business and marketing strategies and are typically taken by senior innovation managers. While novice designers are unlikely to find themselves using the Ansoff Matrix in their daily tasks, a thorough understanding of its basic principles is still valuable because growth is one of the key objectives of companies. From a designer's standpoint, the Ansoff Matrix can be best viewed as a means of goal setting. This is because the design, development and marketing of a company's new products are guided by the overall growth strategy of the company and these activities need to be carried out in the light of the risks associated with the predetermined growth strategy.

Possible procedure

STEP 1
Define the company's current products and markets.
STEP 2
Identify which quadrant best describes the company's current growth strategy.
STEP 3
Define the new products and markets the company can feasibly venture into.
STEP 4
Plot each product/market combination on the 2 x 2 matrix.
STEP 5
Assess the risks and opportunities associated with each product-market combination.
STEP 6
Choose a growth strategy in the light of the company's ambitions and ability to mitigate the risks and exploit the opportunities associated with each option.

Limitations of the method

· The Ansoff Matrix is particularly useful for multi-product organisations or organisations that are planning to increase their market share. It is less applicable for small businesses with a single division or entrepreneurial start-ups.
· In practice, cases typically do not fall neatly into one of the four alternative strategies. For instance, an organisation may primarily use a product development growth strategy but might follow a market penetration strategy in certain markets.

Tips & Concerns

· The Ansoff Matrix does not identify the ideal strategy – it merely provides an outline of alternative methods of achieving growth. It is the decision maker's responsibility to evaluate them in the light of the company's capabilities and external conditions when making the final choice.
· Fruitful use of the Ansoff Matrix relies heavily on a clear definition of what a 'new' product or market is – to do this one must first establish what the current products and markets are.
· The four strategies carry different levels of risk, but that should not be interpreted as an excuse to stick to the least risky strategy. The risks should be assessed not in isolation, but in conjunction with the potential returns.

REFERENCES & FURTHER READING: Ansoff, H.I., 1957. Strategies for diversification. *Harvard Business Review*, September-October, 35(5), pp. 113-124. / Johnson, G. and Scholes, K., 2002. *Exploring Corporate Strategy: Text and Cases*. 6th ed. London: Prentice Hall. / Mullins, J.W. and Walker, O.C., 2013. *Marketing Management, A Strategic Decision-Making Approach.* 8th ed. Singapore: McGraw-Hill/Irwin.

PROSPECTOR	ANALYSER	DEFENDER	REACTOR
STRATEGY	**STRATEGY**	**STRATEGY**	**STRATEGY**
Innovative	*Consolidate*	*Protect turf*	*Copy*
Find new market opportunities	*Maintain current market*	*Hold current market*	*No clear strategy*
Grow	*Moderate innovations*	*Retrench*	*Drift*
Take risks	*Avoid risks*	*No risks*	*No risks*
ENVIRONMENT	**ENVIRONMENT**	**ENVIRONMENT**	**ENVIRONMENT**
Dynamic	*Moderate change*	*Minimal change*	*Conformistic*
Growing	*Stable*	*Stable*	*Any condition*
ORGANISATIONAL	**ORGANISATIONAL**	**ORGANISATIONAL**	**ORGANISATIONAL**
Creative	*Creative*	*Low overhead*	*Low overhead*
Innovative	*Efficient production*	*Efficient production*	*Efficient production*
Flexible	*Flexible*	*Flexible*	*No clear approach*
Decentralised	*Tight control*	*Centralised*	*Depends on current needs*

A changing external environment: according to Moore's Law, processor power doubles every 18 months. The ENIAC Electronic Numerical Integrator And Computer was the first electronic general-purpose computer. When it was announced in 1946, the press heralded it as a 'Giant Brain'. It had a clock speed of 0.1 MHz, 1,000 times that of electromechanical machines. The programming capability of this machine can now be approximated by a small calculator. The rapid progress of computer technology soon made the device obsolete. In the 1950s and 1960s, most computers were large, costly machines that could only be run by trained operators. By the mid-1970s, integrated circuits and microprocessors were small enough and cheap enough for the creation of the Personal Computer. Modern computers now run at about 3,300 Mhz. This trend towards smaller and cheaper computers is still continuing.

MILES AND SNOW BUSINESS STRATEGIES

When can the method be used?

The Miles and Snow typology relates to how the company will compete in a particular industry. Underlying the Miles and Snow typology is the premise that organisations develop relatively stable patterns of strategic behaviour when trying to adapt to their environment. Miles and Snow identify four strategic types: Prospector, Analyser, Defender and Reactor. These four types differ with respect to how they address entrepreneurial, engineering and administrative problems. Prospectors tend to be industry leaders and have a broad product/market domain, but do not usually persevere in any given industry. They are very active in developing new products. Defenders have a limited range of products and serve a limited number of markets. Their focus is on being the best in what they do, which they seek to achieve through constant efficiency and process improvements. Analysers lie midway between prospectors and defenders. Reactors are the organisations that do not have a consistent strategy – they simply respond to changes in the environment.

By identifying which competitive strategy their organisation is following, you can make sure that your project matches the competitive strategy. Or, if you have a very promising project that does not align with the organisation's current posture, you can use the Miles and Snow framework for identifying which strategy would best foster the project.

The Miles and Snow framework is a decision tool that identifies four generic ways in which companies can successfully adapt to, and compete in, an uncertain external environment. It is one of the most widely used typologies of competitive strategy.

How to use the method?

Using the Miles and Snow typology requires little experience or formal training. All that is required is a thorough understanding of (1) the characteristics of the generic strategies and (2) the characteristics of the organisation with respect to its intended product-market development and how it deals with entrepreneurial, engineering and administrative problems. The final step is determining which of the generic strategies best match the organisation's behaviour.

Possible procedure

In order to find which of Miles and Snow's generic strategies best describes an organisation, you can ask questions such as:

- How broad is the product-market domain? Does the organisation focus on a small number of markets or does it serve many different ones?
- Does the organisation remain in a particular product market for a long time or does it move on?
- How regularly and how fast does the organisation release new products?
- Is the focus on innovation or efficiency and process development?
- Does the organisation have a consistent stance with respect to the points above?

Limitations of the method

- The four strategies in the typology are generic. Real-life examples are usually fuzzy so sometimes it can be difficult to say which strategy is the best match for the organisation.
- The framework is not prescriptive in the sense that none of the strategies are ideal or optimal – while Organisation X may thrive as a Prospector, Organisation Y may owe its competitiveness to the Defender strategy and Organisation Z may find that an Analyser strategy is the best option given its strengths and weaknesses and external conditions.

Tips & Concerns

- Different strategies prioritise different performance outcomes. This should be reflected in how a new product development project is evaluated. For instance, a prospector company will be more interested in the level of innovativeness than development costs.
- Projects must fit the competitive strategy. In most cases, it is the project that needs to be changed in line with the competitive strategy. There are, however, instances where organisations rethink their competitive strategies to meet the needs of an exceptionally promising project.

REFERENCES & FURTHER READING: Brunk, S.E., 2003. *From theory to practice: Applying Miles and Snow's ideas to understand and improve firm performance.* The Academy of Management Executive, November, 17(4), pp. 105-108. / McDaniel, S.W. and Kolari, J.W., 1987. *Marketing Strategy Implications of the Miles and Snow Strategic Typology.* Journal of Marketing, July, 51(4), pp. 19-30. / Miles, R.E., and Snow, C.C., 1978. *Organizational Strategy, Structure, and Process.* New York, NY: McGraw-Hill. / Mullins, J.W. and Walker, O.C., 2013. *Marketing Management, A Strategic Decision-Making Approach.* 8th ed. Singapore: McGraw-Hill/Irwin.

PORTER COMPETITIVE STRATEGIES

The Competitive Strategies framework helps companies to characterise their Competitive Strategy and define guidelines for achieving competitive advantage. Porter proposed three Competitive Strategies: focus, differentiation and cost leadership.

When can the method be used?

The Competitive Strategy is defined by the top management and should not be easily modified over time. The Competitive Strategy affects several subsequent decisions and actions, including branding, production, innovation, portfolio management and marketing strategy, as well as shapes the design and development of new products and services accordingly. Choosing the right Competitive Strategy will align marketing activities and design activities with company objectives, improve the coherence of product portfolios and enhance the effectiveness of the marketing mix and innovation.

How to use the method?

The CEO of a company chooses the Competitive Strategy based on two main criteria: the size and composition of the market the company intends to target (*market scope*), and whether the company is better in product differentiation or in reducing the cost of products (*source of competitive advantage*).

As a result, three Competitive Strategies are possible:

· *Cost leadership*: a company makes profits by appealing to cost-conscious or price-sensitive customers in the market, and by producing and operating at a lower cost than its competitors.

· *Differentiation*: a company makes profits by leveraging its unique resources and capabilities to offer products that satisfy customer needs in a way that is distinctive and difficult to imitate.

· *Focus* or *niche strategy*: a company focuses effort and resources on a narrow, defined segment of the market. Products or services are developed specifically for this niche, by using either a differentiation or a cost leadership approach.

Possible procedure

STEP 1
Identify your company's core competences by looking at strengths and weaknesses and by comparing them with your main competitors.
STEP 2
Choose the market scope depending on the size of your company in terms of resources and production capacity as well as the nature and geographical scope of the business.
STEP 3
Select the most appropriate Competitive Strategy.
STEP 4
Develop new products or services according to the selected Competitive Strategy.
STEP 5
Monitor the appropriateness of your Competitive Strategy over time.

Limitations of the method

· The Porter Competitive Strategies framework has been criticised for its lack of specificity and flexibility. Current turbulent market conditions might require the adoption of hybrid Competitive Strategies and/or a more pragmatic approach where the Competitive Strategy is modified depending on the circumstances.

Tips & Concerns

· The choice of a Competitive Strategy should be clear. Do not get 'stuck in the middle' if you want to be profitable and achieve competitive advantage.

· This choice is a long-term decision and should be thought out well. If you are a product manager or a designer, work consistently with the chosen strategy and do not try to change it.

· Choosing a Competitive Strategy should consider the external environment: Industry structure and competitors' strategies might mean that one or more Competitive Strategies are simply not possible – see Porter Five Forces.

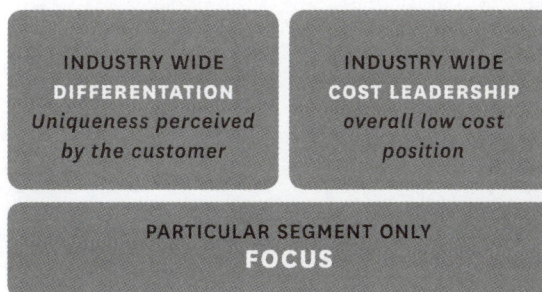

INDUSTRY WIDE **DIFFERENTATION** *Uniqueness perceived by the customer*	INDUSTRY WIDE **COST LEADERSHIP** *overall low cost position*
PARTICULAR SEGMENT ONLY **FOCUS**	

Representation of Porter's Competitive Strategies

REFERENCES & FURTHER READING: Porter, M.E., 1985. *Competitive Advantage: Creating and Sustaining Superior Performance.* New York, NY: The Free Press. / Porter, M.E., 1996. *What is Strategy?* Harvard Business Review, November-December, 74(6), pp. 61-78.

COMPETITIVE IMPLICATION	ECONOMIC IMPLICATION	1. VALUABLE?	2. RARE?	3. INIMITABLE?	4. ORGANISED?
Disadvantage	*Below normal returns*	No	n.a.	n.a.	n.a.
Parity	*Normal returns*	Yes	No	n.a.	Yes
Temporary advantage	*Above normal returns (temporary)*	Yes	Yes	No	Yes
Sustained advantage	*Above normal returns*	Yes	Yes	Yes	Yes

'Example of VRIO Analysis results'

In 1996, then-World Chess Champion Garry Kasparov sat down to the sixth game in his match against Deep Blue, IBM's supercomputer. Kasparov emerged the victor, winning three games, drawing in two, and losing one. When Deep Blue and Kasparov sat down to a rematch a year later, the computer eked out a victory. Photo: Kasparov makes his first move.

VRIO ANALYSIS

VRIO Analysis is a useful method for determining the competitive potential of an organisation's resources and capabilities, that is, WHAT IT HAS and WHAT IT CAN DO. It helps you to identify which of these resources and capabilities the organisation excels at, thereby setting it apart from competitors.

When can the method be used?

VRIO Analysis is a part of internal analysis and should be done during the planning stage of product innovation. It pinpoints the internal strengths that can be used to exploit opportunities and neutralise threats. Knowing which resources/capabilities the organisation excels in is important. If the project demands a resource/capability that the organisation does not have, managers need to take the necessary actions to nurture it, when possible, or obtain it via other means, for example by outsourcing. If these activities are out of the question, the resource needs of the project may need rethinking.

How to use the method?

A VRIO Analysis is fairly structured, so it does not allow much flexibility. It is also linear, meaning that it does not require iteration unless there have been errors.

Possible procedure

STEP 1
Identifying the organisation's resources and capabilities.
STEP 2
Assessing each resource with respect to the following criteria, in the following order: Value, Rarity, Imitability and Organisation.
· Value: Does this resource/capability add value? This can take the form of increased
efficiency, better quality, improved customer responsiveness and greater innovation capacity.
· Rarity: Do many other organisations also possess this resource/capability?

· Imitability: Is it easy for other organisations that currently do not possess this resource/capability to acquire or develop it?
· Organisation: Do the current organisational structure and practices allow this resource/capability to be used to its full potential?
STEP 3
Determining the competitive and economic implications of each resource based on this evaluation. Resources that are valuable, rare, inimitable and organised are sources of sustainable competitive advantage for the organisation.

Limitations of the method

· VRIO Analysis requires individual judgement and, to a certain extent, expertise on part of the user. For example, assessing how imitable a resource is demands a thorough understanding of how this resource is cultivated and this can take many different forms. VRIO Analysis merely facilitates the identification of the current sources of competitive advantage for the organisation. It does not say anything about how new sources of competitive advantage can be fostered.

Tips & Concerns

· It is crucial to come up with an exhaustive list of resources before embarking on the analysis.
· All resources of the company – tangible, intangible and organisational capabilities – should be considered.
· VRIO Analysis should be done individually for each resource/capability. It should not be done on the organisation as a whole.
· A VRIO Analysis should be updated regularly. For instance, the value of a resource can change over time. Or new technological developments may make it easier for competitors to imitate it. Consequently, what was once a source of competitive advantage may now yield only normal returns.
· A resource/capability that is not valuable for the organisation can be a core rigidity if it prevents other resources/capabilities from developing. Since VRIO Analysis originates from the resource-based view of the firm, having a good understanding of the resource-based view will be very helpful for implementing the analysis effectively and efficiently.

REFERENCES & FURTHER READING: Barney, J.B., 1991. *Firm resources and sustained competitive advantage.* Journal of Management, March, 17(1), pp. 99-120. / Johnson, G. and Scholes, K., 2002. *Exploring Corporate Strategy: Text and Cases.* 6th ed. London: Prentice Hall. / Mullins, J.W. and Walker, O.C., 2013. **Marketing Management, A Strategic Decision-Making Approach.** 8th ed. Singapore: McGraw-Hill/Irwin. / Wernerfelt, B., 1984. *A resource-based view of the firm.* Strategic Management Journal, April-June, 5(2), pp. 171-180.

1. *Threat of*
NEW ENTRANTS

2. *bargaining power of*
SUPPLIERS

INDUSTRY COMPETITORS
5. Rivalry among existing companies

3. *bargaining power of*
BUYERS

4. *Threat of*
SUBSTITUTE *products or services*

Porter Five Forces

PORTER FIVE FORCES

Porter Five Forces is a framework for assessing the attractiveness (profitability) of an industry and, subsequently, deciding how the company you work for should position itself and compete in that industry.

When can the method be used?

You can use the Porter Five Forces framework to support your decision to enter a new industry or formulate a clear competitive strategy for your client. The framework sheds light on five competitive forces constraining or creating strategic opportunities in an industry. By assessing the combined effect of these five forces you can answer the following questions: what is going on in my industry or in the industry I want to enter? Of the many things that are happening, which ones matter most for competition?

When companies are deciding whether to enter an industry, this framework is used to compare the attractiveness of different options, such as search fields, and to decide on the most appropriate entry strategy and competitive strategy – for example, should your company pursue a partnership with key players and how much should you differentiate your product from current competitors? In this scenario, the framework is used before starting the idea generation.

How to use the method?

The method is based on the assessment of five competitive forces:

1. Threat of new entrants: the extent to which it is easy to enter an industry, in terms of required knowledge, investments and capabilities.
2. Bargaining power of suppliers: the extent to which key suppliers influence competitive dynamics.
3. Bargaining power of buyers: The extent to which key suppliers influence competitive dynamics.
4. Threat of substitute products or services: the amount of products or services meeting the same basic need as the industry's product in a different way.
5. Rivalry among existing competitors: the amount of competitors and the intensity of competition.

Possible procedure

STEP 1
Define the relevant industry in terms of: Product scope: what products does it include? Which belong to another industry? Geographical scope: is the competition national, regional or global?

STEP 2
Identify the industry players: Who are the buyers? Who are the suppliers? Who are the competitors? Who are the potential entrants? What are the substitute products?

STEP 3
Assess the drivers of each competitive force: Which forces are strong/ unfavourable? Which forces are weak/ favourable? Why?

STEP 4
Consider the combined effect of the five forces and assess the overall industry structure: What is the overall attractiveness of the industry? What are the most important forces determining attractiveness? How are competitors positioned in relation to the five forces?

STEP 5
Analyse recent and likely future changes for each force: Which forces are stable? Which forces are likely to change in your favour or against you?

STEP 6
Position your company in relation to the five forces: Can you use your company's strengths, capabilities and resources to position it where the forces are weakest? Can you use your strengths, capabilities and resources to reshape the structure in your favour?

Limitations of the method

· The five forces identified by Porter are common to any industry. That said, there might be additional forces affecting the attractiveness of a certain industry. For example, the model does not take into account the role of complementary products, strategic alliances and governmental regulations in shaping competition within an industry.
· Presence of increased globalisation and technology may have significantly altered the dynamics of economic growth and competition since the model's inception in 1979.

Tips & Concerns

· Be careful not to define the industry either too broadly or too narrowly.
· Assess each force from the perspective of companies already in the industry.
· Industry structure is dynamic; do not limit your analysis to the current situation but also consider trends in the strength and favourability of the five forces.
· The Five Forces framework is not a tool for declaring an industry attractive or unattractive, but for making strategic choices on how to position your company in an industry by leveraging favourable forces and protecting against unfavourable ones. Do not stop at step four.

REFERENCES & FURTHER READING: Porter, M.E., 1979. *How competitive forces shape strategy.* In P.J. Smit (eds.), Strategic Planning: Readings, pp. 102-117. / Porter, M.E., 2008. *The Five Competitive Forces That Shape Strategy.* Harvard Business Review, January, 86(1), pp. 78-93.

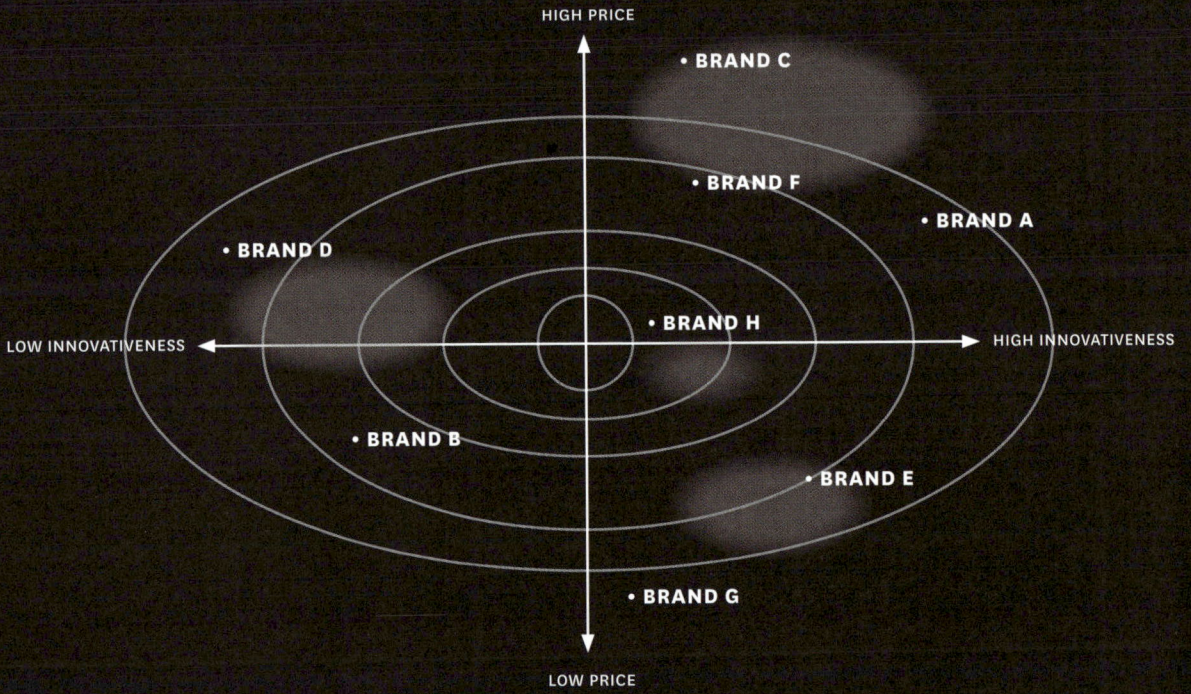

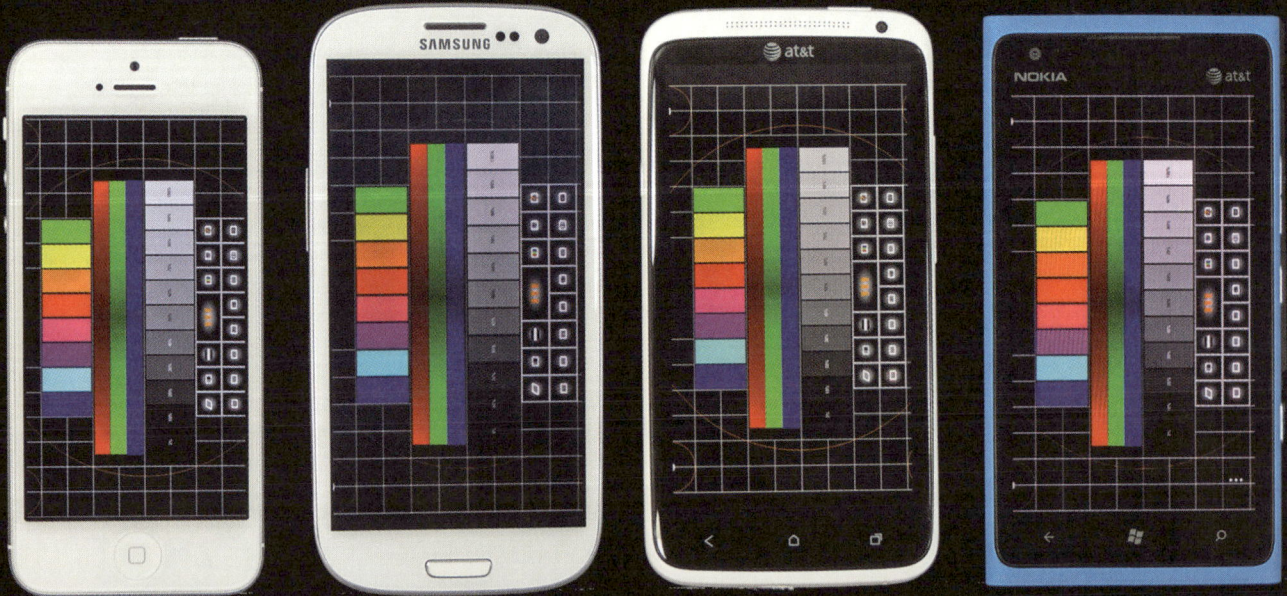

PERCEPTUAL MAP

Perceptual Maps, sometimes called positioning grids, are visual representations of what consumers think about products or brands. They help you assess how consumers view your products or brands in relation to those of competitors.

When can the method be used?
Perceptual Maps are very useful tools for building an effective marketing strategy. They provide you with valuable input for segmentation, differentiation and positioning, and the subsequent decisions on marketing mix elements.

Perceptual Maps can be used for existing products or brands as well as potential new ones. For existing products, they help you to evaluate the strengths and weaknesses of competing offerings with respect to criteria that customers find important and to identify sources of competitive advantage. They can also reveal a need to reposition a brand or product, and show the dimensions along which repositioning should take place.

For potential new brands or products, Perceptual Maps can identify market opportunities. This is typically when there are no current offerings that come close to customers' ideal points. Whether the product in question is existing or new, knowing how customers perceive products and what they would like in an ideal product is very important for you as a designer because you can use this information in the actual design process.

How to use the method?
Putting together a Perceptual Map does not require a lot of expertise and experience. While more advanced forms require the use of statistical methods such as multidimensional scaling, factor analysis and discriminant analysis, basic Excel skills should suffice for creating a simple map. Some reading up on how to word questions and which response formats to use would be good to prevent having to collect the data all over again if the original data is unusable due to misleading wording and use of inappropriate response formats. Doing a pilot run is advisable for refining the data collection instrument.

Possible procedure
The basic steps of creating a Perceptual Map are as follows:
STEP 1
Identify the attributes. For example price and innovativeness. That potential customers are most likely to be aware of and find the most important (determinant attributes).
STEP 2
Identify competing products/brands (competitive set).
STEP 3
Ask potential customers to rate each product/brand with respect to the most important attributes.
STEP 4
Ask potential customers to rate how important these attributes are ("ideal points").
STEP 5
If you got ratings for more than two attributes, select two of them – starting with the two most important ones would be a good idea – and plot the findings from steps 3 and 4 on the map. Repeat with other attribute combinations.

Limitations
· Only two attributes at a time can be represented on a Perceptual Map. When there are more than two attributes, multiple Perceptual Maps or a Value Curve should be used.
· A Perceptual Map represents the perceived position of brands at a specific point in time. They must be updated regularly, particularly when the market is changing rapidly.
· A Perceptual Map can indicate market opportunities, but it says nothing about how long the window of opportunity is and whether or not the organisation has the internal resources and capabilities to realise it.

Tips & Concerns
· Areas on the Perceptual Map where products/brands are located very close together indicate intense competition between them. When they are further apart, this means competition between them is low.
· Areas on the Perceptual Map where there are no products/brands indicate competitive gaps. These gaps can be considered opportunities only if customers want that particular combination of attributes.
· A cluster of ideal points indicates a segment within the target market, for example a group of people with similar preferences in relation to the product of interest. The more ideal points in the cluster, the bigger the segment.

REFERENCES & FURTHER READING: Mohr, J.J., Sengupta, S. and Slater, S.F., 2010. **Marketing of High-Technology Products and Innovations.** New Jersey: Prentice Hall. / Mullins, J.W. and Walker, O.C., 2013. **Marketing Management, A Strategic Decision-Making Approach.** 8th ed. Singapore: McGraw-Hill/Irwin. / O'Shaughnessy, J., 1995. **Competitive Marketing: A Strategic Approach.** New York: Routledge.

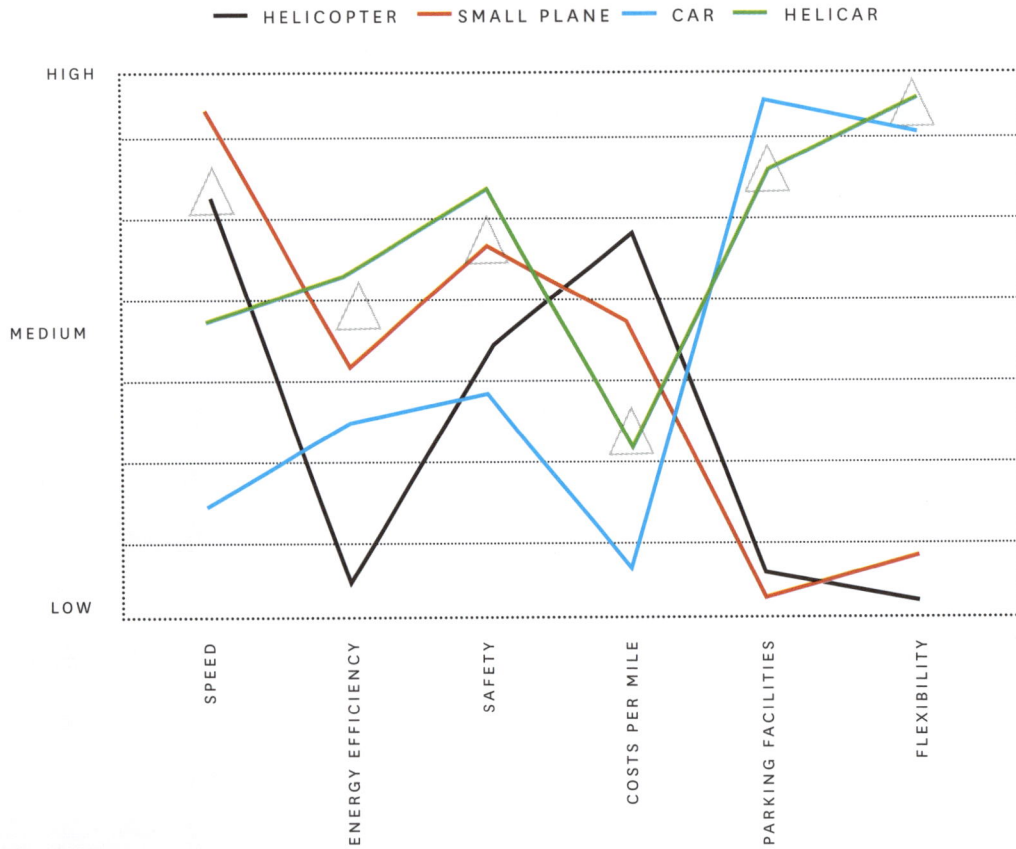

Mobility from door to door – that is the thought behind the PAL-V flying car. Developed and designed in the Netherlands, it made its maiden flight in 2012. Photo: PAL-V. Ideal points in the graph are indicated by triangles.

VALUE CURVE

Value Curves are visual representations of what consumers think about products or brands. In that they are very similar to Perceptual Maps. They help managers assess how consumers view their products or brands in relation to those of competitors.

When can the method be used?

The Value Curve is a useful tool for building an effective marketing strategy. Value Curves provide valuable input for segmentation, differentiation and positioning, and the subsequent decisions on marketing mix elements. They can be used for existing products or brands as well as potential new ones. For existing products, they help you to evaluate the strengths and weaknesses of competing offerings with respect to criteria that customers find important and to identify sources of competitive advantage. They can also reveal a need to reposition a brand or product, and show the dimensions along which repositioning should take place. For potential new brands or products, Value Curves can identify market opportunities. This is typically when there are no current offerings that come close to customers' ideal points. Whether the product in question is existing or new, knowing how customers perceive products and what they would like in an ideal product is very important for designers because they can use this information to focus their design process.

How to use the method?

Putting together a Value Curve does not require a lot of expertise and experience. Basic Excel skills should suffice for creating a graph showing the Value Curves for each product – see example. Some reading up on how to word questions and which response formats to use would be good to prevent having to collect the data all over again if the original data is unusable due to misleading wording and use of inappropriate response formats. Doing a pilot run is advisable for refining the data collection instrument.

Possible procedure

The procedure for creating Value Curves is as follows:

STEP 1
Identify the relevant product attributes, such as 'easy to use', 'price', 'beauty', that potential customers are most likely to be aware of and find most important. These are called determinant attributes.

STEP 2
Identify competing products/brands, forming the 'competitive set'.

STEP 3
Ask potential customers to rate each product/brand on the chosen attributes.

STEP 4
Ask potential customers to rate how important these attributes are. The most important attributes are called 'ideal points'.

STEP 5
Plot the findings from the previous two steps to form Value Curves for each product.

Limitations of the method

· A Value Curve represents the perceived position of brands at a specific point in time. It must be updated regularly, particularly when the market is changing rapidly.

· A Value Curve can indicate market opportunities, but it says nothing about how long the window of opportunity is and whether or not the organisation has the internal resources and capabilities to realise it.

Tips & Concerns

· When lines representing competing products/brands are close together, there is intense competition between them. When they are further apart, competition between them is low.

· Empty areas on the Value Curve indicate competitive gaps. These gaps can be considered opportunities only if customers want that particular combination of attributes.

· A cluster of ideal points indicates a segment within the target market, for example a group of people with similar preferences in relation to the product of interest. The more ideal points in the cluster, the bigger the segment.

REFERENCES & FURTHER READING: Kim, W.C. and Mauborgne, R., 1997. *Value innovation: The strategic logic of high growth.* Harvard Business Review, January-February, 75(4), pp. 103-112. / Kim, W.C. and Mauborgne, R., 1999. *Creating New Market Space.* Harvard Business Review, January-February, 77(1), pp. 83-93. / Mullins, J.W. and Walker, O.C., 2013. *Marketing Management, A Strategic Decision-Making Approach.* 8th ed. Singapore: McGraw-Hill/Irwin.

DEFINE

This section contains methods that can help you to define for whom and for what problem or challenge you are going to design.

Hannah Höch: Cut with the Kitchen Knife through the Last Weimar Beer-Belly Cultural Epoch in Germany. (Schnitt mit dem Küchenmesser durch die letzte Weimarer Bierbauchkulturepoche Deutschlands), 1919-1920. Photomontage and collage with watercolor (1140 x 900 mm) - Staatliche Museen zu Berlin, Nationalgalerie

COLLAGE

A Collage is a visual representation of the context, user group or product category. It helps you to develop visual design criteria and to communicate these criteria to your stakeholders.

When can the method be used?

Collages are mostly used in an early stage of the design process. They are a very suitable means of analysing the current context of use in an early stage of your project. The process of looking for images for your Collage gets you into the right visual mood. Saying 'yes' or 'no' to images helps you to define the desired feeling of the design you are working on. Collages can support you with the generation and communication of an image of your desired context. The term *collage* derives from the French 'coller' meaning 'glue'. This term was coined by both Georges Braque and Pablo Picasso at the beginning of the 20th century when this technique became a distinctive part of modern art.

How to use the method?

Before you start making a Collage you need to determine its purpose. Furthermore, it is important to determine how the Collage will be used: is it instrumental in the design project as a means to generate criteria, for example, or will it be used to communicate a design vision? Analysing Collages helps you to determine the criteria that the solution must meet. Criteria of this kind also set a general direction for idea generation. With a Collage you can find criteria for matters such as the lifestyle of a target group, the visual appearance of a product, the context of use and the interaction with a product. Other criteria can concern the category of products that are comparable to the new design and how the new product will function in its environment. The creation of a Collage is both creative and analytical. After making Collages you can use these images to define a number of characteristic types of colours/textures and materials.

Possible procedure

STEP 1
Determine the most suitable materials (2D and 3D). Intuitively gather as much raw imagery as possible.

STEP 2
Group together the imagery that concerns the target group, environment, handling, actions, products, colour, material and so on.

STEP 3
Decide on the function and meaning of the background: the orientation (landscape or portrait), colours, texture and size.

STEP 4
Experiment by drawing small sketches to set down the structure of the composition, paying attention to the creation of lines and axes.

STEP 5
Think about which imagery should be placed in the foreground and which in the background. Consider the size of the imagery and its relationship with the background.

STEP 6
Make a provisional composition of the Collage with the means at your disposal.

STEP 7
Assess the overall picture: are most of the characteristics represented?

STEP 8
Once the picture meets your expectations, paste the Collage.

Limitations of the method

· A Collage is personal and it is therefore sometimes hard to communicate its meaning to others.
· It takes a lot of time to find the right imagery for a Collage.
· Working from a computer screen and using digital images only limits your freedom.

Tips & Concerns

· If pictures do not meet your expectations, try to identify which element or elements are out of place: imagery (target group, products, et cetera), quantity of material, orientation, relationship, structure of the composition, foreground/background, treatment of material, separation/integration of material or types of colours/shapes.
· Consider the use of zoomed-in details of pictures and scale them up or down according to your needs.
· A mood board is a type of Collage expressing a specific mood or emotion.

REFERENCES & FURTHER READING: Bruens, G.*, 2007. *Form/Color Anatomy.* Utrecht: Lemma./ Muller, W.*, 2001. *Order and Meaning in Design.* Utrecht: Lemma.

PERSONAS

Personas are archetypal representations of intended users, describing and visualising their behaviour, values and needs. Personas help you to be aware of and communicate these real-life behaviours, values and needs in your design work.

When can the method be used?

When the user research is finished, a Persona can be used to summarise and communicate your findings. Personas can also be used during conceptualisation or when evaluating your design together with your team members or with other stakeholders involved in your project. Personas help you to have a consistent and shared understanding of the users' values and needs.

How to use the method?

First, you need to collect information about your intended users, such as by doing qualitative research, using Contextmapping techniques, Interviews and Observations. On the basis of this information, you build up your understanding of the intended users: behavioural patterns and themes, commonalities, particularities and differences. From an overview of the characteristics of your target group, including their dreams and needs and all kinds of insights, you can cluster your users on the basis of their similarities and build the archetypes that represent a specific cluster. When the characteristics of the representatives are clear, they can be visualised, named and described. Usually a limited number of Personas per project, about three to five, is sufficient and still manageable.

Possible procedure

STEP 1
Collect a rich amount of information and insights about your intended users.
STEP 2
Select the characteristics that are most representative of your target group and most relevant to your project.

STEP 3
Create 3 to 5 Personas:
· Give each Persona a name.
· Preferably use a single piece of paper or other medium per Persona to ensure a good overview.
· Use text and a picture of a person representing the Persona and visual elements of his/her material context, including relevant quotes from user research.
· Add some demographics such as age, education, job, ethnicity, religion and family status.
· Include the major responsibilities and goals of the Persona.

Limitations of the method

· Personas cannot be used as an independent evaluation tool. You still need real people to test and evaluate your design.
· Individual representations of Personas do not communicate explicitly the fact that your design will be part of a social context, too. For that reason, 'Socionas' were developed, which represent characteristics typically shared by groups.

Tips & Concerns

· Use quotes that sum up what matters most to the Persona.
· Do not look into details of your research when creating a Persona.
· Make the Personas visually attractive, thereby motivating yourself and others using the Personas during the design process.
· You can use the Personas to make storyboards.
· When making the Personas it helps to focus on a specific intended user, instead of trying to include everyone.

REFERENCES & FURTHER READING: Cooper, A., 1988. *The Inmates Are Running the Asylum*. Indianapolis: Sams. Postma, C.E.*, 2012. *Creating Socionas: Building creative understanding of people's experiences in the early stages of new product-development.* Delft: TU Delft. / Pruitt, J. and Adlin, T., 2006. *The Persona Lifecycle: Keeping People in Mind Throughout Product Design.* San Francisco: Elsevier science & technology.

These storyboards visualise the development and advantages of car sharing (a product-service combination) and service design in general. In this form, storyboards can be used in presentations but they need additional verbal explanation. (Image: SIDx7, Strategic Information Design Group 7, University of Dundee, 2013)

STORYBOARD

A Storyboard is a visual representation of a story or narrative about your design in its context of use over time. A Storyboard helps you to understand your intended users or user groups, context, product use and timing.

When can the method be used?

Storyboards can be used throughout the design process. The reader of a Storyboard will experience the intended interactions and he or she will also reflect on these interactions. In each process the meaning of a Storyboard changes. At the beginning of the process the Storyboard will look sketchy and might evoke comments and suggestions. But throughout the process, the Storyboard will become more detailed and help you in making decisions and exploring ideas. In the final stage of your design you can use a Storyboard to reflect on the product's form, values and qualities.

How to use the method?

Storyboards exploit the powerful aspects of visualisation. The whole setting can be shown at a glance: where and when the interaction happens, the actions that take place, how the product is used, and how it behaves, and the lifestyle, motivations and goals of the users. Storyboards allow you to literally point at elements, which is helpful during the discussion. When used to develop ideas, you start making a Storyboard based on your first idea about the interaction between product and user. The outcome is a good conceptual idea about the interaction, as well as visualisations or written descriptions of the interaction. Both visualisations and written descriptions can be used for communication and evaluation purposes.

Possible procedure

STEP 1
Start from the following elements: ideas, simulations, a user character.
STEP 2
Choose a story and a message: what do you want the Storyboard to express? Limit your story to a clear message, for example with 12 panels.
STEP 3
Create sketchy storylines.
Design the timeline before detailing. Use variations in panel sizes, white space, frames and captions for emphasis and expression.
STEP 4
Create a complete Storyboard.
Use short captions to complement the images, instead of merely describing the content. Do not make all the panels the same: use a hierarchy.

Limitations of the method

· The visualisation style of the Storyboards influences the reactions. Whereas open and sketchy Storyboards elicit comments, sleek and detailed presentations can be overwhelming. Storyboards used for analytical purposes – to map situations, problems and feelings – typically have a factual style of visualisation. Storyboards used to conceptualise ideas have a rough visualisation style. Storyboards used to evaluate design ideas are often open, bringing together different points of view. They have a sketchy, incomplete style of visualisation in order to invite reactions. Storyboards intended to transfer or present concepts often look polished.

Tips & Concerns

· Comics and movies can be a great source of expressive techniques. Some of these can be applied to product design scenarios and storyboards, whereas others are less suitable.
· Think about camera position (for example, close-up versus wide shot), sequence and the style in which you visualise the Storyboards.
· A Storyboard can also be used to make a video clip, for example, about the unique selling points of your design.
· A Storyboard can also help you to communicate with your stakeholders.

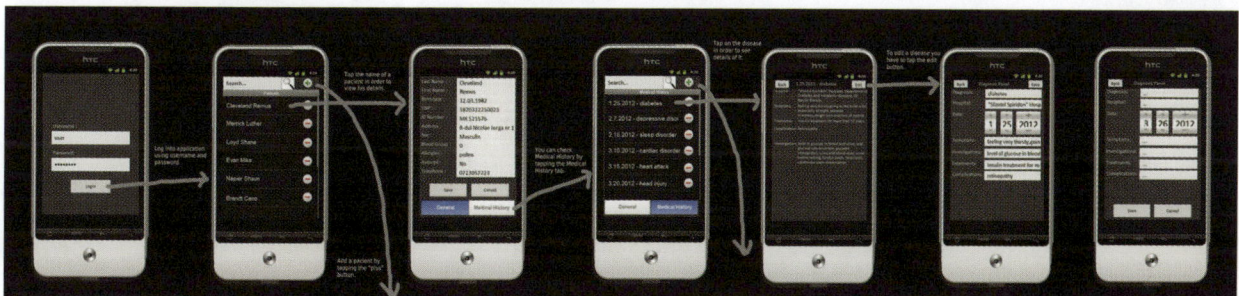

A storyboard depicting actions and resulting stages in the user interface of a smartphone application.

REFERENCES & FURTHER READING: Jacko, J.A. And Sears, A., 2002. *The Human-Computer Interaction Handbook: Fundamentals, Evolving Technologies and Emerging Applications.* New York, NY: Erlbaum and Associates. / Van der Lugt, R., Postma, C.E. and Stappers, P.J.*, 2012. *Photoboarding.* Touchpoint, 4(2), pp. 76-79. / Van der Lelie, C.*, 2005. *The value of storyboards in the product design process.* Personal and Ubiquitous Computing, 22 September, 10(2/3), pp. 159-162.

WRITTEN SCENARIO

When can the method be used?

Similar to Storyboards, Written Scenarios can be used in an early stage of the design process to develop user criteria for interaction with a product/service, and in a later stage to generate ideas. You can also employ Written Scenarios to reflect on a developed concept, to present and communicate ideas and concepts to your stakeholders, and for concept evaluations and usability testing. Furthermore, you can use them to envision future scenarios, describing a desired and imagined new context with new interactions. With your story or narrative you bring your design and intended users to life in a specific context. For example, you can write a scenario about all the possible interactions a mother has with your physical exercise design or some other object, between the moment she wakes up until the moment she leaves her house. You may want to describe a realistic, state-of-the-art scenario, but you can also depict a new, more futuristic and desired one.

How to use the method?

First you need to have input for your scenario. The details you need to know in advance depend on the purpose of your scenario. Before you start, you need to have a basic understanding of your intended user(s) and the interactions within a specific and imagined/intended or real context of use. Scenarios can be derived from data gathered during contextual enquiry activities. You then describe, in simple language, the interaction that needs to take place. Stakeholders can review your

A Written Scenario tells a story about your intended users in a specific situation. Depending on your aim, the story depicts either existing product-user interactions or possible interactions in a future situation.

scenario to ensure that it accurately represents the real world or that they agree on the intended world you propose in your scenario. Use Written Scenarios when designing in order to ensure that all participants understand and agree on the design parameters, and to specify exactly what interactions the system must support.

Possible procedure

STEP 1
Determine the aim of your scenario and the required number of scenarios and length.

STEP 2
Determine the actors, your intended users and the goals the main actor(s) have to complete. The actor has an active role in the scenario. If you have several actors, you should set up more scenarios.

STEP 3
Think about the style of your scenario, for example a neutral sequence of steps or a moving and epic narrative.

STEP 4
Give your scenario an inspiring title and make use of dialogue, spoken by the actors, to bring your story to life.

STEP 5
Define the starting points of the scenario: a trigger or an event.

STEP 6
Start writing. Focus on the most promising or successful scenario.

Limitations of the method

· A scenario is your story. It might be hard to get it across to other people in (your) words only.
· A scenario cannot cover all possible realities.

Tips & Concerns

· Books, comics, movies and commercials are means to tell a story. They can be great sources of inspiration for your Written Scenario.
· The process of writing a scenario is similar to designing a product; it is an iterative process where you need to rewrite your scenario several times and you need to analyse and synthesise, harnessing your creativity.
· It is nice to add variation to your scenario, but do not strive to include everything in the narrative – otherwise your message will get lost.

Jacques Tati was a French screenwriter, film director and actor. In his movies, Tati's characters are often in conflict with infrastructure, modern architecture, products and modernity in general. In 'Jour de Fête', postman François is inspired by a movie about mail delivery by airplane in America. Teased by his fellow villagers, he tries to achieve the same speed of delivery on his bicycle, but of course everything does not go as planned. In his films, Tati shows how people lose track of the changing world around them due to so-called improvements that are often driven by a combination of commerce, overconfidence in technology and wrong assumptions. (Photo by Robert Doisneau, 1949)

REFERENCES & FURTHER READING: Carroll, J.M., 2000. *Five reasons for scenario-based design*. Interacting with Computers, September, 13(1), pp. 43-60. / Jacko, J.A. and Sears, A., 2002. *The Human-Computer Interaction Handbook:* Fundamentals, Evolving Technologies and Emerging Applications. New York, NY: Erlbaum and Associates.

PROBLEM DEFINITION

Designing is often referred to as problem solving. Before you start solving anything, you need to be sure that you are working on the right problem. Finding and defining the real problem is a significant step towards a solution.

When can the method be used?

A Problem Definition is usually set up at the end of the problem analysis phase. A problem always has to do with dissatisfaction about a certain situation. Because satisfaction is a relative concept, problems are also of a relative nature. They are defined from the perspective of a problem owner. The problem owner might foresee problems if nothing is done – but decides to do something to prevent them. For instance, imagine that winter is coming, but you do not have warm clothing. There is nothing you can do to turn back nature's clock, so the winter is not the problem. The real problem is your lack of appropriate clothing. You can avoid getting cold by making or buying a sweater and thick jacket.

For defining a problem this implies that it is not sufficient to describe the current state. As a result, a description of the situation is a description of the current state plus the relevant causal model(s), including the assumed patterns of behaviour of the people and organisations involved. A situation is only a problem if the problem owner can and wants to do something about it. This implies that a situation that is more desirable than the present one must be described: the goal situation. In the case of our example, this goal is to be comfortably warm during the winter.

How to use the method?

Designers often underestimate the work required to find and define problems. As a young and ambitious designer you are probably keen to design an innovative water kettle, car or chair. It takes some experience and courage to discuss with your client that the real problem might be something completely different. For example, a potential car buyer's real problem concerns transportation, not the fact that he does not own a car. So instead of *owning* a car, the *use* of a car can be a solution as well. This kind of thinking has led to a concept like car sharing, where a service replaces the product.

Possible procedure

· Answering the following questions will help to create a Problem Definition:
· What is the problem?
· Who has the problem?
· What are relevant context factors?
· What are the goals?
· What are the side effects to be avoided?
· Which actions are admissible?

The outcome is a structured description of the design problem, with a clear description of the desired end situation (goals) and possibly the direction of idea generation. A well-written Problem Definition provides a shared understanding between you, your client and possible stakeholders.

Limitations of the method

· Defining the problem does not solve the problem.

Tips & Concerns

· When analysing problems there is always a tension between the 'current situation' and the 'desired situation'. By explicitly mentioning these different situations you are able to discuss their relevance with other people involved in your project.
· Make a hierarchy of problems. Start with a big one and divide it into smaller ones by thinking of causes and effects. Use post-it notes to make a problem tree.
· A problem can also be reformulated as an opportunity or 'driver'. Doing this will help you to become active and inspired.

Parking Problem? The most unique features of Volkswagen Autostadt (Wolfsburg, Germany) include the two 60-metre glass silos used to store new Volkswagens. The towers are connected to the Volkswagen factory by a 700-metre underground tunnel. When purchasing a car from Volkswagen, the customer can choose to travel to Autostadt to pick it up. The customer gets free entrance to the museum, meal tickets and a variety of events building up to the point where he or she can follow on screen how the automatic elevator picks up the selected car and lowers it down at 1.5 metres per second. The car is then transported out to the customer without having driven a single metre, and the odometer is thus at "0".

REFERENCES & FURTHER READING: Roozenburg, N.F.M. and Eekels, J.*, 1995. *Product Design: Fundamentals and Methods.* Utrecht: Lemma.

Pugh's checklist for generating design requirements

1. PERFORMANCE: *What main functions does the product need to fulfil? What functional properties should it have (speed, power, strength, precision, capacity, etcetera)?*

2. ENVIRONMENT: *What kind of environmental influences does the product need to withstand during production, transport and use (temperature, vibrations, moisture, etcetera)? What effects of the product to the environment should be avoided?*

3. LIFE IN SERVICE: *With what intensity will the product be used and how long should it last?*

4. MAINTENANCE: *Is maintenance necessary and possible? What parts need to be accessible?*

5. TARGET PRODUCT COST: *Target Product Cost: What is a realistic price for the product, considering similar products? What margin does it need to deliver?*

6. TRANSPORT: *What requirements are set by transport of the product during production and to the location of usage?*

7. PACKAGING: *Is packaging needed? Against what should the packaging protect?*

8. QUANTITY: *What is the amount of units to be produced? In batches or in continuous production?*

9. PRODUCTION FACILITIES: *Should the product be designed for existing production facilities, or is it possible to invest in new production resources? Will (part of) production be outsourced?*

10. SIZE AND WEIGHT: *Are there boundaries to the size and weight of the product due to production, transport or use?*

11. AESTHETIC, APPEARENCE AND FINISH: *Which preferences do buyers and users have? Should the product fit a house style?*

12. MATERIALS: *Should certain materials (not) be used (because of safety or environmental reasons)?*

13. PRODUCT LIFE SPAN: *How long is the product expected to be produced and sold?*

14. STANDARDS, RULES AND REGULATIONS *What standards, rules and regulations (nationally and internationally) apply to the product and to the production process? Should standardisation within the company or within the industry be taken into account?*

15. ERGONOMICS: *What requirements result from observing, understanding, handling, operating (etcetera) the product?*

16. RELIABILITY: *What chance of failure is acceptable? What kind of failure and consequences to the functioning of the product should be avoided at all cost?*

17. STORAGE: *Are there long periods of storing time during production, distribution or usage of the product? Does this call for specific storage measures?*

18. TESTING: *What quality tests are conducted on the product, both inside and outside the company?*

19. SAFETY: *Should specific precautions be taken with regards to the safety of users and non-users?*

20. PRODUCT POLICY: *Are there requirements resulting from the company's current product portfolio?*

21. SOCIETAL AND POLITICAL IMPLICATIONS: *What opinions are there currently in society concerning the product?*

22. PRODUCT LIABILITY: *For what kinds of design, production or usage mistakes can the producer be held accountable?*

23. INSTALLATION AND INITIATION OF USE: *What requirements result from assembly outside the factory, installation, connecting to other systems and learning how to handle and operate the product?*

24. REUSE, RECYCLING: *Can the material cycle be extended by reuse of parts and materials? Are parts and materials easy to separate for recycling or waste processing?*

LIST OF REQUIREMENTS

When can the method be used?

The List of Requirements is drafted on the basis of an analysis of all the information gathered on the design problem. A product design is 'good' insofar as it complies with the stated Requirements. A structured list of Requirements is particularly vital when designing complex products that involve coping with many aspects. In teams, a list is helpful in ensuring that you are all on the same page. This list can even serve as a contract between client and designer whereby you agree on the direction of further development. The Requirements keep evolving during the development process as the design proposals become more concrete and detailed.

How to use the method?

In the beginning it is vital to make a structure that helps you to reach completeness. There are several tools for this. At first, the list will serve as a checklist. You must gather more information to ensure concrete and valid Requirements. For example when designing a playground, you need to know about how children play, ergonomic data, et cetera.

During a design project, new perspectives on the design problem frequently lead to the identification of new Requirements. Therefore, the Requirements should be constantly updated and changed. The outcome is a structured List of Requirements and standards.

Possible procedure

STEP 1

Make a structure based on one of the checklists in order to generate Requirements.

Image left: What started out as a graduation project at the Faculty of Industrial Design Engineering in Delft resulted in a successful product: the main design requirement for the Senz° Umbrella was that it should be able to withstand wind speeds of up to 100 km/h! And it does. Photo: Senz°

A List of Requirements states the important characteristics that your design must meet in order to be successful. A List of Requirements describes concretely all of your design objectives and can be used to select the most promising ideas and design proposal(s) or combinations of proposals.

STEP 2

Define as many Requirements as possible.

STEP 3

Identify gaps in your knowledge, that is, information that needs to be gathered by research.

· Put the Requirements into practice: determine their variables in terms of observable or quantifiable characteristics.

· Not: the price should be as low as possible. But: the consumer price should be between € 100 and € 125 > cost price between € 25 and € 30.

· Make a distinction between demands and wishes: demands must be met, wishes are used to choose between ideas and design proposals.

· Example of demand: the product weight should not exceed 23 kg because of labour rules.

· Example of a wish: the product should be considered 'comfortable' by as many test subjects as possible.

STEP 4

Eliminate Requirements that are similar or do not discriminate between design alternatives.

Identify whether there is a hierarchy of Requirements. Distinguish between lower-level and higher-level Require-ments.

STEP 5

Make sure that your Requirements fulfil the following conditions:

· each Requirement must be valid
· the list must be complete

· the Requirements must be operational
· the list must be non-redundant
· the list must be concise
· the Requirements must be practicable.

Limitations of the method

· Spending too much time on analysing and defining design Requirements can hinder your creative process. Employ an iterative approach, where you switch between sketching and defining criteria.

· Do not overly limit the possibilities of your design by defining too many Requirements.

Tips & Concerns

· To make your Requirements more concrete, define them in numerical terms. For example, change: 'The product should be portable' into: 'The product should weigh less than 5 kg'. Sometimes it takes too long to reliably quantify something or evaluate it numerically. Therefore, this step is not a must.

· Mention the sources in the List of Requirements – publications, experts, own research, et cetera.

· Give your Requirements a structured numbering so that you can easily refer to them. Using Process Tree numbering immediately shows the reason for a certain Requirement.

· Use more than one checklist; checklists complement each other.

REFERENCES & FURTHER READING: Cross, N., 1989. *Engineering Design Methods.* Chichester: Wiley. / Hubka, V. and Eder, W.E., 1988. *Theory of Technical Systems: A Total Concept Theory for Engineering Design.* Berlin: Springer. / Jones, J.C., 1982. *Design Methods: Seeds of Human Futures.* Chichester: Wiley. / Pahl, G. and Beitz, W., 1984. *Engineering Design: A Systematic Approach.* London: Design Council. / Pugh, S., 1990. *Total Design: Integrated Methods for Successful Product Engineering.* Wokingham: Addison Wesley. / Roozenburg, N.F.M. and Eekels, J.*, 1995. *Product Design: Fundamentals and Methods.* Utrecht: Lemma.

KEY PARTNERS	KEY ACTIVITIES	VALUE PROPOSITION	CUSTOMER RELATIONSHIPS	CUSTOMER SEGMENTS
· bicycle shop · sponsors · webprovider · mobile phone provider	· delivering packages on bicycles · maintenance · acquisition · administration · planning	· saving the customer's time by offering an ecofriendly, fast, cost-effective and reliable bicycle courier service · taking care of: internal mail, PO-box delivery, express delivery and one-day service	· face-to-face · telephone · e-mail · newsletter, · website	· anyone who needs packages and letters (max. 1 x 0.5 x 0.5 m and up to 50 kg) to be delivered quickly within a 15 km radius.
	KEY RESOURCES · workspace · personnel · smartphones · website · laptops · bicycles (+ trailers) · bags · cycling clothes · good physical condition		**CHANNELS** · Mouth-to-mouth · (social) media · telephone · pay online · couriers	

COST STRUCTURE	REVENUE STREAMS
· Workspace · maintenance · personnel · laptops · bicycles + equipment · smartphones · insurance · website	· paying customers · shirt sponsoring

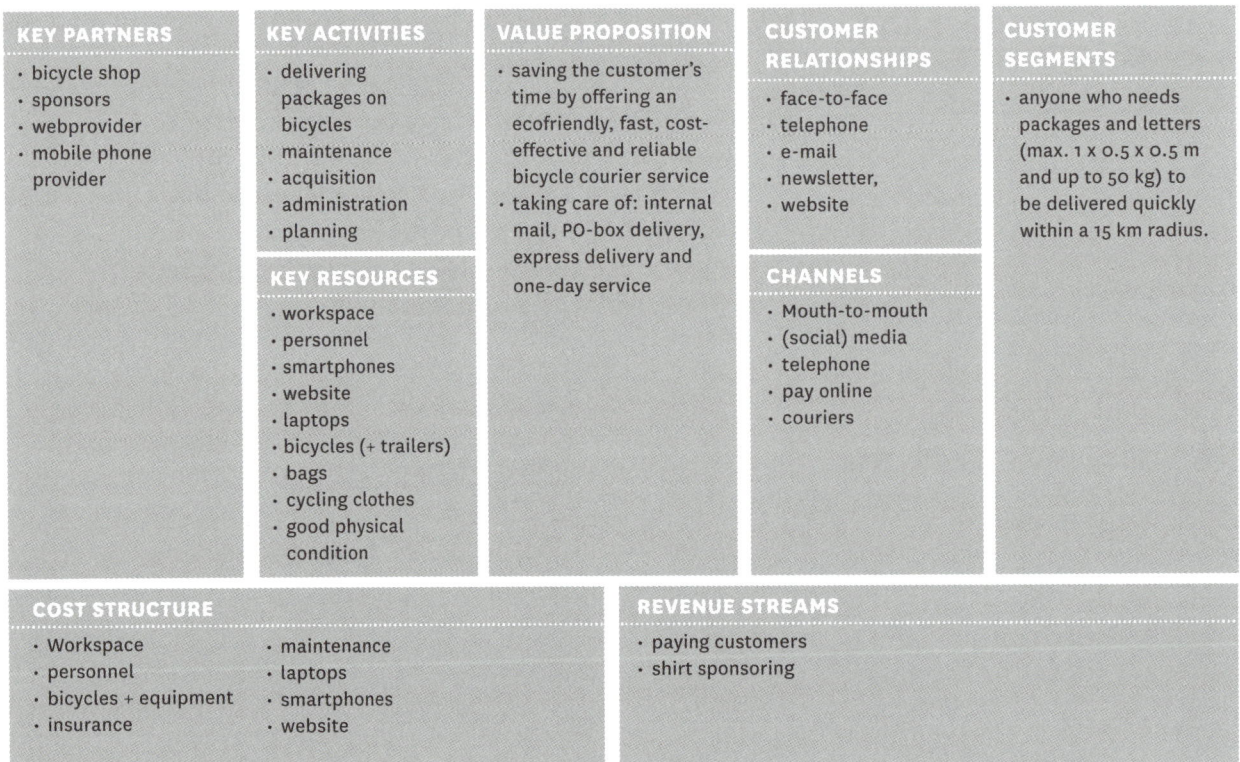

Example of a business model canvas filled in for a bicycle courier service. After Osterwalder and Pigneur, 2010

BUSINESS MODEL CANVAS

When can the method be used?

The Business Model Canvas can be used in many stages of the development process. It enables you to see the economic relevance and context of the product and service that you are developing: what exactly is the added value of the product or service and for whom? In the idea-generation phase it can help in completing ideas or in evaluating them. The same goes for the conceptual phase where you need to choose between several business concepts: which concept can be expected to generate the required turnover and/or profit? Which concept will strengthen the company's competitive position? A perfectly detailed lamp might be your dream as a designer, but if it turns out to be affordable for a handful of buyers only, it might not make a lot of sense from a business point of view, even if it has a high profit margin.

How to use the method? & Possible procedure

A canvas divided into nine areas supports the method. Each area should be defined and the relationship between them can be described using arrows and drawings. Preferably, the template should be printed on a large sheet of paper (minimum A3) so you can work on it with a team in a brainstorm-type setting. This stimulates analysis, discussion and creativity in the group.

These nine key elements should finally be 'aligned' in order to create a well-defined product-service proposal, though not necessarily in this order. The nine key elements can be structured in four clusters:
STEP 1
Offering ('raison d'être'): Value Propositions
STEP 2
Activities (internal): Key Activities, Key Resources and Key Partners

The Business Model Canvas is a comprehensive visual tool to discuss business ideas. It enables you to evaluate business ideas in an early stage and on a conceptual level. It can also support the analysis of the existing business you are in and identify strong and weak spots, threats and opportunities.

STEP 3
Customers (external): Customer segments, Channels and Customer Relationship
STEP 4
Finances (input-output): Cost Structure versus Revenue Streams In a further stage, the external context of the business idea can be drawn up around the Canvas and more Canvases can be drafted to communicate the development of the new business over time.

Limitations of the method

· Compared to a business plan, the Business Model Canvas represents a more conceptual level of thinking about new business. At this level of thinking you should not try to put in exact numbers like expected turnover or running costs. On the other hand, it is wise to ensure that the order and magnitude of the numbers are realistic. This could be a first step in working out several business ideas.

Tips & Concerns

· Like in a brainstorm, you need to postpone criticism. New ideas and approaches should be welcomed and if needed adapted in order to improve them.
· If an idea is not realistic, add a new idea to make it realistic or change it in such a way that it becomes more realistic. Often the trick is to turn a 'problem' into a possibility.
· When a business concept is finally chosen to be detailed, a more exact business plan can be drawn up.

REFERENCES & FURTHER READING: Osterwalder, A. and Pigneur, Y., 2010. *Business Model Generation.* New Jersey: John Wiley & Sons Inc.

PRODUCT

- What does the customer want from the product?
- What features does it have to meet these needs?
- How and where will the customer use it?
- What does it look like?
- What size or colour should it be?
- What is it to be called?
- How is it branded?
- How is it differentiated from its competitors?

PRICE

- What is the value of the product or service to the buyer?
- Are there established price points for the products or services in this area?
- Is the customer price sensitive?
- What discounts should be offered to trade customers?
- How will your price compare with your competitors?

PROMOTION

- Where and when can you get across your marketing messages to your target market?
- Will you reach your adience by advertising in the press, on tv, radio, billboards, other media?
- When is the best time to promote?
- How do your competitors do their promotion and how does that influence your choice of promotional activity?

PLACE

- Where do buyers look for your product or service?
- If they look in a store, what kind of store?
- How can you access the right distribution channels?
- Do you need to use a sales force?
- What do your competitors do, and how can you learn or differentiate from them?

Prada Marfa is an art installation by American artists Elmgreen and Dragset (2005) near Marfa, Texas. It was intended to be not repaired or maintained so it would slowly degrade. Prada provided 14 right-footed shoes and six bags, but they were stolen three days after the opening. The artists decided to restore and repair the installation. Photo: Marshall Astor, Creative Commons.

MARKETING MIX OR 4PS

The Marketing Mix is a combination of four instruments – Product, Price, Place and Promotion – with which a product manager or strategic product designer can influence a marketing strategy.

When can the method be used?

The Marketing Mix can be used for developing a marketing plan for an existing product or a new product concept. The former typically takes place in the commercialisation phase of new product development, the latter in the fuzzy front end. The product manager commonly uses the method as a checklist for decision-making. It indicates the four instruments with which a product manager can influence the marketing strategy for a product. The use of the Marketing Mix is often considered to be relevant for tactical or short-term decision-making and typically requires information from previous phases of the New Product Development process. However, the method can also be beneficial for strategic product designers by assisting them in articulating value propositions or new product concepts in the fuzzy front end.

How to use the method?

The use of the Marketing Mix typically starts with a positioning statement for the new product, including information about the target market and competitive advantage. Based on the positioning, decisions can be made for each of the 4Ps. The most important decisions focus on:

· Product: for example, its features, branding, packaging, assortment, services and guarantee.
· Price: for example, the retail price, discounts and price structure.
· Place: for example, the distribution channel, retail stores and shelves and channel management.
· Promotion: for example, the target audience, communication media, message, objectives and budget.

Decisions about each marketing instrument should be consistent and integrated with decisions concerning the other 3 Ps. The decisions together form the core of the marketing plan. In addition, a marketing plan also contains statements about the finances, sales forecast and responsibilities.

Possible procedure

STEP 1
Depending on the type of product and market, you first have to decide for each 'P' which marketing elements are relevant. For example, for a certain product offering, packaging and retail price might be more relevant than the guarantee. Check if you need to add elements to the list above.

STEP 2
Generate and map possible solutions for each element – for example, for 'packaging' you can think of possible solutions such as blister packaging, single or bulk packaging, et cetera.

STEP 3
Determine the best solution, consisting of a relevant and coherent Marketing Mix for your product offering.

Limitations of the method

The Marketing Mix should be considered to be a steppingstone towards a full-fledged marketing strategy. The advantage of this framework is its simplicity, yet its use alone may be insufficient for new market situations or complex product/service offerings. Alternative classifications exist for different situations and products, for example:

· For services: 7Ps, adding Participants, Physical evidence and Process.
· For a stronger focus on the consumer: 4Cs, namely, Customer needs, Convenience, Cost and Communication.
· For B2B or Industrial Marketing: an emphasis on collaboration and personalisation.
· For E-marketing: 4Ps with minor changes, for example, Price is changed to greater Transparency.

Tips & Concerns

· Before you apply the method yourself, it may be helpful to analyse how companies have used the Marketing Mix for products that are already on the market.
· The different instruments are often treated separately, but are in practice strongly related to each other and are equally important.
· During the Product Life Cycle, you have to monitor the product closely and, if necessary, adapt your decisions in line with the 4Ps.
· Check if the different elements are consistent and convey the same message – for example, low-quality packaging is not a good fit for an expensive, high-quality product.
· Finally, the price component of the Marketing Mix deserves special attention: price delivers revenue, while the other Ps create value for the consumer and require investments.

REFERENCES & FURTHER READING: Mullins, J.W. and Walker, O.C., 2013. *Marketing Management, A Strategic Decision-Making Approach.* 8th ed. Singapore: McGraw-Hill/Irwin. / Borden, N.H., 1964. *The Concept of the Marketing Mix in Science in Marketing.* New York: John Wiley. / Constantinides, E., 2006. *The Marketing Mix Revisited: Towards the 21st Century Marketing.* Journal of Marketing Management, April, 22(3/4), pp. 407-438.

DEVELOP

This section contains methods that can help you to develop
ideas and concepts while designing.

BASIC
STRUCTURE

TYPE SB

TYPE SA

TYPE FA

TYPE FB

TYPE MA

CRITERIA — CRITERIA — CRITERIA

Generate

Alternatives on
a topological level

Categorize

Generate

Alternatives on
a typological level

Categorize

Generate

Alternatives on
a morphological level

Categorise

BASIC STRUCTURE

STRUCTURAL CONCEPT

FORMAL CONCEPT

MATERIAL CONCEPT

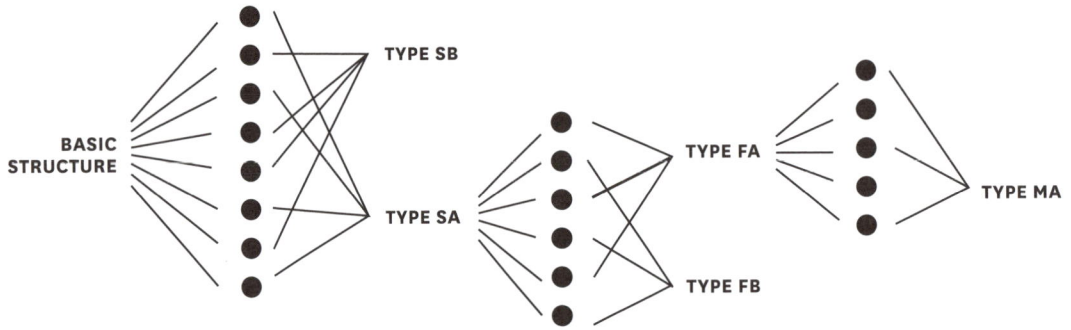

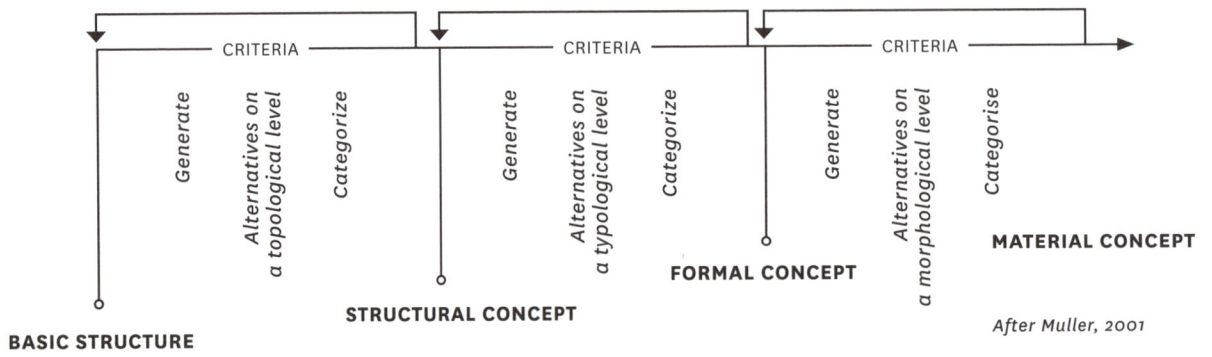

After Muller, 2001

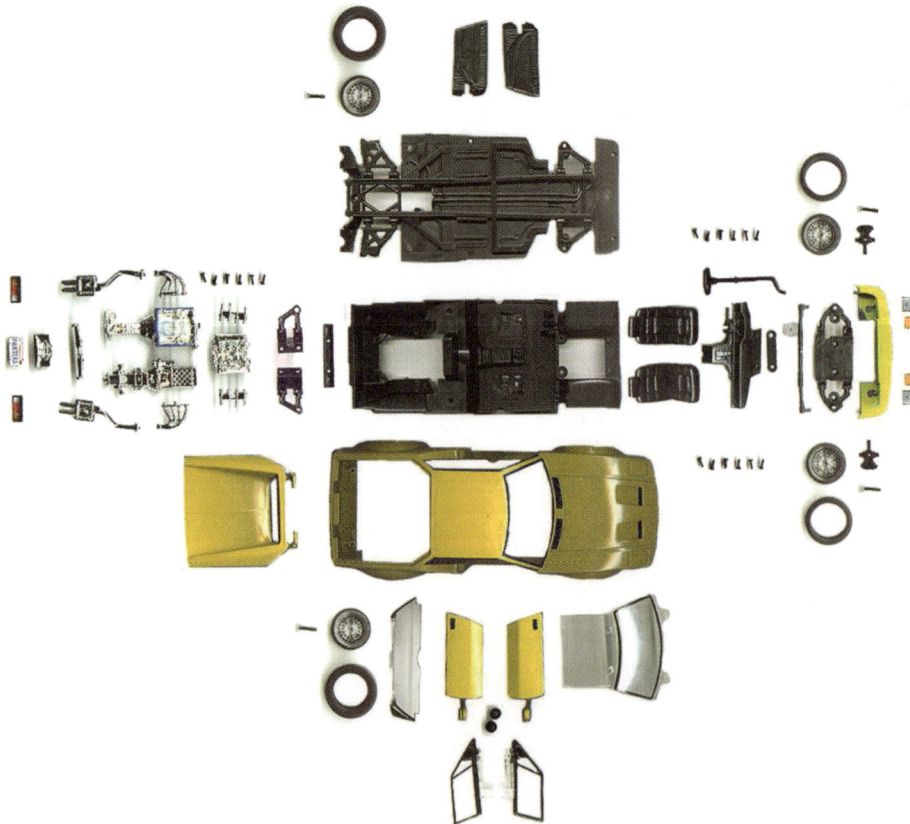

FISH TRAP MODEL

The Fish Trap Model helps you in generating and developing material concepts that determine the geometrical form of your design. It prescribes a process of converging, diverging and categorising, metaphorically referring to a 'fish trap' for 'catching a final solution'.

When can the method be used?

The starting point for the use of the Fish Trap model is a basic structure of the intended functions of the product and the components required to fulfil these functions. The method ends at the material concept stage (sketch plan or preliminary design), which describes how a product's subassemblies are embodied, detailed and formed into a coherent whole. An essential aspect of the model is the simultaneous development of design criteria with the generation of concepts. Furthermore, the Fish Trap model emphasises visiospatial thinking. That is, stimulation of the imagination and exploration through sketching are seen to be essential for developing design criteria and concepts. Initially, the criteria are derived from the visual exploration and analysis of the context, which involves the users, use and the use environment. The design space is then explored by means of both visualisation techniques such as sketching & collages and three-dimensional sketch models or mock-ups.

How to use the method?

You systematically explore alternative solutions on three subsequent levels of increasing detail and meaning. Exploring alternatives on each of these levels yields three types of concepts:
STEP 1
Topological level, resulting in a structural concept;
STEP 2
Typological level, resulting in a formal concept;
STEP 3
Morphological level, resulting in a material concept.

On each level, you generate a large variety of design alternatives (or variants), cluster them in groups and evaluate them. After selecting the most promising concepts, you proceed to the next, more detailed generation phase.

Possible procedure

STEP 1
Develop a Structural Concept. Start by defining the basic functional components. These components, or ordering elements, are technical parts or sub-assemblies that embody working principles or use functions. Develop many topological variants that differ in terms of the spatial ordering of the components. Cluster the variants and develop them into structural concepts that represent each topological type, such as open, compact or horizontally structured. Select one or more structural concepts using the simultaneously developed preliminary criteria.
STEP 2
Develop a Formal Concept. Focus on the overall form of the whole structural concept. Sketch a variety of possible geometric forms. Evaluate the viability of the rough formal concepts (in terms of construction, integration of components, needed material) and categorise them in groups with the same form type. Cluster the variants and develop them into one or more formal concepts that represent each form type. Show the formal features and the typical intended

product-user interactions, like 'cool', 'childish' or 'playful'. Select one or more formal concepts, using the simultaneously developed criteria.
STEP 3
Develop a Material Concept. Materialise one or more formal concepts, looking for detailed solutions, including aspects such as manufacturing, assembly, specification of materials, finishing, texture and colours.

Limitations of the method

· The Fish Trap model is especially useful when you can start with a clearly defined function structure and functional components. These are not always clearly defined in advance. Whether or not you like to work using a systematically defined and prescriptive method like the Fish Trap model depends on your personal preferences.

Tips & Concerns

· In his book, Muller describes the Fish Trap model and presents a useful overview of possible ways of ordering the structural components and the meanings they could articulate.
· It is important for you to contextualise the structural concepts and evaluate them by imagining the possibilities for the interaction with the intended user. By doing so, you can identify new ways in which the product-user interaction can appear.

REFERENCES & FURTHER READING: Macey, S. and Wardle, G., 2008. H-Point, *the fundamentals of car design and packaging.* Pasadena: Art Centre College of Design. / Muller, W.*, 1997. *Vormgeven: ordening en betekenisgeving.* 2nd ed. Utrecht: Lemma. / Muller, W.*, 2001. *Order and meaning in design.* Utrecht: Lemma.

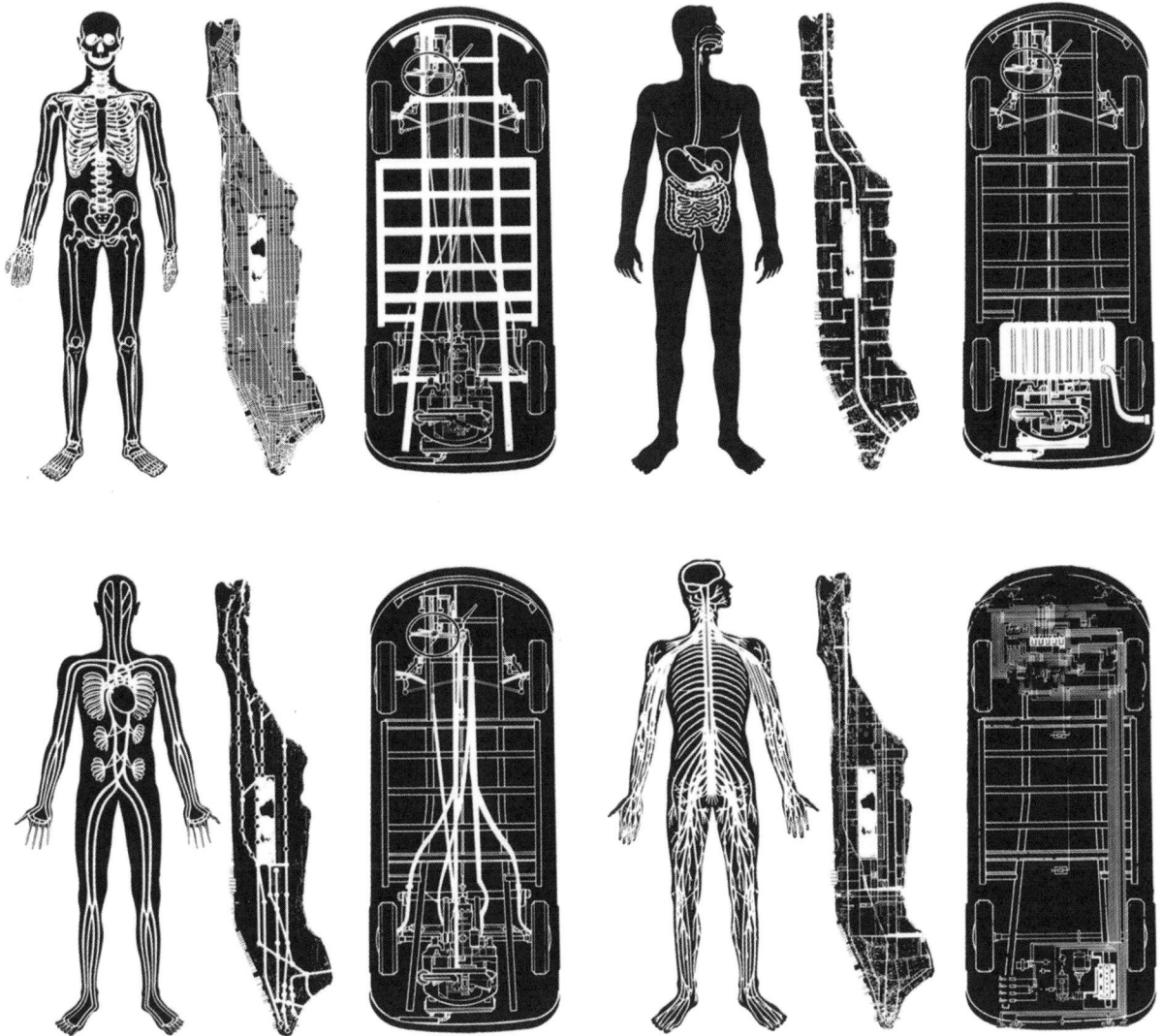

First published in 1982, German architect Oswald Mathias Ungers' City Metaphors juxtaposes more than 100 various city maps throughout history with images of flora and fauna and other images from science and nature. Ungers assigns each a title--a single descriptive word printed in both English and German. In Ungers' vision, the divisions of Venice are transformed into a handshake and the 1809 plan of St Gallen becomes a womb. Ungers writes in his foreword: "Without a comprehensive vision reality will appear as a mass of unrelated phenomenon and meaningless facts, in other words, totally chaotic. In such a world it would be like living in a vacuum; everything would be of equal importance; nothing could attract our attention; and there would be no possibility to utilize the mind." A classic of creative cartography and visual thinking, City Metaphors is also an experiment in conscious vision-building.

ANALOGIES & METAPHORS

You can use Analogies and Metaphors to find inspiration for new solutions derived from a mapping process between inspirational sources and a target domain, which is the problem to be solved.

When can the method be used?

Analogies and Metaphors are especially helpful during idea generation. Seeing an existing problem through the lens of another domain supports the creation and exploration of novel solutions. Analogies are typically used for conceptualisation, starting from a clear problem definition, and Metaphors for early problem framing and analyses.

When using an Analogy, inspirational sources can be closely or distantly-related to the current problem. For example, a close Analogy for a new office air conditioning system might be air conditioning systems in cars, hotels or airplanes. A distant Analogy might be a self-cooling termite mound. Metaphors, on the other hand, are mainly helpful for communicating particular messages to users. They typically do not help in solving practical problems, but represent the meaning a product evokes. For example, you can attribute a personality – like adventurous, feminine or trustworthy – to a solution concept and evoke particular emotions. When using metaphors, the source of inspiration should be from distantly related domains.

How to use the method?

Start by searching for inspirational material. If you want to come up with more creative and innovative thoughts, search in distant domains. When finding material, ask yourself why you associate that particular inspirational source with your design. Then you can decide whether to implement the Analogy or Metaphor by asking yourself how you will employ it in the new design solution. When using Analogies, be careful not to simply copy the physical attributes of a given source to your problem. You need to identify relevant relationships in the remote domain and turn them into

potential solutions through abstraction and transformation. The better you abstract from the relationships you observe, the more inspiration you are likely to get.

Possible procedure

STEP 1 – FRAMING:

Analogy: Frame the design problem to be solved.

Metaphor: Frame the qualities of the experience you want to provide to users through the new design solution.

STEP 2 – SEARCHING:

Analogy: Search for situations where that problem has been successfully solved.

Metaphor: Search for a distinct concrete entity that already has the quality you intend to convey.

STEP 3 – APPLYING:

Analogy: Retrieve the relationships from the existing components and processes in the inspirational domain. Abstract from what you see and capture the essence of that relationship. Transform and transfer the abstracted relationships to fit your new problem situation.

Metaphor: Retrieve the physical properties of the inspirational domain. Abstract the essence of these properties. Transform them to match the inherent constraints of the product or service at hand.

Limitations of the method

· When trying to establish analogies you might take a lot of time to identify an appropriate source domain, with no guarantee of arriving at a useful search. You might get stuck when the inspirational material you are trying to use does not help you to find a solution. Therefore, it is important to have a good knowledge about the source domain you are exploring so that you can recognize such situations early on.

Tips and concerns

· *Analogies:* It is important to play with both close and distant domains. When you choose only close domains you risk finding only obvious and unoriginal solutions. Your success depends partly on how you abstract and transform inspiration into innovative solutions.

· *Metaphors:* It is fruitful to look for qualities that you want to emphasise in your concept and find Metaphors that encapsulate these qualities. When applying a metaphor, try to establish subtle yet identifiable references to the original entity. However, avoid making very obvious connections otherwise you could end up with a 'kitsch' product.

REFERENCES & FURTHER READING: Casakin, H. and Goldschmidt, G., 1999. *Expertise and the use of visual analogy: Implications for design education.* Design Studies, 1 March, 20(2), pp. 153-175. / Hey, J., Linsey, J., Agogino, A.M. and Wood, K.L., 2008. *Analogies and metaphors in creative design.* International Journal of Engineering Education, March, 24(2), pp. 283-294. / Madsen, K.H., 1994. *A Guide to Metaphorical Design.* Communications of the ACM, December, 37 (12), pp. 57-62. / Van Rompay, T.J.L.*, 2008. *Product expression: Bridging the gap between the symbolic and the concrete.* In H.N.J. Schifferstein & P. Hekkert (eds.)*, Product experience, pp. 333-352. Amsterdam: Elsevier.

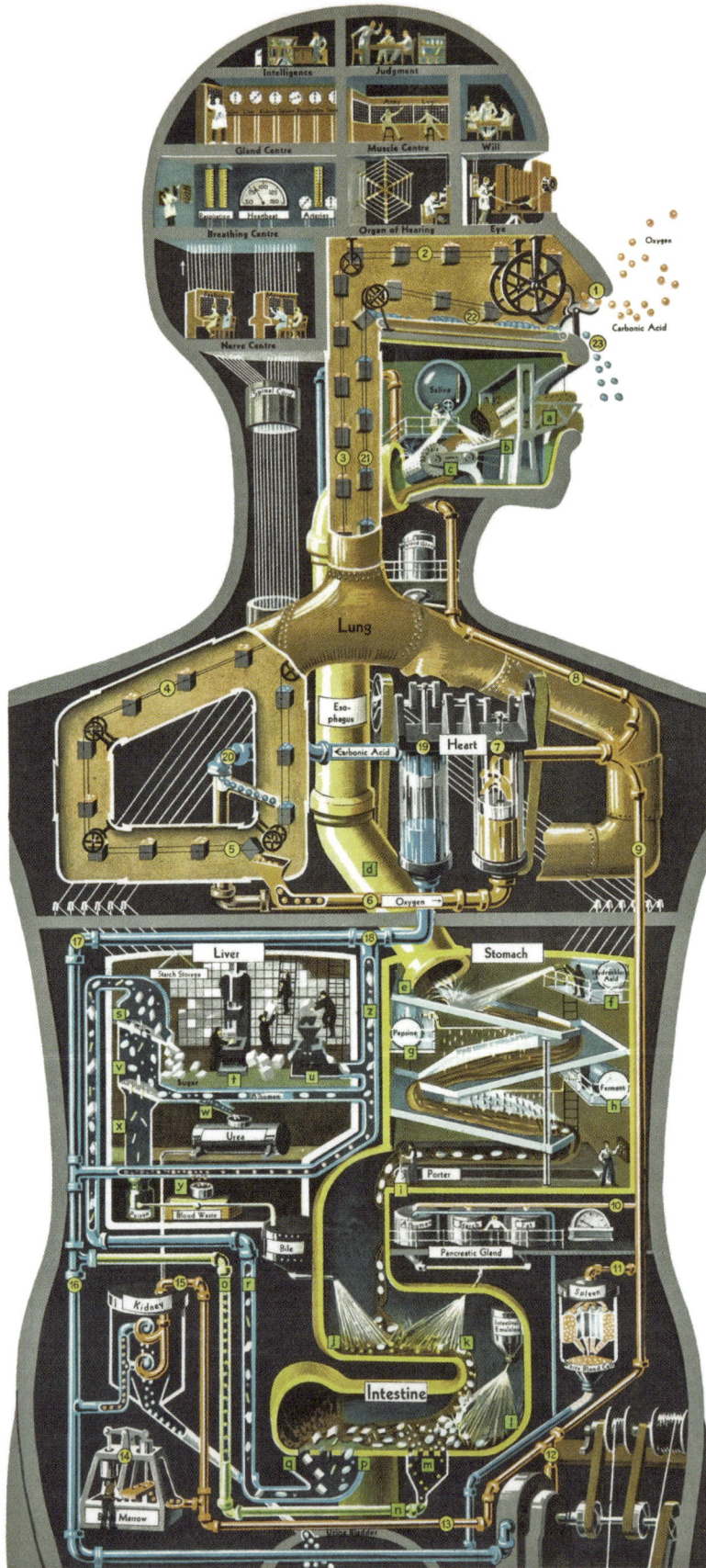

Fritz Kahn: The Man as Industrial Body. Fritz Kahn (1888-1968) is considered by many to be the founder of conceptual medical illustration. Kahn produced a series of books during the 1920s on the inner workings of the human body using metaphors of modern industrial life. His modernist visualisation was fitting since he was writing during a time of great industrial and technological change, especially in Germany.

SYNECTICS

Synectics is a comprehensive method to facilitate creative problem solving using analogies and joining together different and apparently irrelevant elements. It typically helps you to generate a limited set of preliminary yet surprisingly high-quality ideas.

When can the method be used?

Synectics is best applied for complex and intricate problems, because the procedure is systematic and requires a relatively large investment of time and effort. Synectics can be used in teams and individually. The method contains guidelines for executing a problem analysis, idea generation and selecting from alternative solutions. The starting point for using Synectics could be a preliminary problem statement.

How to use the method?

The Synectics method requires you to use analogies to come up with design ideas. The use of analogies allows you to move away from the original problem statement and existing solutions by force-fitting the analogies to the problem statement. The process of force-fit allows you to develop ideas based on the analogies, instead of solely based on the problem definition. The Synectics procedure relies on the processes of (1) preparation, (2) incubation, (3) illumination and (4) verification. The incubation and illumination stages are brought about through the use of analogies or metaphors to make the strange familiar and the familiar strange.

In the preparing stage, the problem owner typically articulates a problem statement/ briefing. Based on this, users of Synectics will go through an extensive problem analysis phase, if possible including discussion between participants. The problem analysis should lead to a single concrete target. After this, a purging phase takes place in which known and immediate ideas are collected and recorded. This phase is also called 'shredding the known'. From this point on, analogies are used to estrange oneself from the original problem statement and come up with inspirations for new solutions and approaches.

There are different types of analogies you can think of, for example direct from nature, personal, for example imagining that you are the product yourself, symbolic via the meaning that an object elicits (for example 'the humour of a bicycle') and fantasy analogies that do not exist in real life yet. In order to select between alternative solutions, Itemised Response can be used.

Possible procedure

STEP 1
Start with the original problem statement. Invite the problem owner to present and discuss the problem briefly.
STEP 2
Analyse the problem. Restate the problem. Formulate the problem as a single concrete target.
STEP 3
Generate, collect and record the first ideas that come to your mind, shredding the known.
STEP 4
Find a relevant analogy or metaphor.
STEP 5
Ask yourself questions in order to explore the analogy. What types of problems occur in the analogous situation? What types of solutions are there to be found?
STEP 6
Force-fit various solutions to the reformulated problem statement and generate, collect and record the ideas.
STEP 7
Test and evaluate the ideas. Use the Itemised Response method or another selection method to select ideas.
STEP 8
Develop the selected ideas into concepts.

Limitations of the method

· With an untrained group, the facilitator will have to work one small step at a time; he or she must have enough experience to inspire the group through such a process.
· Synectics can be quite demanding for inexperienced participants.

Tips & Concerns

· Visual and auditory Synectics is a variation on the common Synectics procedure. In this case, soothing images and music are introduced to induce an incubation phase in which the participants daydream calmly. After some time you switch to much more active music and images, which stimulate your participants to generate ideas. This last step is similar to Brainstorm or Brainwriting methods.

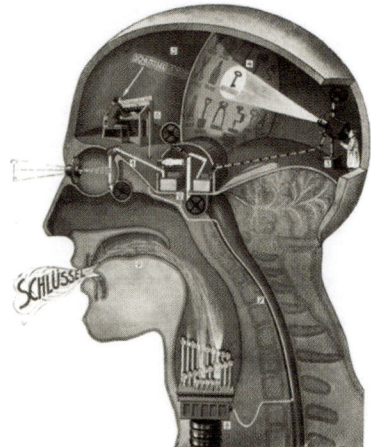

REFERENCES & FURTHER READING: Gordon, W., 1976. *Synectics, the Development of Creative Capacity*. New York, NY: Collier. / Roozenburg, N.F.M., Eekels, J.*, 1995. *Product Design: Fundamentals and Methods*. Lemma, Utrecht. / Tassoul, M.*, 2006. *Creative Facilitation: a Delft Approach*. Delft: VSSD. / Wallas, G., 1926. *The art of thought*. In P.E. Vernon (eds.), Creativity. Penguin.

BRAINSTORM

Brainstorm prescribes a specific approach with rules and procedures for generating a large number of ideas. It is one of many methods used in creative thinking, based on the assumption that quantity leads to quality.

When can the method be used?

Brainstorming can be useful during each phase of the design process, but especially when starting up the generation of ideas after defining the design problem and the first set of design requirements. Brainstorming is based on the principle of the avoidance of premature criticism. That is why during a Brainstorm, the list of requirements can be temporarily 'forgotten'. On the other hand a Brainstorm can be dedicated to one requirement: for example, 'how can we make our product more energy efficient?'

How to use the method?

A Brainstorm is usually carried out with a group of people. In practice, any number between 4 to 15 people will work. Several strict rules must be followed during a Brainstorm:

- Criticism is postponed: during the session you should try not to think about utility, importance, feasibility and the like, and should not make any critical remarks. This rule should lead to many and unexpected associations. It also ensures that participants will not feel they are being attacked or their suggestions are being overruled.
- 'Freewheeling' is welcomed: you can express any idea you can think of – 'the wilder the idea, the better'. An atmosphere must be created where the participants feel safe and secure.
- 1+1=3: combinations and improvements of ideas are sought: you should endeavour to come up with better ideas by building upon the ideas of others.
- Quantity is wanted: the underlying idea is that 'quantity breeds quality'. Due to the rapid succession of associations, there is little opportunity to be critical.

Possible procedure

STEP 1
- Define the problem. Develop a problem statement, for example by formulating a 'How-To'. Select a team of participants. Draw up a plan for the Brainstorm session, including a timeline and the methods to be used.
- Have a preparatory meeting with the team to explain the method and the rules. The problem is redefined if necessary, and a so-called warm-up is held.
- At the beginning of the actual session, write the problem statement and the four rules on a blackboard or flip chart.
- The facilitator asks a provocative question and writes down the group's responses on a flip chart.

STEP 2
Diverge from the problem.
Once many ideas have been generated, the group selects the most promising and interesting ideas or clusters of ideas. Usually, some criteria are used in this selection process.

STEP 3
Make an inventory, evaluate and group your ideas.

STEP 4
Converge: choose ideas or clusters of ideas to take along to the next phase of the design process. See, for example, the C-Box technique.

STEP 5
These steps can be carried out using three different media:
- Speaking: Brainstorm
- Writing: Brain writing – see Brain Writing
- Drawing: Brain drawing – see Brain Drawing

Limitations of the method

- Brainstorming is suited for solving relatively simple problems with an 'open' formulation. For more complex problems, it would be possible to Brainstorm about sub-problems, but this might lead you to lose sight of the problem as a whole.
- Brainstorming is not very well suited to problems that require highly specialised knowledge.

Tips & Concerns

- Do not criticise any outcomes of the Brainstorm during the session.

REFERENCES & FURTHER READING: Roozenburg, N.F.M. and Eekels, J.*, 1995. *Product Design: Fundamentals and Methods.* Utrecht: Lemma. Tassoul, M.*, 2006. *Creative Facilitation: a Delft Approach.* Delft: VSSD. / Higgins, J.M., 1994. *101 Problem Solving Techniques.* New York: New Management Publishing Company.

What is portable? When radio-cassette players became smaller, lighter and more portable in the 1980s, a subculture developed where youngsters would carry around large ghettoblasters, heavily packed with batteries. In the streets they shared their musical tastes and showed off dance moves. Also known as boom boxes, special models were designed by JVC, Hitachi, Panasonic and others. The trend eventually disappeared during the 1990s.

BRAINWRITING AND BRAIN DRAWING

When can the method be used?
Brainwriting and Brain Drawing are especially useful when starting up idea generation, after defining the design problem and the first set of design requirements. Like Brainstorming these methods are based on the principle of avoiding premature criticism. The list of requirements can thus be temporarily 'forgotten'. On the other hand a session can be dedicated to one requirement: for example, 'how can we make our product portable?'

How to use the method?
Brainwriting and Brain Drawing are usually carried out in a group of 4 to 8 people. During the session, these rules must be followed:

1. Criticism is postponed: try not to think about utility, importance, feasibility and the like, and do not make critical remarks. This rule should lead to many and unexpected associations. It also ensures that participants will not feel they are being attacked or ignored.
2. Freewheeling is welcomed: you can express any idea you can think of – the wilder, the better. Create an atmosphere where the participants feel safe and secure.
3. 1+1=3: seek combinations and improvements of ideas: endeavour to come up with better ideas by building upon the ideas of others.
4. Quantity is wanted: the underlying idea is that 'quantity breeds quality'. Due to the rapid succession of associations, there is little opportunity to be critical.

In these alternatives to the Brainstorm method, participants write or draw their ideas on a sheet of paper. They pass the papers to each other several times so that they can all build upon each other's ideas. Like in Brainstorming, it is assumed that quantity leads to quality.

Possible procedure

STEP 1 – DEFINE THE PROBLEM
Develop a problem statement, for example by formulating a 'How-To'. Select a team of participants and draw up a plan for the Brainstorm session, including a timeline and the methods to be used. Have a preparatory meeting with the team to explain the method and the rules. Redefine the problem if necessary and hold a warm-up session.

STEP 2 - DIVERGE FROM THE PROBLEM
At the beginning of the actual session, write the problem statement and the four rules on a blackboard or flip chart. Plenty of A4 or A3 sheets of paper should be available together with pens, pencils or markers, depending on the method to be used:

· *Brainwriting (6-5-3 method)*
Each participant writes down some ideas on a piece of paper. After a few minutes each paper is passed to the next participant. As an idea is passed from one participant to another, it is elaborated or serves as a steppingstone for new ideas. A well-known version is the 6-5-3 method: 6 participants take 5 minutes to generate 3 ideas and pass them around, generating 6 x 3 x 5 = 90 ideas in 25 minutes.
· *Brain Drawing*
Each participant draws one idea on a sheet of paper. Every 3 minutes, each paper is passed around to the next team member, who adds drawings or ideas to the initial drawing. This process can be repeated several times.

STEP 3 - MAKE AN INVENTORY, EVALUATE AND GROUP YOUR IDEAS
Once many ideas have been generated, the group selects the most promising and interesting ideas or clusters of ideas. Usually, some criteria are used in this selection process.

STEP 4 – CONVERGE
Choose ideas or clusters of ideas to take along to the next phase of the design process. See for example the C-Box method.

Limitations of the method
· Brainwriting and Brain Drawing are suited for solving relatively simple problems with an 'open' formulation.
· For Brain Drawing the participants need to have good drawing skills so that their drawings communicate the essence of the ideas effectively.

Tips & Concerns
· Do not criticise the outcomes of the Brainstorm during the session.
· Part of Osborn's way to put theory into practice was to have a coffee break after the idea generating phase. In his opinion, the break is important to indicate the switch from the phase of no criticism to the phase of evaluation and selection.

REFERENCES & FURTHER READING: Higgins, J.M., 1994. *101 Problem Solving Techniques.* New York, NY: New Management Publishing Company. Roozenburg, N.F.M. and Eekels, J.*, 1995. *Product Design: Fundamentals and Methods.* Chichester: John Wiley & Sons. Tassoul, M.*, 2006. *Creative Facilitation, a Delft Approach.* Delft: VSSD Delft.

Morphology originates from the biological study of animals and their functional body parts.
Below: example of of a morphological chart for a pedal kart.

SOLUTIONS	1	2	3	4	5	6
Support kart	4 wheels A	4 wheels B	3 wheels A	3 wheels B	3 wheels C	
Put kart into motion	Direct drive	Chain drive	Belt drive	Drive shaft	Crankshaft	
Stop kart	Disk brakes	Rim breaks	Brakes on tire	Brake with feet	Parachute	Anchor
Control direction	Central axis	Ackermann				
Support driver's body	Saddle	Chair	Plank	Cloth		

SUB FUNCTIONS

principal solution 1 ←········
> starting point for ideation

principal solution 2 ·······→
> starting point for ideation

principal solution 3 ·······→
> starting point for ideation

MORPHOLOGICAL CHART

When can the method be used?

The Morphological Chart is usually applied at the beginning of the idea generation phase after some ideas have been sketched. A function analysis is used as a starting point to break down the overall product function into sub-functions – see Function Analysis. Often a number of solutions to these sub-functions are already known, while others still need to be generated. The morphological method results in a matrix of sub-functions and solutions, also referred to as parameters and components. Functions are abstract and solutions are concrete but do not need to have a definitive shape or size yet. The matrix enables you to describe possible principal solutions by combining solutions for each sub-function.

How to use the method?

The starting points of a Morphological Chart are a well-defined main function of the product and a function analysis of the product; the product should be described in terms of its function and sub-functions. The sub-functions describe the characteristics that a product normally has to have in order to serve its overall function. For example, a teapot has the following sub-functions: containing tea (container), filling water (opening in the top), pouring tea (snout) and operating teapot (handle).

The description of a function always contains a verb and an object. In a Morphological Chart, functions and sub-functions are independent and have no reference to material features. Through careful selection and combination of a set of solutions, a 'principal solution' is formed. Generating solutions is thus a process of systematically combining solutions.

The Morphological Chart helps you to generate principal solutions in an analytical and systematic way. It is based on the deconstruction of the overall function of a product into sub-functions.

Possible procedure

STEP 1
Formulate the main function of the product.
STEP 2
Identify all the functions and sub-functions that are needed in the solution.
STEP 3
Construct a matrix with these sub-functions as rows. For the design of a pedal kart this could be, for example: put kart into motion / stop kart / control direction / support the driver's body.
STEP 4
Fill the rows with solutions for a particular parameter. Solutions can be found by analysing similar products or by thinking up new principles for these sub-functions. For example: stopping a pedal kart can be done with disc brakes / cantilever brakes / brake on the tires / feet on tires / feet on the ground / stick in the ground / parachute / and probably more. Use evaluation strategies to limit the number of principal solutions.
STEP 5
Create 'principal solutions' by combining one solution per row for each sub-function.
STEP 6
Carefully analyse and evaluate all solutions with regard to the design requirements and choose at least three principal solutions.
STEP 7
Sketch possible ideas for the whole product based on each principal solution.
STEP 8
Further detail a selection of the ideas into design proposals.

Limitations of the method

· The Morphological Method is not suitable for all design problems. It is best suited to design problems in the field of engineering design, but with some imagination it can also be applied to form-related design problems.

Tips & Concerns

· The possible combinations for solutions increase fast; a 10 x 10 matrix yields 10,000,000,000 solutions. In order to limit the number of options, analyse the rows critically and group the solutions before making the combinations.
· For the analysis of the rows you can rank the solutions per sub-function in order of first and second preference, using the design requirements.
· Group the sub-functions in groups of decreasing importance. As a first step, only evaluate the most important sub-function group. After you have chosen one or more combinations of solutions, only these are involved in the evaluation. When a combination of solutions has yielded a principal solution, be sure to draw all the solutions or components when developing the solution principle into an idea or design proposal.
- Challenge yourself by making counterintuitive combinations of solutions.

REFERENCES & FURTHER READING: Roozenburg, N.F.M. and Eekels, J.*, 1995. *Product Design: Fundamentals and Methods.* Utrecht: Lemma. / Cross, N., 1989. *Engineering Design Methods.* Chichester: Wiley.

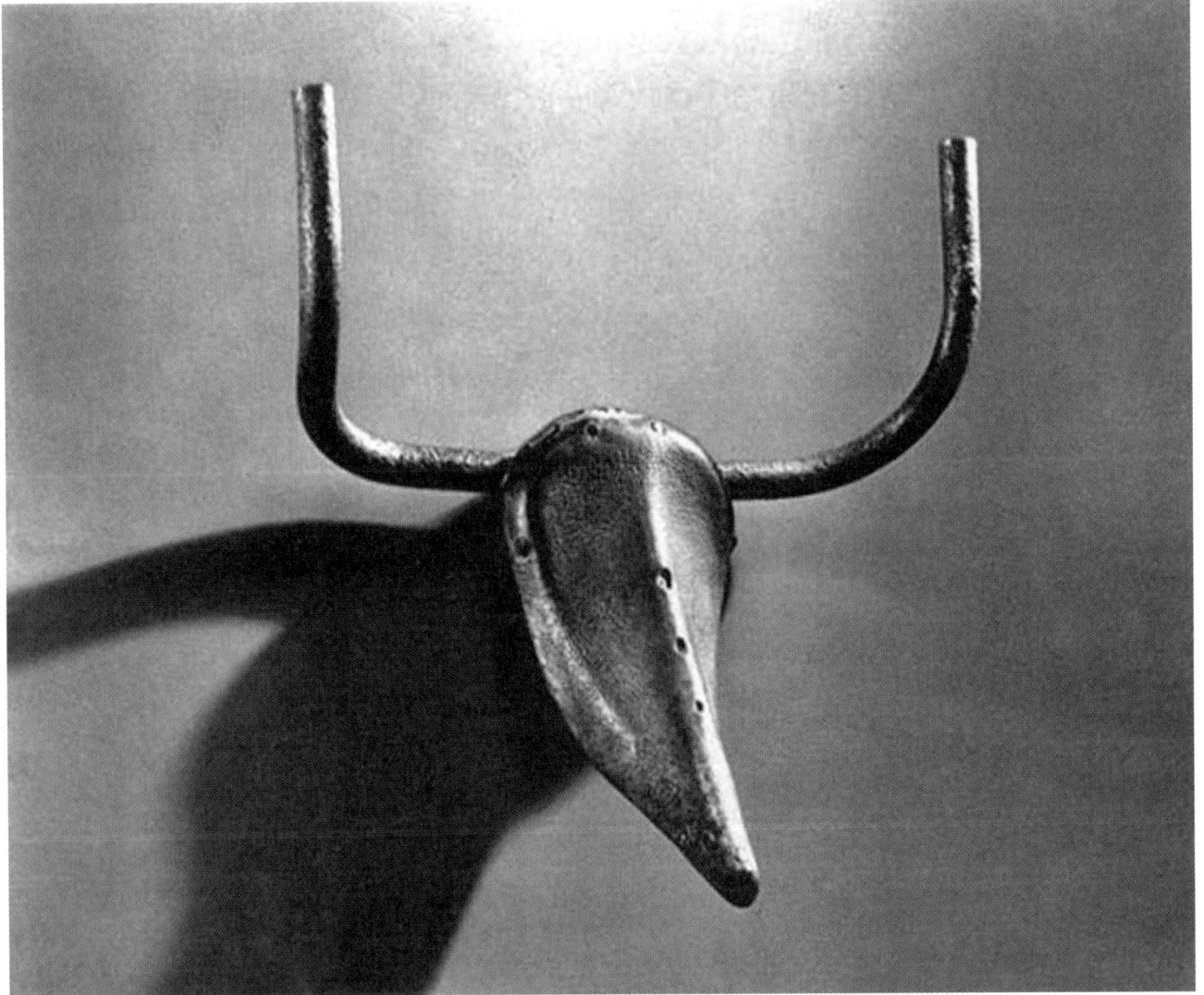

Pablo Picasso: Bull's Head, 1942

SCAMPER

SCAMPER is a creativity method that can help with creating ideas through the application of seven heuristics: Substitute, Combine, Adapt, Modify, Put to another use, Eliminate and Reverse.

When can the method be used?

The SCAMPER method can be used in a late stage of idea generation, when initial ideas or concepts already exist. The method is typically used after you have 'run out' of ideas. By creating possibilities with SCAMPER, without considering feasibility or relevance at first, you can create unexpected ideas or steppingstones to new ideas and concepts. SCAMPER is often used as part of a Brainstorming session, when it can elicit a new range of ideas based on what is already on the table. Individuals can also use this method.

How to use the method?

When using the SCAMPER method, you will typically confront each product idea or concept with the seven heuristics by asking a number of questions per heuristic. After you have generated a satisfying number of new ideas, you can proceed by clustering the ideas, like in a Brainstorm session, and select the most promising ones for further detailing.

STEP 1
· What can be substituted (S) in the idea/ concept to improve it?
· What materials or resources can you substitute or swap?
· What other product or process could you use to achieve the same outcome?

STEP 2
· What can be combined (C) to improve the idea/concept?
· What would happen if you combined a product with another to create something new?
· What if you combined the purposes or objectives of the ideas/concepts?

STEP 3
· What aspects of the idea/concept can you adapt (A) to improve it?
· How could you adapt or adjust the product to serve another purpose or use?
· What else is like your product that you could adapt?

STEP 4
· How could you modify (M) your idea or concept to improve it?
· How could you change the shape, look or feel of your idea or concept?
· What would happen if you magnify or minimise the size?

STEP 5
· How can the idea or concept be put to another use (P)?
· Can you use the idea/concept somewhere else, perhaps in another industry?
· How would the product behave differently in another setting?
· Could you recycle the waste to make something new?

STEP 6
· What aspects of the idea or concept can be eliminated (E)?
· How could you streamline or simplify the idea or concept?
· What features, parts or rules could you eliminate?

STEP 7
· What about the idea or concept can be reversed (R)?
· What would happen if you reversed the use process? Or if you changed the sequence of use?
· What if you were to try to do the exact opposite of what you are trying to do now with the idea or concept?

Limitations of the method

· The SCAMPER method might suggest that by applying the seven heuristics, creativity is guaranteed. This is not the case, as a lot depends on the designer's use of the heuristics. Therefore, the SCAMPER method is not very suitable to untrained designers.

Tips & Concerns

· The heuristics of the SCAMPER method are at the core of creative thinking; these kinds of questions should occur again and again in the mind of a designer. The key to effective use of the method lies in asking challenging – and sometimes radical – questions. If you want to reap the greatest benefits from the SCAMPER method, you should be willing to challenge your own creativity. Sometimes you might want to go a little crazy and ask questions like 'what does this idea look like from the perspective of a fly?'
· Like in any creative process, avoid criticism or discarding seemingly unrealistic ideas. Evaluation should be done in a separate stage when you can evaluate ideas, cluster them, eliminate unfeasible or irrelevant ideas and proceed with detailing selected ideas or concepts. It might take a few rounds of SCAMPER until successful results can be achieved.

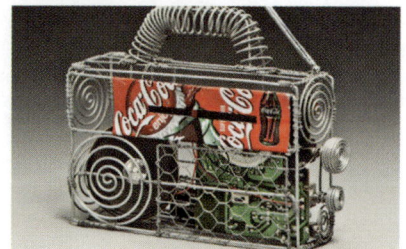

Ghana Radio, 1995/1996

REFERENCES & FURTHER READING: Eberle, B., 1996. *Scamper On: More Creative Games and Activities for Imagination Development.* Waco: Prufrock Press Inc. / Osborn, A., 2007. *Your Creative Power.* Meyers Press.

From The Book to just books. In the Netherlands, Christianity has been losing 'business' for many decades now, resulting in a large number of abandoned churches. Bookshops face difficult times as well: people read fewer books as they are spending more time online, and readers now tend to order books online or read them as e-books. The Selexyz bookshops chain tries to reinvent their bookshops by adding attractive features and services such as lunch corners and art galleries. In Maastricht, they converted an abandoned church building into a much-appreciated venue for adoring books.

WWWWWH: WHO, WHAT, WHERE, WHEN, WHY, AND HOW

When can the method be used?

Problem analysis is one of the activities you typically do in an early stage of a design process, when you have read the design brief. WWWWWH is a checklist to be used when defining your design problem – see Problem Definition. WWWWWH helps you to formulate the problem in a structured and complete way. This WWWWWH checklist is also useful in other stages of the design process, for example, when preparing and designing user research activities and presentations or writing reports.

How to use the method?

An important notion in problem analysis is the deconstruction of the problem. First, define the preliminary problem or draft a design brief. By asking yourself a multitude of questions about the stakeholders, facts and more, you can deconstruct the problem systematically. Consequently, you can review the problem and set priorities. You can expect to gain greater clarity about the problem and its context and a better understanding of the stakeholders, facts and values of the problem. You also will have greater insight into other problems underlying the initial problem.

- *WHO: Stakeholder: Selexyz bookshop chain (now called: Polare)*
- *Book lovers who like to browse in bookshops*
- *WHAT: Sales of bookshops are decreasing dramatically. Fewer bookshops means a decline in book-browsing experiences*
- *WHERE: Shopping areas losing shops In the bookshops*
- *WHEN: Ongoing for several years; 2005-2012*
- *WHY: There is a significant shift going on in the book business*
- *HOW: More online sales*
- *More time is dedicated to Facebook instead of reading books. Rise of e-books, e-readers, tablets*

WWWWWH (Who, What, Where, When, Why, How) is a checklist of the most important questions to be asked to analyse your design problem, which means obtaining a thorough understanding of the problem, its stakeholders and the facts and values involved.

Possible procedure

STEP 1
Write down the initial design problem or task in brief statements.

STEP 2
Ask yourself the following WWWWWH questions in order to analyse the initial design problem. Perhaps you can come up with more questions yourself.

- Who has the problem? Who have an interest in finding a solution? Who are the stakeholders?
- What is the problem? What has been done to solve it?
- Where is the problem? Where is a possible solution?
- When did the problem occur? When should it be solved?
- Why is it a problem? Why is there no solution?
- How did the problem come about? How did the stakeholders try to solve the problem?

STEP 3
Review the answers to the questions. Indicate where you need more information.

STEP 4
Prioritise the information: What is most important and what less? Why?

STEP 5
Rewrite your initial design problem – see Problem Definition.

Limitations of the method

- WWWWWH is one of several techniques available for analysing a problem systematically. Another technique is to break down the original problem into means-ends relationships, questioning what are the goals and with which means are they achieved.

Tips & Concerns

- Who: Mention as many people as possible who are involved in the problem.
- What: Also think about the problems behind the problem and try to find the essence of the problem.
- You can also use WWWWWH, replacing the term problem with the term 'challenge' to widen your scope. For example: Who could be challenged with the innovation? When and in which situation could that person be challenged?
- You can also ask 'What for?'

REFERENCES & FURTHER READING: Tassoul, M.*, 2006. *Creative Facilitation: a Delft Approach.* Delft: VSSD.

How to expand your mind? Olafur Eliasson (1967) is a Danish-Icelandic artist known for his sculptures and large-scale installation art employing elemental phenomena such as light, water and air temperature to enhance the viewer's experience. Photo: Pedestrian Vibes Study (2004).

HOW-TOS

How-Tos are problem statements written in the form of questions that support idea generation. How-To questions reflect the different life phases and stakeholders of a product-to-be.

When can the method be used?

How-Tos are most helpful at the start of idea generation. With How-Tos the problem is reformulated in many different ways to stimulate you or your team to come up with ideas easily. For example, 'How should I carry luggage in an airport? Or how should I transport deep-frozen food to a shop?'

The How-To way of phrasing is dynamic and inviting and is very suitable for use in groups. The idea is to create a wide variety of problem descriptions. In this way, different perspectives on the design problem become clear to everyone involved. When using the How-To method, it is important to follow rules such as 'postpone judgment', 'associate on the ideas of others' and 'strive for quantity rather than quality'. How-Tos are open questions that are intended to stimulate your creativity almost immediately. By asking a wide variety of How-To questions you can gain a comprehensive overview of the problem that you are working on.

How to use the method?

The starting point for using How-Tos is a problem formulation, which is often the result of a problem analysis phase. It is typically a short description of the problem or a problem statement. By formulating many different How-To questions, you can quickly generate many different design ideas. Each question is typically associated with a certain stakeholder or life phase of your product-to-be. For example, if you expect transportation will be a crucial issue in the product's life, you might ask, 'How can I fit as many products as possible in a standard shipping container?' The precision of your How-To questions is important. If you do not find it easy to come up with ideas, it might be a good idea to change

your How-To formulation: either more precise or more abstract. For example, to make questions more precise, you should distinguish more concrete sub-problems within your design problem, and work on those. But this works both ways of course; if you need more holistic/integrated ideas, you could try to formulate your problem in more abstract ways! The How-Tos generate design ideas.

Possible procedure

STEP 1
Provide a short description of the problem and invite the group to name all the important stakeholders and aspects of the problem typically associated with the different life phases of a product-to-be. You could use a Mindmap.
STEP 2
Invite the group to formulate as many How-To questions as possible from different stakeholders' points of view and concerning different life-phases. You can use a flip chart or post-it notes to write down the How-Tos.
STEP 3
Evaluate the most important common elements of the How-Tos.
STEP 4
Select a number of How-Tos that cover the different points of view, that is, the ones that best cover the different stakeholders and product life-phases.
STEP 5
Start generating ideas with the whole group, starting with a How-To question until no more new ideas are generated. Then skip to the next How-To question until you have covered all the selected questions.

Limitations of the method

· The How-To method is suitable for idea generation in early conceptual design when the design problem is still formulated in a rather open fashion with a large design space.
· The How-To method requires participants who are familiar with the design problem at hand, and preferably know about some of its stakeholders and/or life phases.

Tips & Concerns

· Be careful in formulating the How-To questions. If ideas do not come easily, it might be wise to vary the precision of your How-To questions until productivity increases.

How to make a bicycle portable? Dutch bicycle manufacturer Koga developed the Bergmönch, a compact mountain bike that can be carried like a rucksack for hiking uphill and wheeling downhill.

REFERENCES & FURTHER READING: Tassoul, M.*, 2006. *Creative Facilitation: a Delft Approach.* Delft: VSSD.

EVALUATE & DECIDE

This section contains methods that can help you to evaluate design proposals and make decisions while designing.

Above: a quick cardboard model gives the designer feedback on how the design works and how users react and interact. Right: about 200 units were built of the Apple 1 (1976). They were originally sold without keyboard, monitor or even a housing for $666.66 each. After working with this prototype-style machine, a client asked for a protective cover. Apple founder Steve Jobs delivered it with a keyboard and a wooden case. This marked the beginning of Apple computers as we know them today.

INTERACTION PROTOTYPING AND EVALUATION

When can the method be used?

Interaction Prototyping and Evaluation can be used throughout your design project, but is typically employed in low-fidelity prototyping during concept development. Designers often tend to assume that future users will interact with the product in the intended way. Interaction prototypes enable you to quickly try out concepts and check if your assumptions are feasible. In doing so, you can develop and iterate concepts at a fast pace based on actual user feedback. Interaction prototypes can even be used to enhance discussion with clients about users' future interactions with the product.

Interaction prototypes can help you to generate scenarios of product-user interactions. These scenarios can inform the design brief and requirements by providing insight into use situations, sequences of use and the geometrical and material qualities that influence a user's experiences.

How to use the method?

Creating interaction prototypes is a skill that is developed by doing. You can use the method flexibly to envision, detail, check and communicate aspects of your design that will affect future interactions with it. The method orients you and your team to focus on future interactions. Use it on a small scale, either one-off or repeatedly.

Interaction Prototyping and Evaluation is a method that helps you to simulate and test how people will experience future interactions with your design. It helps you to evaluate concepts at an early stage of development, facilitating quick learning cycles during concept development.

You test and observe the users' experience of specific aspects of your design. These observations help you to decide on design characteristics, such as the physical shape and use sequence of a product, and to identify knowledge gaps.

Possible procedure

STEP 1
Make a quick scenario sketch – a Storyboard – of expected future interactions.

STEP 2
Create an interaction prototype, a rough and simple version of the design aspects you wish to explore.

STEP 3
Users or actors use the prototype and act out the interactions as if using a final design. Tweak the prototype. Repeat the process until you are satisfied and ready to resume developing the concept. During this step:
· Focus on the user's behaviour, not words.
· Make sure that observers are recording the interactions.

STEP 4
Evaluate the experienced interaction qualities you saw when the prototype was used. An example of an interaction quality is 'the user interacts with the product *gracefully*'. Link these qualities to the design's properties and revise it as necessary.

Limitations of the method

· Users may mistake this method for Usability Evaluation. However, the method generates insights into the desired and experienced interaction qualities of product concepts. Its results should help you to develop your concept further and feed into a more comprehensive list of design requirements. A final design still needs to be evaluated in terms of a user's actual experience of the product and its usability.

Tips & Concerns

· Give yourself space to develop and explore various prototypes. Building the prototypes is a quick process, especially with more practice. As your skill improves, you can use the method in more collective situations such as client meetings.
· Try to involve someone with experience in improvisation/theatre techniques. However, you do not need to be a good actor or improviser to use this method. Anybody can build simple prototypes and observe how a user's or actor's interaction with it unfolds.
· Try to enact the interactions in gestures, behaviour and events rather than verbally in conversations.
· Developing, enacting and evaluating interaction prototypes should typically take you 2 to 4 hours per prototype.

REFERENCES & FURTHER READING: Boess, S.U., Pasman, G.J. and Mulder, I.J.*, 2010. *Seeing things differently: prototyping for interaction and participation.* DeSForM 2010: Design and Semantics of Form and Movement, 3-5 November, pp.85-97 / Boess, S. U., Van der Bijl-Brouwer, M., & Harkema, C.*, 2012. *Envisioning Use. A workshop technique to share use-related knowledge in product development teams.* In J. van Kuik and R. Staats (Eds.), Design for Usability Methods & Tools, pp. 72-83. Delft: Delft University of Technology / Brandt, E. and Grunnet, C., 2000. *Evoking the Future: Drama and Props in User Centered Design.* Proceedings on the Participatory design Conference, pp.11-20. / Buchenau, M. and Fulton Suri, J., 2000. *Experience Prototyping.* Proceedings of the 3rd conference on Designing Interactive Systems, 17-19 August, pp.424-433.

PRODUCT USABILITY EVALUATION

When can the method be used?

Product Usability Evaluations are typically conducted at several points of the design process. In each stage of the process, different things can be evaluated:

1. At the start you test and analyse the use of existing similar products.
2. In an early stage you can evaluate ideas and concepts using sketches, scenarios or storyboards for simulation.
3. Throughout, you evaluate the use of intermediate or final designs using three-dimensional models that can simulate specific functionalities and forms.
4. Towards the end you evaluate the use of almost fully functioning prototypes.

The outcomes of the evaluations help you to generate requirements for efficiency, effectiveness and satisfaction. Additionally, you discover useful issues, such as errors and misunderstandings, possible improvements to resolve those issues and opportunities to improve the safety and the user experience of your design.

How to use the method?

Using a representation of your design, observe intended users in a realistic situation. Observe which 'usecues' they perceive and encounter during usage (their perception), how they understand them (their cognition), and how their perception and cognition help them achieve their goal. Observe intended and unintended use.

Usability evaluation requires good preparation with the appropriate materials and participants. For a simple qualitative evaluation you need about 4 to 10 participants.

The result is a list of requirements for the redesign. The evaluations can be recorded (voice, photos, video) for analysis and communication.

Product Usability Evaluation serves to validate product usability, enabling you to understand the quality of your designs (ideas or concepts) in actual use conditions. You can modify your design on the basis of the outcomes.

Possible procedure

STEP 1
Make a storyboard of the expected, realistic users and usage of your design.
STEP 2
Decide which parts of product use you need to evaluate, how and in which context.
STEP 3
Describe your assumptions in detail: which product characteristics will users perceive, understand and operate in a specified situation? (Characteristics in use = usecues.)
STEP 4
Formulate open research questions, such as 'How do people use the product?' and 'What do they use as usecues?'
STEP 5
Set up your research: representations of your product (storyboards, models), the research environment, instructions and questions for the participants.
STEP 6
Prepare your participants, managing their expectations, including privacy issues, and do the research. Record the activities. Observe intended and unintended use.
STEP 7
Analyse the results qualitatively (issues and opportunities) and/or quantitatively (for example, by counting occurrences).
STEP 8
Communicate results and redesign the product accordingly. Ideas for improvements often emerge during the evaluation.

Tips & Concerns

· Ask someone less involved in the design to conduct the actual evaluation to avoid influencing your users.
· The validity of your results will increase over time as you gain research experience.
· You can ask a limited number of qualitative questions about your design direction and desired improvements, but only at the end of the evaluation session. Do not sidetrack your participants from their primary tasks.
· You often do not need formal recruiting or testing facilities. Use your personal network to find unbiased participants. Use a conference room or private residence as a test lab. Any testing is better than none at all. Do 'guerrilla testing' if money and time are limited.
· Handle privacy issues in advance.
· Exercise caution when working with inexperienced researchers. Without experience and the right attitude, it is difficult to be objective. The observed use can even be confrontational.
· Specialists in some disciplines, for example marketing and management, sometimes need to be convinced that valid results can be derived from small samples of participants. Video has great value as a communication tool.

REFERENCES & FURTHER READING: Boess, S.U., De Jong, A.M. and Kanis, H.*, 2004. *Usage research in the Delft Design Project* Ontwerpen 4. In P. Lloyd, N.F.M. Roozenburg, C*. McMahon and L. Brodhurst (Eds.) Procs. EPDE, pp. 577-584. Delft: Fac IDE, TU Delft. / Boess, S.U. and Kanis, H.*, 2008. *Meaning in product use: a design perspective.* In H.N.J. Schifferstein and P.P.M. Hekkert (Eds.)*, Product experience, pp. 305-332. Amsterdam: Elsevier. / Kanis, H.*, 1998. *Usage centred research for everyday product design.* Applied Ergonomics, February, 29(1), pp. 75-82. / Kanis, H., Rooden, M.J. and Green, W.S.*, 2000. *Usecues in the Delft Design course.* Contemporary Ergonomics, 6 April, pp.75-82

Bear-resistant containers come in all sizes and shapes, from ultra-light backpacker food containers weighing a few ounces to dumpsters able to hold 20 tons. Some of these products have been tested by trial and error through direct experience with bears, and actually meet the criteria for 'bear-resistance'.

PRODUCT CONCEPT EVALUATION

When can the method be used?

Product Concept Evaluations take place throughout the design process. Concept screenings usually involve large numbers of product ideas and concepts, and therefore are more frequently used in the beginning of the design process. Concept optimisation takes place near the end of the design process, when aspects of the concept need to be improved.

How to use the method?

Typically, these evaluations are carried out in a controlled environment, where a panel of people judge product concepts based on a list of predetermined issues. The starting point of a Product Concept Evaluation is a number of concepts to be judged and a reason for conducting the evaluation. Often, concept screenings are conducted by experts such as managers, engineers and marketers instead of representatives from the user group. Concept optimisation aims to judge parts or elements of product ideas and concepts. The assumption is that preferred aspects or elements of the individual product concepts can be connected with each other, yielding a concept that is regarded as optimal. Go/no-go decisions usually involve the choice between two or three product concepts. The types of concept representations that you can use for Product Concept Evaluations are:

· Textual concepts: Written scenarios describing how people can use the product, or an enumeration of the aspects of the product idea.
· Pictographic concepts: Visual representations of the product ideas. Depending on the stage of development these can be sketches or highly detailed 3D-CAD models.

Product Concept Evaluation helps you to understand how intended users or other stakeholders value your concept design. This will enable you to determine which aspects should be optimised. You can then make a go/no-go decision or select concepts (concept screening).

· Animations: Moving visual representations of the product idea or a user scenario.
· Mock-ups (dummies): Three-dimensional, tangible representations of the product idea.

Possible procedure

STEP 1
Describe the aim of the Product Concept Evaluation.
STEP 2
Determine what type of Product Concept Evaluation you want to conduct, for example personal interviews, focus groups or discussion groups.
STEP 3
Create the appropriate concept representations.
STEP 4
Create a plan that includes: The aims and type of evaluation, a description of the respondents, questions you want to ask the respondents, aspects of the product concept that need to be evaluated, a description of the test environment, the means of recording the evaluation, a plan for how you will analyse the results.
STEP 5
Search for and invite respondents to the evaluation.
STEP 6
Set up the test environment, including recording equipment.
STEP 7
Conduct the concept evaluation.

STEP 8
Analyse the results, and present the results concisely, using for example a report or a poster.

Tips & Concerns

· The selection of respondents is an important aspect of Product Concept Evaluations. The invited respondents belong to one or more of the pre-formulated user groups.
· You can select them based on sociocultural characteristics or demographic characteristics.
· An important issue to be taken into account is the respondents' level of knowledge of the product category. To assess this level of knowledge, you could simply ask respondents about their experiences with similar products.
· Another important issue when selecting respondents is related to psychological aspects such as tolerance and innovativeness. One important question is: how tolerant are the respondents towards new products and new situations?
· Another important question is how innovative, or conservative, are the respondents? Such psychological aspects have a big influence on the results of the Product Concept Evaluations.
· Do not forget to provide the respondents with some form of compensation.
· Make sure you structure the evaluation systematically with the questions you want to ask.

REFERENCES & FURTHER READING: Antonides, G., Oppedijk – Van Veen, W.M., Schoormans, J.P.L. and Van Raaij, W.F.*, 1999. *Product en Consument.* Utrecht: Lemma. / Roozenburg, N.F.M. and Eekels, J.*, 1995. *Product Design: Fundamentals and Methods.* Utrecht: Lemma. / Schoormans, J. and De Bont, C.*, 1995. *Consumentenonderzoek in de productontwikkeling.* Utrecht: Lemma.

EMOTION MEASUREMENT (PREMO)

When can the method be used?
PrEmo helps you to answer the question: what emotions are evoked by a particular stimulus such as a product, package or fragrance? It can be used in various stages of a design process to assess the emotional impact of existing designs or new (concept) designs. Respondents use animated characters to express their emotional responses. PrEmo measures 12 emotions: six positive and six negative emotions. The result is a detailed emotional profile.

How to use the method?
The method has been developed for designers who are not experienced with measuring emotional responses to products or product concepts. It runs on an online platform that supports the generation of quantitative data. Some knowledge or experience is required for the analysis of this data. The analysis results can be used for different purposes: as input for new product design to formulate an emotional benchmark, as input for concept selection to select the concept that evokes the most positive emotions and as a communication method in design teams to achieve a shared understanding of the emotional impact of given products, to name but a few.

The Product Emotion Measurement Instrument (PrEmo), is a non-verbal self-report instrument that measures users' emotional responses to products.

Possible procedure
You can design your own emotion-measure experiments in the online platform. The platform includes a design module and an experiment module.

DESIGN MODULE:
STEP 1
Create your experiment by uploading the stimuli – either text, images or both – that you want to measure
STEP 2
Select the emotions that you want to measure
STEP 3
Determine the experiment language
STEP 4
Formulate introduction and instruction texts. Respondents will have access to the experiment module.

EXPERIMENT MODULE:
STEP 1
Test your experiment.
STEP 2
Send your participants an Internet link for individual participation.

Limitations of the method
· The method can only measure emotions, such as attraction, fascination, boredom and dissatisfaction, and only in relation to defined stimuli, such as products or fragrances.

Tips & Concerns
· Use the method if you want quantitative emotion data only. If you need qualitative insights, it is not advised to use PrEmo. PrEmo is available for free under a student licence agreement.
· The instrument has been validated in various cultures, runs online and can be used for a wide variety of stimulus types.

· pleasant surpirise
· satisfaction
· desire
· fascination
· amusement

· unpleasant surpirise
· dissatisfaction
· disgust
· contempt
· boredom

After Desmet, 2003

REFERENCES & FURTHER READING: Desmet, P.M.A.*, 2003. *Measuring emotion; development and application of an instrument to measure emotional responses to products.* In: M.A. Blythe, A.F. Monk, K. Overbeeke, & P.C. Wright (Eds.), *Funology: from Usability to Enjoyment*, pp. 111-123. Dordrecht: Kluwer Academic Publishers. / Desmet, P.M.A., & Schifferstein, N.J.H.*, 2012. *Emotion research as input for product design.* In J. Beckley, D., Paredes, & K. Lopetcharat (Eds.), Product Innovation Toolbox: A Field Guide to Consumer Understanding and Research, pp. 149-175. Hoboken, NJ: John Wiley & Sons.

STAPLE

	--	-	+	++
Speed			■	
Costs (variable + fixed) 100 reports				■
Amount of sheets per report			■	
Durability			■	
Looks		■		
Environment / material use			■	

↑ BEST CONCEPT

PAPERCLIP

	--	-	+	++
Speed				■
Costs (variable + fixed) 100 reports			■	
Amount of sheets per report	■			
Durability	■			
Looks		■		
Environment / material use		■		

WIRE-O

	--	-	+	++
Speed	■			
Costs (variable + fixed) 100 reports		■		
Amount of sheets per report				■
Durability				■
Looks		■		
Environment / material use		■		

↑ *Importance of criteria*

STAPLE

	--	-	+	++
Environment / material use			■	
Durability			■	
Looks		■		
Costs (variable + fixed) 100 reports				■
Amount of sheets per report			■	
Speed			■	

↑ BEST CONCEPT

PAPERCLIP

	--	-	+	++
Environment / material use		■		
Durability	■			
Looks		■		
Costs (variable + fixed) 100 reports			■	
Amount of sheets per report	■			
Speed				■

WIRE-O

	--	-	+	++
Environment / material use		■		
Durability				■
Looks		■		
Costs (variable + fixed) 100 reports	■			
Amount of sheets per report	■			
Speed			■	

↑ *Importance of criteria*

↑ CLOSE SECOND

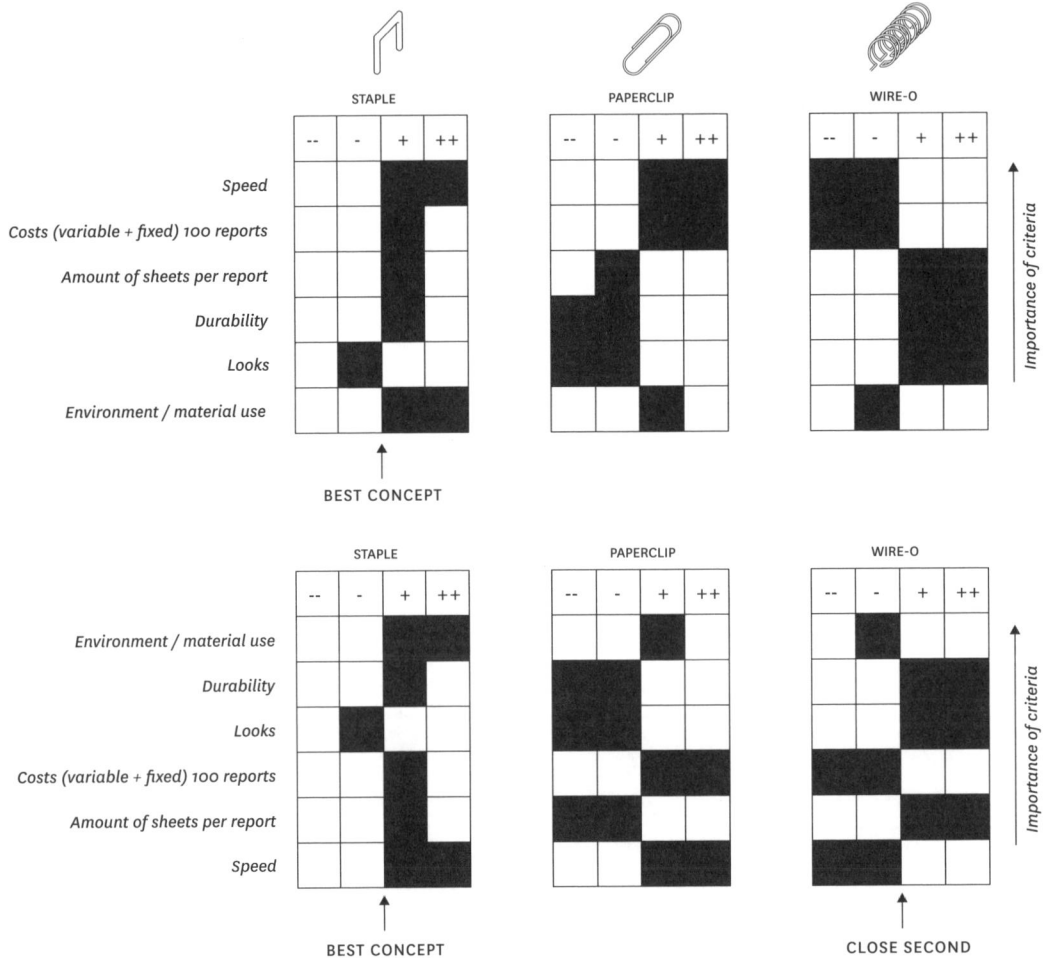

In a Harris profile, the main design requirements are ranked in order of importance with the most important one on top. An even number of possible scores are used to prevent neutral scoring. This way of evaluating is helpful when ideas and designs are still conceptual and not worked out in detail: imagine the black squares are building blocks of a tower. By viewing 'which way the tower of blocks would fall', a choice can be made. Colours should not be used and scores can not be added up. In general, all decision making methods are meant to initiate discussion within the development team and to structure the process of chosing. In the lower example, another design prevails because the design requirements are listed in another order. It shows how another team could have a different view on what is important.

HARRIS PROFILE

A Harris Profile is a graphic representation of the strengths and weaknesses of design concepts with respect to predefined design requirements. It is used to evaluate design concepts and facilitate decisions on which concepts to continue with in a design process.

When can the method be used?

A Harris Profile is based on the design requirements for your design. Whenever a number of alternative product concepts need to be compared and evaluated, the Harris Profile can be used to make your – or your team's – evaluation explicit. As designers make some of their evaluations intuitively, the Harris Profile can help you to make those intuitions explicit so that you can discuss them with other stakeholders.

A Harris Profile can be useful during each phase of the design process, but typically it is used after an idea generation phase when ideas or concepts need to be eliminated.

How to use the method?

Create a Harris Profile for each alternative design concept. A Harris Profile consists of an assessment of how the concept meets each of the listed design requirements. The evaluations are relative, comparing the different concepts in terms of their performance in each criterion. A four-point scale is typically used to score the concepts. You should interpret the meaning of the scale positions: -2 = bad, -1 = moderate, et cetera. Thanks to the visual representation, decision makers can quickly view the overall score of each design alternative for all the criteria, and compare them easily.

An important role of the Harris Profile is to make your evaluation explicit and easy to understand: it can help to stimulate discussion with your project's stakeholders in the early phases of design, when design requirements typically change as the concepts evolve and you gain a greater shared understanding of the design problem.

Possible procedure

STEP 1
List the design requirements as fully as possible and rank them according to their importance for the design project.
STEP 2
Create a four-point scale matrix next to each requirement, coded -2, -1, +1, and +2.
STEP 3
Create a Harris Profile for each of the design alternatives by evaluating the relative performance of each alternative with respect to the requirements.
STEP 4
Draw the profile by marking the scores in the four-point scale matrix for all the criteria.
STEP 5
Present the profiles next to each other to allow discussion with stakeholders and to determine which design concept has the best overall score.

Limitations of the method

· The four-point scales should be interpreted differently for each requirement and are not necessarily comparable.

· It is tempting to interpret Harris Profiles as 'true' representations of the performance of design alternatives. However, it is important to realise that the performance assessment of design concepts is typically an intuitive prediction of performance, with low reliability.

· The primary function of the profile is to communicate the evaluations that you have made after careful discussions and deliberations, and if necessary to open up discussion to sharpen the definitions of requirements or improve design concepts.

Tips & Concerns

· Use drawings to represent concepts in each profile – this will enhance the communicability of your profiles.
· If possible, cluster the criteria.
· Design is not a linear process, so you might discover new design requirements while evaluating concepts. You can add those requirements to your Harris Profile and enhance the accuracy of your evaluation.
· When attributing the -2 or +2 values to a criterion, be sure to colour all the blocks in the Harris Profile. Only then can you create a quick visual overview of the overall score of a design alternative.

REFERENCES & FURTHER READING: Harris, J.S., 1961. *New Product Profile Chart.* Chemical and Engineering News, 17 April, 39(16), pp.110-118. / Roozenburg, N.F.M. and Eekels, J.*, 1995. *Product Design: Fundamentals and Methods.* Utrecht: Lemma.

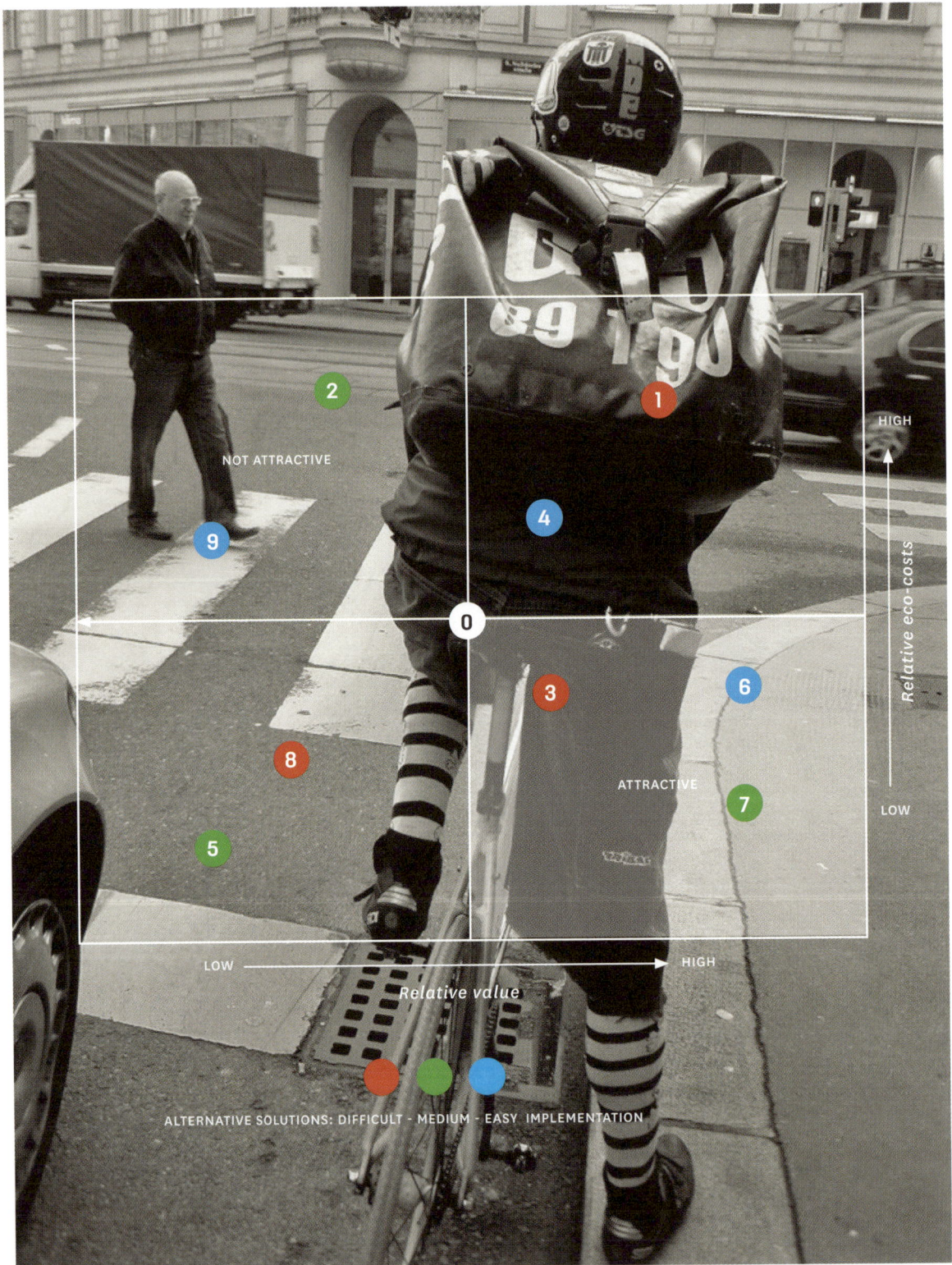

HIGH

Relative eco-costs

LOW

NOT ATTRACTIVE

ATTRACTIVE

LOW → HIGH

Relative value

ALTERNATIVE SOLUTIONS: DIFFICULT - MEDIUM - EASY IMPLEMENTATION

A courier service on bicycles offers equal value to the client compared to a courier service with cars. In case of quicker delivery in busy city centres, the value is even higher. The ecocosts are a lot lower, resulting in a lower EVR (Ecocost Value Ratio). Another strategy to lower the EVR is to create more value with equal ecocosts. After Vogtländer, 2011

EVR DECISION MATRIX

EVR refers to Eco-costs-Value Ratio. The EVR Decision Matrix is a decision tool to select the most promising sustainable solution from a number of design alternatives on the basis of the eco-costs and the expected market value of the product. EVR is a fast method to discuss and select the most promising designs.

When can the method be used?

The EVR Decision Matrix is typically used in the fuzzy front end of the design during the concept development stage, especially when the selection of materials is an issue. It might be considered in other stages of product development as well in order to structure team-based decision taking.

How to use the method?

The basis of the tool is the product portfolio matrix, which is used to position design alternatives in terms of eco-cost and value:
· The eco-burden, such as the eco-costs or carbon footprint of a product, is on the y-axis.
· The value (Willingness To Pay, WTP) is on the x-axis.

The matrix has four quadrants with a reference product in the middle. The reference product can be an existing product that the new design will compete with. The design objective is to obtain a high value with a low eco-burden. Your team assesses the value of each solution. The eco-burden can be based on gut feelings, but it is better to make a quick-and-dirty assessment of the eco-cost on the basis of the materials used, manufacturing processes and the end-of-life scenario.

Possible procedure

STEP 1
Rank the product solutions in order of relative value (WTP).
STEP 2
Rank the product solutions in order of relative eco-burden, for example, relative eco-costs.
STEP 3
Characterise the product solutions in terms of an important issue, for example, expected market volume, ease of implementation (see figure), ease of production, costs, et cetera.
STEP 4
Draw the EVR Decision Matrix on a white board or flip chart, and draw a red, green or blue dot at the right spot for each product solution and label each solution.
STEP 5
Discuss the result and decide on the most attractive solutions.

Limitations of the method

The EVR method is not applicable for:
· assessing the most profitable design solution, since costs are not known at the fuzzy front end.
· benchmarking of products with a major energy demand in the use phase.

Tips & Concerns

· You can use either the LCA databook or the Excel lookup tables of the Idemat database at www.ecocostsvalue.com.
· Each solution has a position in the matrix. Sometimes it is handy to give a further indication of the characteristics of the solutions by labelling each solution with a colour to indicate how difficult it is to implement them.

REFERENCES & FURTHER READING: Vogtländer, J.G.*, 2011. *A quick reference guide to LCA DATA and eco-based materials selection.* Delft: VSSD. / Vogtländer, J.G.*, Baetens, B., Bijma, A., Brandjes, E., Lindeijer, E., Segers, M., Witte, F., Brezet, J.C. * and Hendriks, Ch.F., 2010. *LCA-based assessment of sustainability: The Eco-costs/Value Ratio: EVR.* Delft: VSSD. / Vogtländer, J.G., Mestre, A., Van der Helm, R., Scheepens, A. and Wever, R.*, 2013. *Eco-efficient Value Creation for sustainable design and business strategies.* Delft: VSSD.

How feasible is it to scale down? Studying future Smart Grids, Siemens expects that electricity will no longer be centrally generated in large power stations but increasingly in small, local units. Even residential buildings will become producers of electricity. In addition, intelligent building technology will ensure a reduction in building power consumption, for example with more needs-based air conditioning and ventilation technology. (Source: Siemens Electronics)

C-BOX

A C-Box is a matrix that helps you categorise and evaluate large numbers of ideas. The ideas are mapped based on innovativeness and feasibility.

When can the method be used?

A C-Box is commonly used in early idea generation when a Brainstorm session has generated a surplus of early ideas, for example more than 40. Making a C-Box with a development team opens up discussion on the ideas and enhances the understanding of the solution space. It also helps you to reach agreement on the direction of the design process.

How to use the method?

The starting point of a C-Box is a multitude of early ideas (40-60). The outcome of a C-Box is an overview of these early ideas, clustered in four groups based on criteria set to the axes of the C-Box. Essentially you create a rough distinction between the ideas in four groups.

Possible procedure

STEP 1
Create two axes on a large sheet of paper and construct a 2 x 2 C-Box matrix:
x-axis = innovativeness: familiar ideas are at one end, highly innovative ones at the other end.
y-axis = feasibility: one end is not feasible, the other end represents immediate feasibility.

STEP 2
Make sure all ideas are written down or drawn on small pieces of paper, for example on post-it notes or A5 sheets.

STEP 3
In your group, review and discuss the ideas, and place each idea in one of the four quadrants.

STEP 4
Make sure that ideas in one quadrant are situated closely to the criteria they meet best.

Once you have placed all the ideas in the C-Box, you have created a first overview, and can proceed to the next steps. These steps consist of working out the most promising ideas and dropping the bad ideas that are not innovative and not feasible.

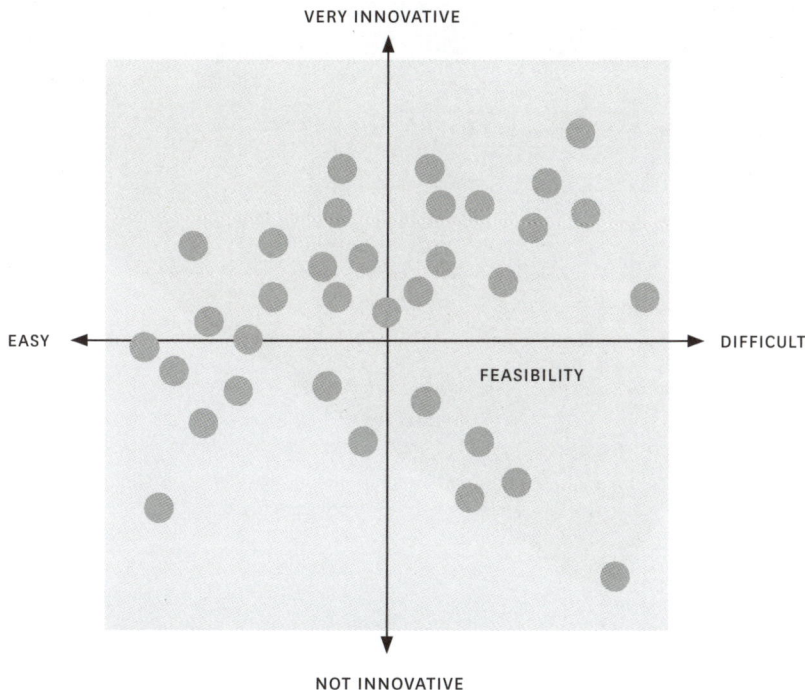

VERY INNOVATIVE

EASY — FEASIBILITY — DIFFICULT

NOT INNOVATIVE

REFERENCES & FURTHER READING: Tassoul, M.*, 2006. *Creative Facilitation – a Delft Approach*, Delft: VSSD.

ITEMISED RESPONSE AND PMI

The Itemised Response Method is a simple means of judging ideas quickly and intuitively. With PMI, which means 'Plus-Minus-Interesting', you can evaluate early design ideas in a systematic way.

When can the method be used?

The Itemised Response Method and PMI essentially help to bring structure to a set of early ideas and can be used to select ideas for concept development. PMI works best when you need to screen a manageable number of ideas. It is essentially used in brainstorm settings. Because of its quick and intuitive nature, the PMI method is best applied at the beginning of the design process, during early idea generation.

How to use the method?

List the positive and negative features of each idea. By examining these positive and negative features, you can develop the positive aspects of the ideas to make them stronger. Also, you can evaluate the negative aspects and improve upon them. The goal of the method is to gain a better understanding of the solution space, for example more insight into valuable directions for solution finding. The results will give you and your design team not only a better understanding of interesting and promising ideas, but also an overview of your bad ideas.

Possible procedure

STEP 1

For each idea, list the positive features and the negative features in the form of a list with pluses and minuses.

For each idea, answer the following questions:

· What is good about the idea (Plus)?
· Which aspects would you need to improve (Minus)?
· What makes the idea interesting (Interesting)?

STEP 2

For each idea, you now have:

· Plus: these are the good aspects of the idea, worth developing further into concepts or harnessing.
· Minus: these are bad aspects of the idea, not worth developing further.
· Interesting: these are interesting aspects of the idea, but they need more development in order to become good ideas.

STEP 3

Decide upon your course of action: Are you going to develop the good ideas into concepts? If so, how many concepts? Perhaps you should combine some of the good ideas? Or will you continue with the early idea generation and seek more ideas? Combine interesting ideas with the good ideas? Explore the interesting ideas further?

Tips & Concerns

· Working with Pluses and Minuses invites people to take decisions, but do not do so too quickly. Decision methods such as PMI, C-Box, Itemised Response and vALUe are all meant to help you become acquainted with all possible ideas without deciding on which ones to discard.

In its modern form, the useless machine appears to have been invented by MIT professor and artificial intelligence pioneer Marvin Minsky, while he was a graduate student at Bell Labs in 1952. Minsky dubbed his invention the Ultimate Machine, but that sense of the term did not catch on. Minsky's mentor at Bell Labs, information theory pioneer Claude Shannon, made his own versions of the machine. He kept one on his desk, where science fiction author Arthur C. Clarke saw it. Clarke later wrote: "There is something unspeakably sinister about a machine that does nothing - absolutely nothing - except switch itself off", and he was fascinated by the concept. From: Abigail Pesta: Looking for something Usefull to do with your Time? Don't Try This, Wall Street Journal p.1 Retrieved 14 March 2013.

REFERENCES & FURTHER READING: Gordon, W.J.J., 1961. *Synectics.* New York, NY: Harper and Row. / De Bono, E., 1970. *Lateral Thinking: Creativity Step by Step.* New York, NY: Harper and Row. / Tassoul, M.*, 2006. *Creative Facilitation: a Delft Approach.* Delft: VSSD.

	STAPLE	PAPERCLIP	WIRE-O		STAPLE	PAPERCLIP	WIRE-O
Speed	S	•	-		•	S	-
Costs (variable + fixed) 100 reports	S	D	-		D	S	-
Amount of sheets per report	+	A	+		A	-	+
Durability	+	T	+		T	-	+
Looks	S	U	+		U	S	+
Environment / material use	+	M	-		M	-	-
Σ +	3	•	3		•	0	3
Σ -	0	•	3		•	3	3
Σ S	3	•	0		•	3	0

BEST CONCEPT? 2 CONCEPTS WITH EQUAL SCORE

The Japanese term 'chindogu' describes a product that is un-useless. That is, by solving one problem it creates another one. The Mug-a-Tron 8000 solves the age-old problem of how to hand someone a hot cup of tea or coffee without either person getting burned. However, its eight handles make it rather difficult to drink the hot tea or coffee. (Rosanna Martlew, 2013)

DATUM METHOD

The Datum Method enables you to evaluate design alternatives using design criteria. One design is randomly chosen to be the 'datum'; it represents by definition a neutral performance on each criterion. You evaluate each criterion to determine if your design alternatives are less effective, the same or better than the datum.

When can the method be used?

The Datum Method can be used whenever you need to compare a number of design proposals and have to arrive at a consensus or an intuitive decision is needed. Typically it is used after an idea-generation phase in the design process. The method aims to provide you with confidence through a systematic discussion of the criteria and by determining the advantages and disadvantages of the alternative designs.

How to use the method?

The value of the alternative designs is determined on the basis of your 'intuitive' judgements. Three judgements can be given: less good, the same or better, expressed as '-', 'S' and '+'. The sum of each of these three values will help you to make a decision. The best alternative design is the one in which you or your design team have the most confidence. The method starts with product concepts, developed to an equal, and therefore comparable, level of detailing and with a list of criteria suitable for use in this stage and in relation to the level of development. The expected outcome is a reasoned selection of design concepts suitable for further development. Thanks to this procedure, you and the project stakeholders can be confident that you have selected the correct design concept.

Possible procedure

STEP 1
Arrange all the design alternatives and criteria in a matrix.
STEP 2
Choose the datum, for example a similar existing product.
STEP 3
Compare the properties of the other designs with those of the datum:
= less good than the datum
+ = better than the datum
s = same as the datum
STEP 4
Compare scores: many pluses and few minuses indicate that your alternative design is good. An equal spread of pluses, minuses and sames may indicate vague and ambiguous criteria.
STEP 5
Choose a new datum, and iterate steps 3 and 4. For example, take a 'strong design' from step 4 and see if it remains strong.
STEP 6
Repeat steps 3, 4, and 5 until you reach consensus about the best design.
STEP 7
To save time, weak designs can be left out after the first session.

Limitations of the method

· The method should not be seen as a sort of mathematically justified process, but as a decision-making aid. You can not only look at each score individually, but also add up the totals. Each "+" for a particular concept is offset by each "-" given to the same concept. A concept with two "+", one "S" and two "-" will have an end score of zero (0). Although this delivers an attractive outcome, you must realise that this will nullify the results and does not help the discussion of the concepts or criteria.

Tips & Concerns

· The alternatives need to be developed to an equal level, and visualised as realistically as possible.
· A criterion stating that the product should cost no more than € 15 or weigh no more than 800 grams cannot be judged in an early stage of the design process. Still, you may have some ideas about the differences in the cost prices of your design proposals. When you have formulated more general criteria, limit your number of criteria to no more than 10.
· When step 4 does not provide a strong profile, reformulate the criteria and make sure that a strong profile emerges.

REFERENCES & FURTHER READING: Pugh, S., 1981. *Concept selection: a method that works.* In: Hubka, V. (ed.), Review of Design Methodology, pp. 497 – 506. Zürich: Heurista. / Roozenburg, N.F.M. and Eekels, J.*, 1995. *Product Design: Fundamentals and Methods.* Utrecht: Lemma.

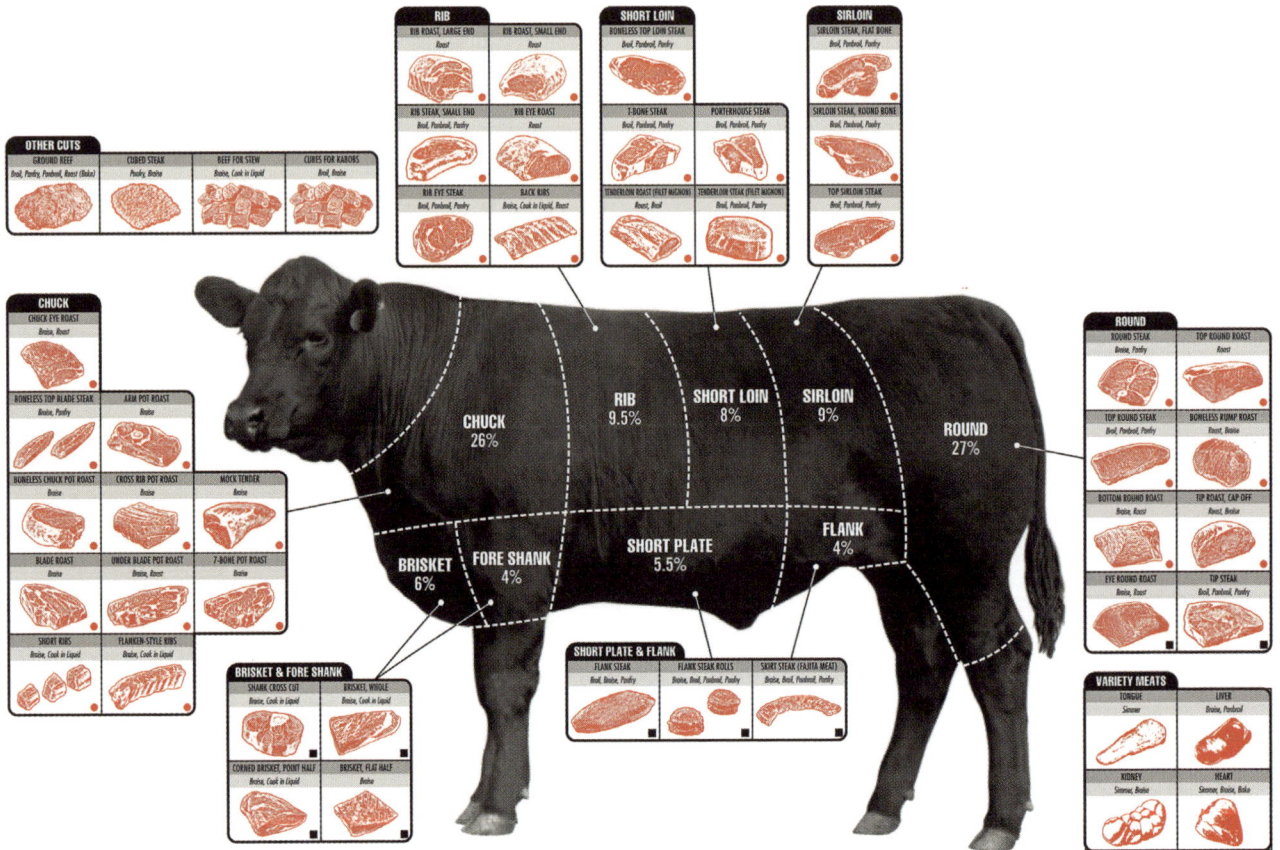

OTHER CUTS

GROUND BEEF	CUBED STEAK	BEEF FOR STEW	CUBES FOR KABOBS
Broil, Panfry, Panbroil, Roast (Bake)	*Panfry, Braise*	*Braise, Cook in Liquid*	*Broil, Braise*

RIB

RIB ROAST, LARGE END	RIB ROAST, SMALL END
Roast	*Roast*
RIB STEAK, SMALL END	RIB EYE ROAST
Broil, Panbroil, Panfry	*Roast*
RIB EYE STEAK	BACK RIBS
Broil, Panbroil, Panfry	*Braise, Cook in Liquid, Roast*

SHORT LOIN

BONELESS TOP LOIN STEAK	
Broil, Panbroil, Panfry	
T-BONE STEAK	PORTERHOUSE STEAK
Broil, Panbroil, Panfry	*Broil, Panbroil, Panfry*
TENDERLOIN ROAST (FILET MIGNON)	TENDERLOIN STEAK (FILET MIGNON)
Roast, Broil	*Broil, Panbroil, Panfry*

SIRLOIN

SIRLOIN STEAK, FLAT BONE	
Broil, Panbroil, Panfry	
SIRLOIN STEAK, ROUND BONE	
Broil, Panbroil, Panfry	
TOP SIRLOIN STEAK	
Broil, Panbroil, Panfry	

CHUCK

CHUCK EYE ROAST	
Braise, Roast	
BONELESS TOP BLADE STEAK	ARM POT ROAST
Braise, Panfry	*Braise*
BONELESS CHUCK POT ROAST	CROSS RIB POT ROAST	MOCK TENDER
Braise	*Braise*	*Braise*
BLADE ROAST	UNDER BLADE POT ROAST	7-BONE POT ROAST
Braise	*Braise, Roast*	*Braise*
SHORT RIBS	FLANKEN-STYLE RIBS
Braise, Cook in Liquid	*Braise, Cook in Liquid*

ROUND

ROUND STEAK	TOP ROUND ROAST
Braise, Panfry	*Roast*
TOP ROUND STEAK	BONELESS RUMP ROAST
Broil, Panbroil, Panfry	*Roast, Braise*
BOTTOM ROUND ROAST	TIP ROAST, CAP OFF
Braise, Roast	*Roast, Braise*
EYE ROUND ROAST	TIP STEAK
Braise, Roast	*Broil, Panbroil, Panfry*

BRISKET & FORE SHANK

SHANK CROSS CUT	BRISKET, WHOLE
Braise, Cook in Liquid	*Braise, Cook in Liquid*
CORNED BRISKET, POINT HALF	BRISKET, FLAT HALF
Braise, Cook in Liquid	*Braise*

SHORT PLATE & FLANK

FLANK STEAK	FLANK STEAK ROLLS	SKIRT STEAK (FAJITA MEAT)
Broil, Braise, Panfry	*Braise, Broil, Panbroil*	*Braise, Broil, Panbroil, Panfry*

VARIETY MEATS

TONGUE	LIVER
Simmer	*Braise, Panbroil*
KIDNEY	HEART
Simmer, Braise	*Simmer, Braise, Bake*

CHUCK 26%

RIB 9.5%

SHORT LOIN 8%

SIRLOIN 9%

ROUND 27%

BRISKET 6%

FORE SHANK 4%

SHORT PLATE 5.5%

FLANK 4%

The Value Method is an inventorying method.

VALUE

vALUe stands for: Advantage, Limitation, Unique Elements. This method is used to evaluate a large set of early design ideas in a quick and systematic way.

When can the method be used?

The vALUe method allows ideas to be described in common terms. Therefore, it is best applied during early idea generation, often in a Brainstorm setting. This method works best just after you have selected or clustered ideas from a large number of ideas – five to nine ideas or clusters of ideas from a group of 50 or more. Using the vALUe method yields a better understanding of the solution space. It gives more insight into valuable directions for solution finding and a better understanding of interesting and promising ideas, but also of bad ideas.

How to use the method?

The vALUe method is an inventorying method: it allows designers to review and validate ideas. By explicitly writing down the ideas in terms of advantages, limitations and unique elements, the designers impose a common vocabulary on the ideas, making further selection easier. After applying this method, the decision maker has to decide what to do next: look for more ideas, or make a decision as to which ideas will be developed into concepts.

Possible procedure

STEP 1
Generate a large set of early ideas or principal solutions.
STEP 2
For each idea, answer the following questions:
STEP 3
What are the advantages of the idea (A)?
STEP 4
What are the limitations of the idea (L)?
STEP 5
What are the unique elements of the idea (U)?

Limitations of the method

· vALUe is not a selection tool because it does not provide you with a set of requirements that is independent of your ideas. Note that ideas might provide advantages in different areas. For example: idea 1 has the advantage of being lightweight. Idea 2 is not lightweight but is very cheap to manufacture. With this knowledge, you cannot compare these ideas and select one. First you need to draft a list of requirements. Following the example you should include criteria concerning the weight and the price of the product, limiting both to either a maximum or a range. vALUe helps you to determine the importance of these requirements.

Selecting design ideas is like selecting the right golf club with the right performance. Which choice is the best depends on what is needed to get the job done.

REFERENCES & FURTHER READING: Buzan, T., 1996. *The Mind Map Book: How to Use Radiant Thinking to Maximize Your Brain's Untapped Potential*. New York, NY: Plume. Tassoul, M.*, 2006. *Creative Facilitation: a Delft Approach*, Delft: VSSD.

	Weight	STAPLE		PAPERCLIP		WIRE-O	
		Score	Total	Score	Total	Score	Total
Speed	30	9	270	9	270	3	90
Costs (variable + fixed) 100 reports	25	7	175	8	200	2	50
Amount of sheets per report	20	6	120	2	40	10	200
Durability	10	6	60	3	30	10	100
Looks	10	4	40	3	30	9	90
Environment / material use	5	9	45	7	35	4	20
Total score	100		710		605		550

↑
BEST CONCEPT

	Weight	STAPLE		PAPERCLIP		WIRE-O	
		Score	Total	Score	Total	Score	Total
Environment / material use	30	9	270	7	210	4	120
Durability	25	6	150	3	75	10	250
Looks	25	4	100	3	60	9	225
Costs (variable + fixed) 100 reports	10	7	70	8	80	2	20
Amount of sheets per report	5	6	30	2	10	10	50
Speed	5	9	45	9	45	3	15
Total score	100		665		480		680

↑   ↑
CLOSE SECOND   BEST CONCEPT

By attributing weight factors to design requirements, the choice of a certain design can be precisely motivated. Design proposals should be worked out in detail so that they can be scored. Like all methods for evaluation, the main aim is to initiate a structured discussion and to communicate the processes of choice within a development team. The highest-scoring proposal is not necessarily the winner. By analysing the scores, strong features of different proposals can be combined into a new one.

WEIGHTED OBJECTIVES

The Weighted Objectives Method is an evaluation method for comparing design concepts based on the overall value of each design concept.

When can the method be used?

The Weighted Objectives Method is best used when a decision has to be made between a selected number of design alternatives, design concepts or principal solutions. Usually, the Weighted Objectives Method is used when evaluating design concepts, and to make a decision as to which design concept should be developed into a detailed design. The Weighted Objectives Method enables you to sum up the scores of all criteria into a numerical value for each design alternative.

How to use the method?

The Weighted Objective Method assigns scores to the degree to which a design alternative satisfies a criterion. However, the criteria that are used to evaluate the design alternatives might differ in their importance. For example, the cost price might be of less importance than appealing aesthetics. The Weighted Objectives Method allows you to take into account the difference in importance between criteria by assigning weights according to their importance for the evaluation. You can rank each of the weights on a scale from 1 to 5 or decide on a total sum of the weights of the criteria, for example 100.

Possible procedure

STEP 1
Select the criteria according to which the selection will be made.
STEP 2
Choose three to five concepts for evaluation.
STEP 3
Assign weights to the criteria.
Step 4
Construct a matrix, with the criteria in rows and the concepts in columns.
STEP 5
Attribute values to how each concept meets a criterion. Rank the scores of the concepts from 1 to 10.
STEP 6
Calculate the overall score of each concept by summing up the scores on each criterion (make sure you take into account the weight factor).
STEP 7
The concept with the highest score is the preferred concept.

Tips & Concerns

· This method should be carried out coherently, while discussing and reviewing both the weights assigned to the criteria and the scores of the concepts according to all the criteria.
· To determine the weight factors of the criteria it is recommended that you compare the criteria in pairs to attribute a weight factor to each of them.

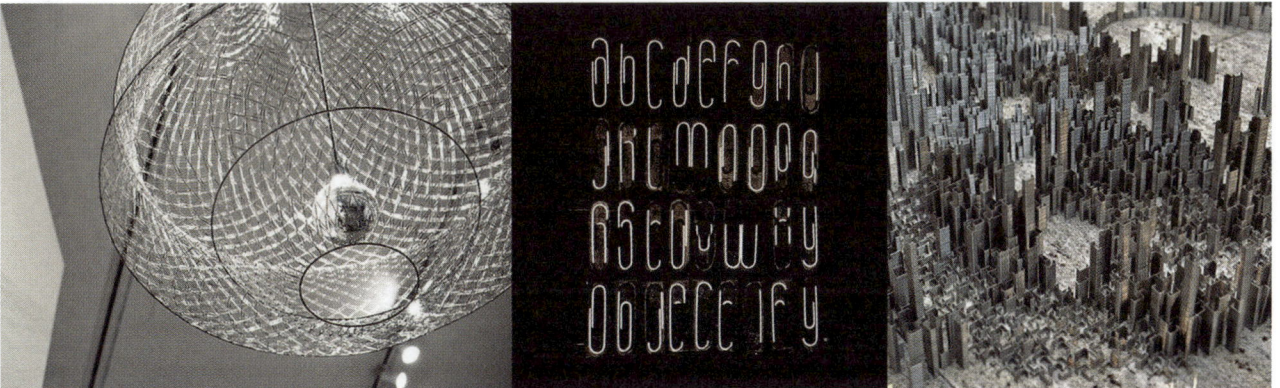

From left to right: paperclip lamp, paperclip alphabet, staple city.

REFERENCES & FURTHER READING: Roozenburg, N.F.M. and Eekels, J.*, 1995. *Product Design: Fundamentals and Methods*. Utrecht: Lemma. / Roozenburg, N.F.M. and Eekels, J.*, 1998. *Product Ontwerpen: Structuur en Methoden*. 2nd ed. Utrecht: Lemma.

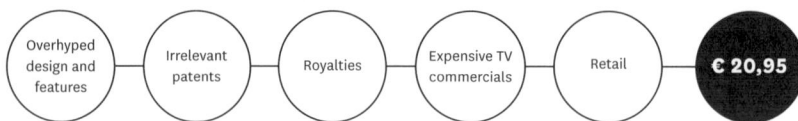

SAMPLE REGULAR RAZORS

Manufacturing cost price (incl. patents, materials, assembly, packaging)	€	6,10
Overhead costs / factory running costs 15%*	€	0,92
Selling costs 5%*	€	0,31
Factory margin (profit/risk) 25%*	€	1,53
Factory selling price	**€**	**8,86**
Distribution and wholesale margin 30%*	€	2,66
Buying price for retailer (Retail margin 50%**)	**€**	**11,52**
Selling price excl. VAT	€	17,28
VAT	€	3,63
Selling price for customer	€	20,91
Round off pricetag to:	**€**	**20,95**

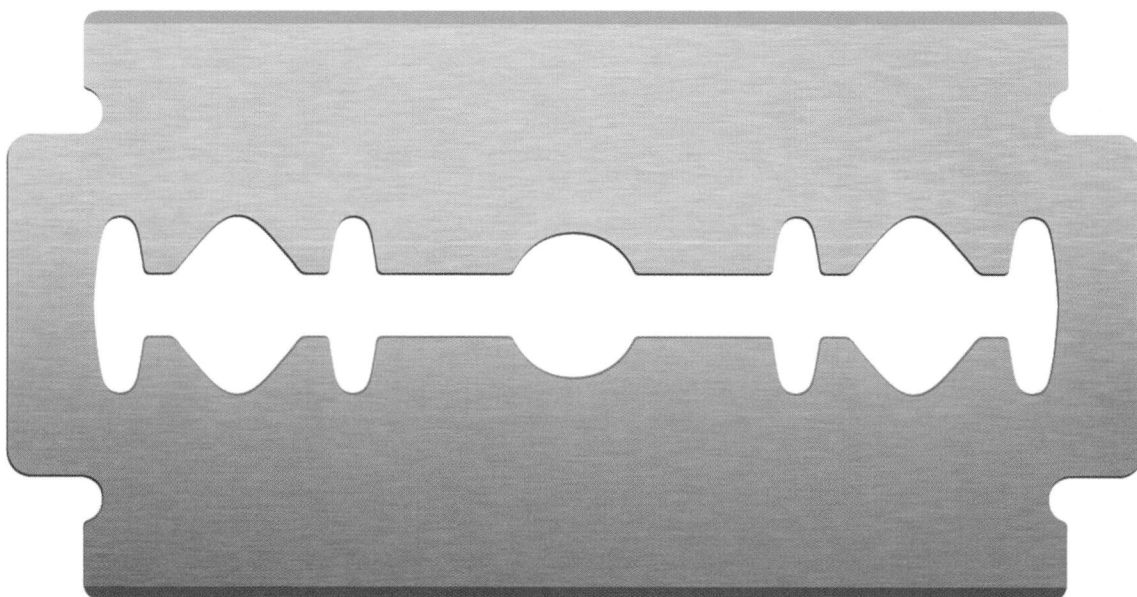

Cutting the price: razor blades sell for anything up to € 21,- per pack. A Dutch company called Boldking cuts prices by more than 50% without cutting corners when it comes to quality. See the calculation below.

SAMPLE PRICE CUT RAZORS BY *BOLDKING*

Manufacturing cost price (no excessive design features, no patents)	€	4,40
Overhead costs / factory running costs 15%*	€	0,66
Selling costs 5%	€	0,22
Factory margin (profit/risk) 25%*	€	1,10
Factory selling price	€	6,38
Distribution and wholesale margin 0% (no wholesale in between)	€	0,00
Buying price	**€**	**6,38**
Boldking retail margin 30%* (website, online payment, profit/risk)	€	1,91
Selling price excl. VAT	€	8,29
VAT (in the Netherlands: 21%)	€	1,74
Selling price for customer	€	10,03
Round off pricetag to:	**€**	**10,00**

* average value, varies from case to case ** varies per branch, brand or shop from 20-300%

COST PRICE ESTIMATION

When can the method be used?

This method helps you estimate the cost price and provides you with a checklist of additional costs that should not be overlooked. For this, you need a lot of detailed information, such as material choices, dimensions, packaging and serial numbers. One problem you might encounter in design education is that you overlook cost aspects that are hidden in the production and distribution chain: after buying the prototyping materials in the workshop for € 8.50 you might expect that the product could be sold in shops for € 10.00, yielding a profit of € 1.50 for you as its designer. That is not at all realistic. With some basic rules of thumb, you can estimate the selling price realistically within a certain range. You can also estimate what kinds of parts, materials, details and extra features would make the design more or less costly than your target figure.

How to use the method?

You can estimate cost price qualitatively and quantitatively. The qualitative approach is based on existing products: you can compare your design proposal to what is already on the market. The quantitative approach is based on adding up all the cost factors and margins that are needed to build and sell your product. With some rules of thumb, it is possible to estimate the cost price.

Possible procedure

QUALITATIVELY
· Compare your design proposal to what is already on the market. If you design a bicycle with an electric motor, it is probably more expensive than a normal bicycle but less expensive than a scooter. A bigger engine and bigger batteries would increase the cost, as would any added functionalities like gears and lightweight wheels.

The Cost Price Estimation method helps you to roughly define the cost price of your design in an early stage of your design process.

· Usually, using expensive materials makes the product more expensive. Examples are titanium, carbon-reinforced epoxy and veneer. Over time, the cost of labour has become a much bigger component in the cost price, so labour-intensive parts or connections, such as welding instead of bending a tube, make products more expensive. Finishing steps like grinding away mould marks or polishing are particularly costly steps.
· Industrial Design often involves producing designs in series, from small series of several hundred to mass production in the millions. Each series has a specific production method and manufacturing cost. The key is to find a balance between fixed costs (moulds) and variable costs (material, labour cost per product). Injection moulding involves expensive moulds, but in mass production they only add a few cents per product to the cost price, and clever design can save on costs.

QUANTITATIVELY
· Start by estimating how much your material will cost. You can do this with the Cambridge Engineering Selector program or search for the material on the Internet. Also think of the packaging. A very rough estimate can be made with this rule of thumb: the consumer price is seven to eight times the material cost. Or, to be more exact: the consumer price is three to four times the manufacturing cost. The manufacturing cost (factory selling price) includes labour, packaging and the manufacturer's profit.

· This checklist can help you estimate the cost price more precisely. Novice designers often overlook cost components like packaging, transport, wholesale and value added tax.

Tips & Concerns
· Design schools often overlook Cost Price Estimation, but it is important to gain experience with this subject as soon as possible, preferably during study projects.

Limitations
· Always be aware that these cost calculations are estimates. The method can give you an idea of the selling price within a margin that might be hard to predict. If your estimate for the material price is off by 10%, your final estimate might be off by 70 or 80%.
· Estimates from producers can show differences of 100%, leading to a difference of 300% in the consumer price. For this reason, experience is very important. After going through this process several times, you will know better what surprises lie ahead.

REFERENCES & FURTHER READING: Buiting-Csikós, C., Kals, H.J.J., Lutterveld, C.A., Moulijn, K.A. and Ponsen, J.M., 2012. *Industriële Productie.* Den Haag: Academic Service.

ARTICULATE & SIMULATE

This section contains methods that can help you to articulate and simulate design proposals while designing.

Researchers at the Delft University of Technology use one or more layers of sandwich bags as a simple and effective way to simulate different degrees of blurred vision.

ROLE-PLAYING

Role-playing is a form of simulation that helps you to develop and determine the interaction between your design and its intended users.

When can the method be used?

Role-playing is just like theatre acting: by acting out the tasks your intended user has to perform, you reach a better understanding of the complexity of the interaction, and can develop different ideas for the interaction.

You can use Role-playing throughout the design process in order to develop ideas about how people would interact with the product you are developing. You can also engage in Role-playing to understand the interaction qualities of an existing product or in a later stage when evaluating a concept. It can be particularly useful to put yourself in the role of your intended user when you do not belong to that user group. For example, by putting on semi-covered eyeglasses and taping up your joints, you can get a sense of how a person who cannot see and move experiences the world.

How to use the method?

One of the major advantages of Role-playing is that you use your entire body; it is more like real interaction as compared to using storyboards or scenarios. Role-playing techniques enable you to explore the tangibility of the interaction, as well as the appearance and attractiveness of elegant movements. Also, by Role-playing you can simulate an interaction walkthrough. Role-playing is usually captured using photography or video. Role-playing starts with a first idea about the interaction between product and user.

The outcome of using Role-playing techniques is a good conceptual idea about the interaction, as well as visualisations or written descriptions of the interaction. Both visualisations and written descriptions can be used for communication and evaluation purposes.

Possible procedure

STEP 1
Determine the actors and the goal of the actors or the interaction.

STEP 2
Determine what you want to portray through Role-playing. Determine the sequence of steps.

STEP 3
Make sure that you record the Role-playing.

STEP 4
Divide the roles amongst the team members.

STEP 5
Play the interaction and improvise. Be expressive in your movements. Think aloud when enacting motivations.

STEP 6
Repeat the Role-playing task several times until different sequences have been enacted.

STEP 7
Analyse the recordings: pay attention to the sequences of tasks, motivations and factors that could influence the interaction.

Tips & Concerns

· Start with a small research on how it is done, watch example videos.
· Sometimes it takes hours, days or even weeks before you really experience your role.
· Do not try to win an Oscar, the acting itself is not the goal.

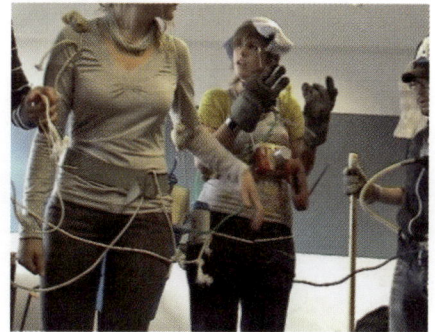

By wearing restrictive clothes like straps, extra weights, gloves and vision-blocking glasses, designers experience how it feels to live with arthritis and limited eyesight.

REFERENCES & FURTHER READING: Jacko, J.A. and Sears, A., 2002. *The Human-Computer Interaction Handbook: Fundamentals, Evolving Technologies and Emerging Applications.* New York, NY: Erlbaum and Associates.

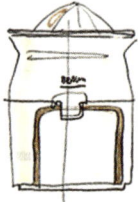
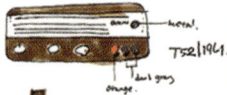
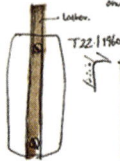
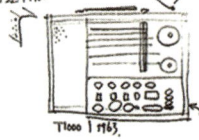
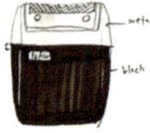
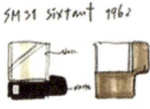

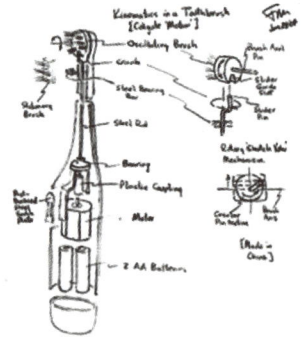

Gutes Design is langlob
Good design is durable

T52/1961.

Gutes Design ist Unaufdringlich
Good design is unobtrusive

T22/1960

SM 31 sixtant 1962

T1000/1963

MPZ 2/21/22 citromatic 1972.

LESS but better

FS1000/1962.

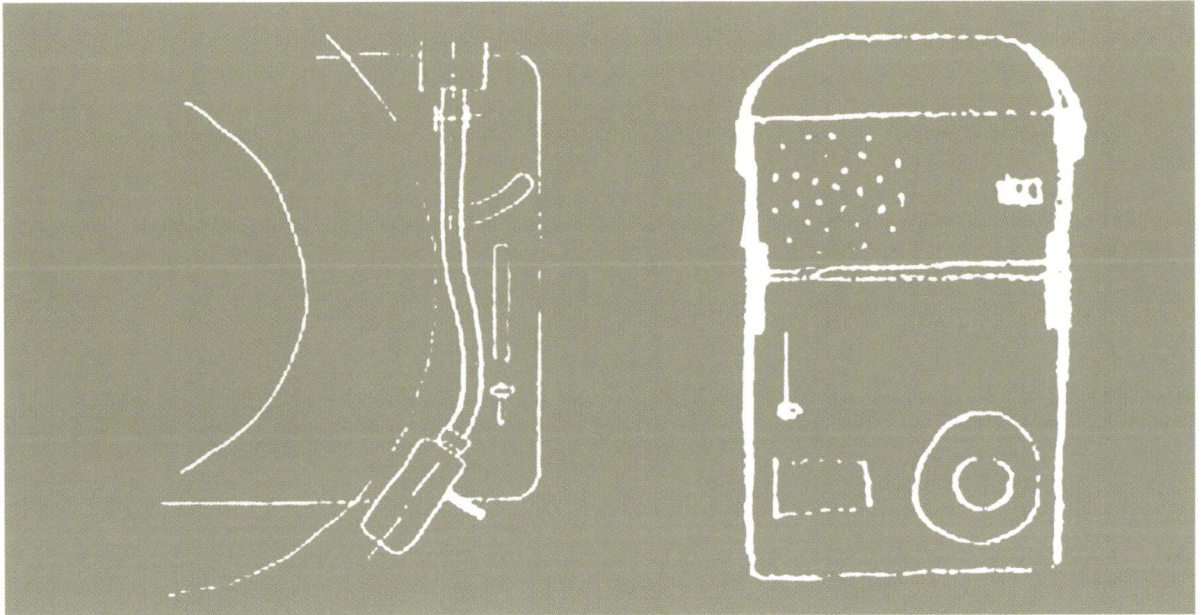

ENTL HINTEN (BEILE

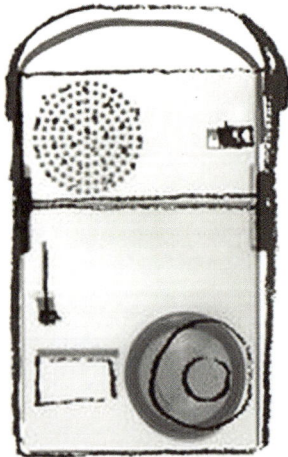

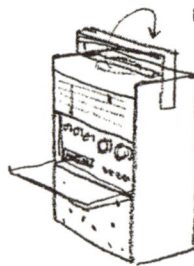

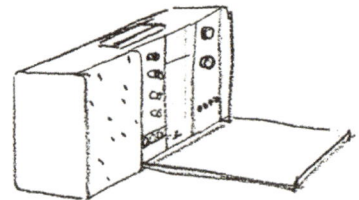

Design drawings by Dieter Rams made for Braun Electronics

DESIGN DRAWING

Design Drawing by hand is a versatile and powerful tool for both design exploration and communication. It is an integral part of the decision-making process, used in the early stages of design, in brainstorm sessions, in the phase of researching and exploring concepts and in presentation.

When can the method be used?

In the early phase of the design process, drawings tend to be simple: basic shapes or configurations, shading and casting shadows. These kinds of drawings incorporate the basic skills and rules of perspective, construction of 3D shapes, shading and constructing cast shadows. Colour is not always used and very often this kind of drawing will suffice for idea sketching or structural concepts.

When several ideas are combined to develop preliminary concepts, the designer has a general idea about the materials being used, the shape of the product, its function and how it will be manufactured. The colour and expression of the materials – for example matt or reflective plastic – become more important and the drawings become more elaborate.

Side-view sketching can be a quicker and easier way of making variations in shape, colour and details.

How to use the method?

Sketching can play a role in different phases of the design process.

Explorative drawing enables you to analyse visually and to generate and evaluate ideas throughout the entire product design cycle, particularly in the synthesis phase.

· Sketching can help you in analysing and exploring the perimeters of the problem definition.

· You can use drawings as a starting point for new ideas by means of association.

· Sketching can help you to explore shapes and their meaning, function and aesthetics.

Along with verbal explanations, you use drawings to interact and communicate with several groups of people who have different levels of understanding of professional jargon.

Limitations of the method

· You need to be a trained and experienced design drawer to be able to communicate your designs effectively.

· In some cases three-dimensional models will communicate your design more effectively than any drawing and make it easier to explain.

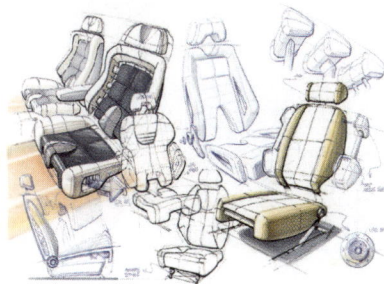

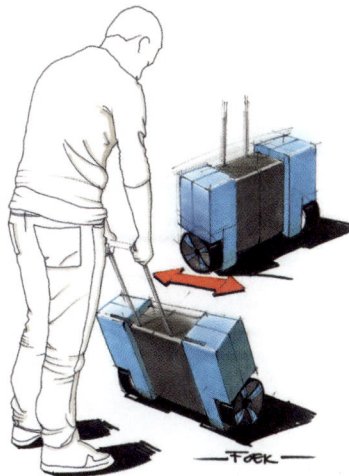

Tips & Concerns

· Define the purpose of your drawing.

· Make sure that you define the purpose of your drawing before you start sketching. Choose a drawing technique based on your purpose, time, skills and tools define the kind of drawing

· The significance of a drawing depends on the context in which it is made. A drawing serves its purpose when it is effective. Therefore, a certain phase in the design process may require a certain type of drawing. Since time is an issue, a quick sketch is in many cases preferable to a more time-consuming rendering.

· For generating and evaluating ideas, hand drawing is more versatile than CAD rendering and prototyping. A rendering can look very definite and unchangeable, which is not appropriate, for example, when you are still conferring with your client about design directions and possibilities.

· A brainstorm sketch can also easily be upgraded into a more presentable drawing, either on paper or digitally by using a tablet and software such as Adobe Photoshop or Corel Painter.

· Drawing by hand is also beneficial for the development of your visual perception, your imaginative capacities and perceptiveness of form in general.

REFERENCES & FURTHER READING: Eissen, J.J. and Steur, R.*, 2007. *Sketching: Drawing Techniques for Product Designers.* Amsterdam: BIS. / Eissen, J.J. and Steur, R.*, 2011. *Sketching: The Basics.* Amsterdam: BIS. / Eissen, J.J., Van Kuijk, E. and De Wolf, P.*, 1984. *Produkt Presentatietechnieken.* Delft: DUP. / Van den Herik, Y. and Eissen J.J.*, 2005. *Intuitive sketching: a new and explorative medium in generating ideas.* Congress CAID&CD Applications of digital techniques in industrial design engineering. May, pp. 708-713.

MOTOR VEHICLE — DYMAXION CAR, United States Patent Office no. 2,101,057, filed October 18, 1933, serial no. 694,068, granted December 7, 1937, inventor: Buckminster Fuller

The Dymaxion car in technical drawings projected over the prototype. The Dymaxion car was a concept car designed by American inventor and architect Richard Buckminster Fuller in 1933. The word Dymaxion is a brand name that Fuller gave to several of his inventions to emphasise that he considered them part of a more general project to improve humanity's living conditions. The car had a fuel efficiency of 7.8 L / 100 km. It could transport 11 passengers. While Fuller claimed it could reach speeds of 190 km/h, the fastest documented speed was 140 km/h. The Dymaxion car was a three-wheeler, steered by a single rear wheel, and could do a U-turn in its own length. However, the rear-wheel steering made the car somewhat counterintuitive to operate, especially in crosswind situations. The teardrop-shaped body was designed by Aurel Persu and was naturally aerodynamically efficient. Measuring 6.1 metres in length, the car was twice as long as a conventional automobile.

TECHNICAL DOCUMENTATION (TECDOC)

When can the method be used?

TecDoc is closely related to the materialisation phase. This is the stage after the generation of concepts when research is needed to determine what production techniques and specific materials can be applied to manufacture a desired component or product. However, TecDoc can also provide support in an earlier stage, when it can be used to quickly generate concept variants or to determine what production processes, means or techniques are possible. TecDoc can be used to model basic components, such as batteries or an internal frame that will be applied in the design (bottom-up design). Paper prints of these models can serve as an underlay when doing a form study, making clear the geometrical design space limitations of your design. Tangible models can be created through rapid manufacturing techniques to support moulded shells or housings. Finally, TecDoc can be applied when using digital 3D models of outer parts such as product housings (top-down design).

How to use the method?

Design software such as SolidWorks is used to generate parametric digital 3D models. These models must be based on the feature-modelling concept: separate parts are built by combining or extracting basic forms, such as cylinders, spheres or more organically shaped bodies. The 3D shapes can be not only solids (volume-based geometries) but also surfaces (zero thickness), especially when organic shapes are required. A 3D model of a product, an assembly, can be built from the separate parts. Parts, assemblies and features in parts are dependent on each other, linked through their relations. If you have good spatial visualisation abilities you can develop basic modelling skills in about 60-80 hours. To guarantee and certify quality and tolerances, technical

Technical Documentation is the unambiguous recording of designs, using standards-compliant digital 3D models and technical drawings. The 3D-model data can also be used to simulate and control manufacturing processes and the assembly of products or parts (components). Rendering techniques or animations can be applied for presentation purposes.

drawings must be made according to valid standards. To this end, you must have the skills to 'read, write and speak' the 'manufacturing language'.

Possible procedure

STEP 1
Make a first digital 3D model during the conceptualisation phase. In earlier stages the 3D model can be used to study the behaviour of possible mechanisms through animations.
STEP 2
Within the materialisation phase, use the software to choose sustainable materials, to do additional simulations to predict a component's behaviour during manufacturing processes such as mould filling or cooling, to do failure analysis such as strength calculations, and to study form, colours and texture.
STEP 3
At the end of the design process, generate an evolved digital 3D model and a final set of technical drawings to safeguard the manufacturing processes and valid product properties and functions.
STEP 4
After completion, use the digital 3D model to control production machines or to produce production-related tools. Finally, you can generate renderings, 'exploded views' of the (de)assembled product and animations to support product presentations, manuals or develop and produce packaging.

Tips & Concerns

· Develop a modelling strategy and time schedule in advance.
· Develop a strategy for Product Data Management – file management, part or product revisions, et cetera.
· Build your 3D models of parts and assemblies as symmetrically as possible.
· Think about manufacturing at an early stage.
· Start with completely new 3D-CAD models when entering the materialisation phase, that is, final detailing.
· Be careful with relations between part features, parts, subassemblies and drawings.
· Use drawing standards to produce proper technical drawings that are legally sound.
· Make backups very often.
· A combination of 3D modelling and sketching can be very useful. While stepping through the design the level of detailing increases and both modelling and drawing will take more time accordingly.

REFERENCES & FURTHER READING: Bertone, G.R. and Wiebe, E.N., 2002. *Technical Graphics Communication*. Blacklick, OH: McGraw-Hill College. / Breedveld, A., 2011. *Producttekenen en –documenteren: van 3D naar 2D*. The Hague: Academic Service. Bremer, A.P.*, 2004. *Technisch documenteren*. Delft: Delft University of Technology.

Sketch model of a transport device for heavy loads.

THREE-DIMENSIONAL MODELS

A Three-Dimensional Model is a physical manifestation of a product idea, a hand-built physical model that represents a final product. In the design process, Three-Dimensional Models are used to express, visualise and materialise product ideas and concepts.

When can the method be used?

Models are often used in the practice of design and they play a vital role in the product development process. The process of design happens not only in your head, but also in your fingers and hands. In industry, models are used to test product aspects, change constructions and details, and to reach consensus within the company on the final form of a product. In mass production, working prototypes are used to test functionality and ergonomics. Changes that need to be made after the production preparation phase are often expensive and time-consuming. The final prototypes thus facilitate the preparation and planning of production. The first phase in the production process is called the null series: these first products, which are to a certain extent still prototypes, are used to test the production process.

How to use Three-Dimensional Models?

3D models can be useful for three reasons:

1. *Generating and developing ideas and concepts*
   Sketch models are used frequently when generating ideas and concepts. Simple materials are used, such as paper, cardboard, foam, wood, tape, glue, wire and solder. With sketch models you can quickly visualise early ideas and develop them into better ideas and concepts. An iterative process often occurs between sketching, making sketch models, drawing, and making a second generation of sketch models.
2. *Communicating ideas and concepts in design teams*
   A dummy mock-up is a 1:1 scale model of the product idea. A dummy only has the external characteristics of the product idea, and not the technical working principles. It is often built at the end of the idea generation phase to visualise and present final concepts. A dummy is also called a VISO: a Visual Model.

A detailed model is used in the concept generation phase to show particular details of the concept. A detailed model is much like a dummy; both are 1:1 scale models with predominantly external characteristics of high quality. A detailed model can also have some limited functionality. The final model is a prototype that has a high-quality look. Built of wood, metal or plastic, it features real buttons and high-quality paint or finishing. The final model should preferably also include some of the technical working principles.

3. *Testing and verifying ideas, concepts and solution principles*
   Proof-of-concept prototypes are used to verify whether certain technical principles actually work. They are simplifications; often details are left out, and only rudimentary forms and working principles are built. They are also known as FUMOs: Functional Models. The level of detail and materials are determined based on what is required at that stage of the idea generation phase.

Richard Buckminster Fuller with dome models.

Possible procedure

· It is vital to determine the purpose of your model before you start building.
· The required level of detail has to be chosen prior to collecting materials, devising a plan and building the model.
· Simple sketch models at the beginning of idea generation can be made with the materials that you find around you, while working prototypes or presentation models require a detailed plan for how to build them.

Limitations of the method

· Building models might be seen as a time-consuming and costly process. However, spending resources on model building during the development phase can bring to light design mistakes that would otherwise cost a lot more time and money.

Tips & Concerns

· Look for examples of sketch models for inspiration.
· Paper-and-tape sketch models are often very helpful during idea generation when the two dimensions of drawing are not enough.
· In design schools, you can often find examples of presentation models on display or in the workshop.
· Harness the expertise of the people working in model workshops.
· Practice makes perfect: practice and practice some more.

REFERENCES & FURTHER READING: Hallgrimsson, B., 2012. *Prototyping and Modelmaking for Product Design.* London: Laurence King. / Thompson, R. 2011. *Prototyping and Low-Volume Production.* London: Thames & Hudson.

New York made instruction videos on how to use their Citi Bike Share bicycles.

VIDEO VISUALISATION

Video Visualisation enables you to visualise future experiences or scenarios that show how a new design concept could potentially be used in or affect people's lives.

When can the method be used?

Video Visualisation is typically used to show the richness and detail of future contexts of use, through its ability to mix concrete images, people and sensations with virtual elements. Carefully staging an imagined context of use enables you to present the functioning of a proposed design and show the value it should bring to this specific context. Video can not only depict the tangible parts of a design idea, such as a physical product, but also show the intangible parts, such as people's responses and emotions. Video Visualisation offers great possibilities to conceptualise, formulate and visualise solutions that are not yet available, particularly for the upcoming domain of service design, which deals with the relationships and interactions between people, artefacts and activities.

How to use the method?

Video Visualisation is best applied in cases where the overall experience of a future product or service needs to be communicated. Crafting convincing videos is something that needs to be practiced frequently, since it requires the integration of various skills, techniques, media and equipment. Making the video involves several iterations, starting with creating a scenario and storyboard, continuing to staging and shooting the video footage, and ending with editing and producing the final version. Going through this process continuously challenges you to frame and present your concept within the envisioned context of use, which significantly contributes to the design value of the method.

Possible procedure

Video Visualisation involves three successive phases:
STEP 1
Pre-production, which is the process of preparing all the elements of the video.
· Create a storyboard and/or a shot list
· Arrange materials – the product, camera, lights, etc.
· Arrange actors
· Arrange location
STEP 2
Production, in which the actual video is shot.
STEP 3
Post-production, in which the raw video footage is edited and effects are added.

Limitations of the method

· Video Visualisation can easily become very resource-intensive, requiring special software, equipment or skills.
· A potential pitfall of the method is that you might be tempted to spend too much time on the technical quality of the video in order to impress a potential client. The main focus, however, should be on the value of the video for the design task at hand.

Tips & Concerns

· First think of the story you want to tell
· What is/are the unique selling point(s) of your concept?
· What are your resources and skills?
· Do you want to focus on product features/product use, context/ atmosphere or service/experience?
· Carefully select the music, since it will heavily influence the mood of the video.
· Be very careful about putting humour into your movie. You can all-too easily overdo it, thereby ruining the professional quality of your production.
· Show people's faces in close-ups to convey emotions and experiences
· Pay special attention to the end of the video, as it is the last thing people will see.
· Do not forget the credits – you deserve to get applauded at the end.

Google uses video demos to inform people about the functions of the Google Glasses.

REFERENCES & FURTHER READING: Buxton, B., 2007. *Sketching User Experiences: Getting the Design Right and the Right Design.* London: Morgan Kaufman. / Mackay, W.E., Ratzer, A.V., and Janecek, P., 2000. *Video artifacts for design: bridging the gap between abstraction and detail.* Proceedings of the 3rd Conference on Designing Interactive Systems: processes, practices, methods, and techniques (DIS '00), pp.72-82. Pasman, G.*, 2012. *From different angles: exploring and applying the design potential of video*, Proceedings of the 14th International Conference on Engineering and Product Design Education, 31 December. / Ylirishu, S. and Buur, J., 2007. *Designing with video.* London: Springer-Verlag.

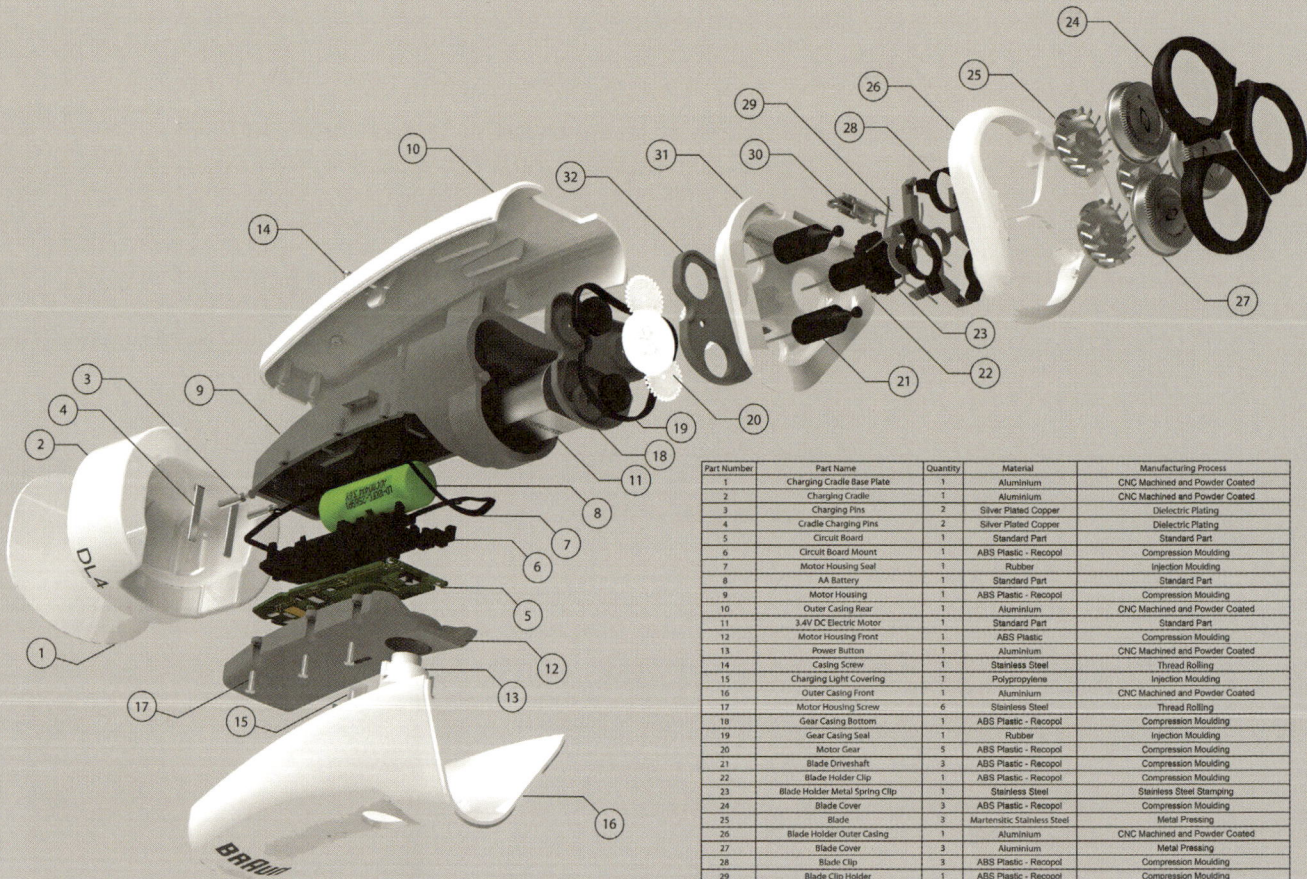

Part Number	Part Name	Quantity	Material	Manufacturing Process
1	Charging Cradle Base Plate	1	Aluminium	CNC Machined and Powder Coated
2	Charging Cradle	1	Aluminium	CNC Machined and Powder Coated
3	Charging Pins	2	Silver Plated Copper	Dielectric Plating
4	Cradle Charging Pins	2	Silver Plated Copper	Dielectric Plating
5	Circuit Board	1	Standard Part	Standard Part
6	Circuit Board Mount	1	ABS Plastic - Recopol	Compression Moulding
7	Motor Housing Seal	1	Rubber	Injection Moulding
8	AA Battery	1	Standard Part	Standard Part
9	Motor Housing	1	ABS Plastic - Recopol	Compression Moulding
10	Outer Casing Rear	1	Aluminium	CNC Machined and Powder Coated
11	3.4V DC Electric Motor	1	Standard Part	Standard Part
12	Motor Housing Front	1	ABS Plastic	Compression Moulding
13	Power Button	1	Aluminium	CNC Machined and Powder Coated
14	Casing Screw	1	Stainless Steel	Thread Rolling
15	Charging Light Covering	1	Polypropylene	Injection Moulding
16	Outer Casing Front	1	Aluminium	CNC Machined and Powder Coated
17	Motor Housing Screw	6	Stainless Steel	Thread Rolling
18	Gear Casing Bottom	1	ABS Plastic - Recopol	Compression Moulding
19	Gear Casing Seal	1	Rubber	Injection Moulding
20	Motor Gear	5	ABS Plastic - Recopol	Compression Moulding
21	Blade Driveshaft	3	ABS Plastic - Recopol	Compression Moulding
22	Blade Holder Clip	1	ABS Plastic - Recopol	Compression Moulding
23	Blade Holder Metal Spring Clip	1	Stainless Steel	Stainless Steel Stamping
24	Blade Cover	3	ABS Plastic - Recopol	Compression Moulding
25	Blade	3	Martensitic Stainless Steel	Metal Pressing
26	Blade Holder Outer Casing	1	Aluminium	CNC Machined and Powder Coated
27	Blade Cover	3	Aluminium	Metal Pressing
28	Blade Clip	3	ABS Plastic - Recopol	Compression Moulding
29	Blade Clip Holder	1	ABS Plastic - Recopol	Compression Moulding
30	Blade Casing Hinge	1	Stainless Steel	Stainless Steel Stamping
31	Blade Holder Bottom	1	Aluminium	CNC Machined and Powder Coated
32	Gear Housing Case Top	1	ABS Plastic - Recopol	Compression Moulding

INDEX

COLOPHON

Publisher
BIS Publishers
Building Het Sieraad
Postjesweg 1
1057 DT Amsterdam
The Netherlands
T +31 (0)20 515 02 30
F +31 (0)20 515 02 39
bis@bispublishers.com
www.bispublishers.com

ISBN 978 90 6369 327 5

3ʳᵈ printing 2016

Editors
Annemiek van Boeijen
Jaap Daalhuizen
Jelle Zijlstra
Roos van der Schoor

Graphic design & Image editing
Yvo ZIjlstra / Antenna-Men

English (style) correction
Joel Kuntonen

Reference
A.G.C. van Boeijen, J.J. Daalhuizen, J.J.M. Zijlstra and R.S.A. van der Schoor (eds.)
(2013) Delft Design Guide. Amsterdam: BIS Publishers.

Revised 2nd edition 2014 - Copyright © 2013 BIS Publishers, TU Delft

While every effort has been made to trace all present copyright holders of the material in this book, any unintentional omission is hereby apologised for in advance, and we should of course be pleased to correct any errors in acknowledgements in any future editions of this book.

For questions and suggestions please contact us via ddg@tudelft.nl.